Oscar Wilde's
Scandalous Summer

Oscar Wilde's
Scandalous Summer

THE 1894 WORTHING HOLIDAY
AND THE AFTERMATH

ANTONY EDMONDS

AMBERLEY

To Donald Mead
a Wildean of some importance

First published 2014

Amberley Publishing
The Hill, Stroud
Gloucestershire, GL5 4EP

www.amberley-books.com

Copyright © Antony Edmonds, 2014
The quotations from the letters of Oscar and Constance Wilde and from *Son of Oscar Wilde* are © the estates of Oscar and Constance Wilde and of Vyvyan Holland.

The right of Antony Edmonds to be identified as the Author of this work has been asserted in accordance with the Copyrights, Designs and Patents Act 1988.

All rights reserved. No part of this book may be reprinted or reproduced or utilised in any form or by any electronic, mechanical or other means, now known or hereafter invented, including photocopying and recording, or in any information storage or retrieval system, without the permission in writing from the Publishers.

British Library Cataloguing in Publication Data.
A catalogue record for this book is available from the British Library.

ISBN 978 1 4456 3618 4 (hardback)
ISBN 978 1 4456 3646 7 (ebook)

Typesetting and Origination by Amberley Publishing.
Printed in the UK.

Contents

Introduction: 'Scandal is gossip made tedious by morality'   7

1   'Three is company and two is none': A Disruptive Friendship   11

2   'Anything is better than London': The Haven in Worthing   27

3   'The beauty and grace of everything': Oscar Wilde and the Worthing Festivals   37

4   'You will come, won't you?': Bosie   59

5   'A happy, good-humoured companion': Alphonse   69

6   'No-one to talk to': Constance   87

7   'My play is really very funny': *The Importance of Being Earnest*   109

8   'Absurd and silly perjuries': The Dramatist in the Dock   124

Notes   151

Appendices ... 170

    A: Chronology of the Worthing Holiday of 1894 (with notes) ... 170

    B: Four Letters from Oscar Wilde to Lord Alfred Douglas ... 176

    C: Speech Given by Oscar Wilde on 13 September 1894 ... 182

    D: Three Extracts from the Transcript of the Queensberry Libel Trial ... 184

    E: The Location of the Haven ... 193

    F: Alphonse Conway's First Name ... 199

    G: Alphonse Delahay ... 201

    H: Alphonse Conway and the Australian Connection ... 205

    I: The Ballad of Worthing Beach (with notes) ... 212

Sources of Illustrations ... 217

Acknowledgements ... 220

Index ... 221

INTRODUCTION

'Scandal is gossip made tedious by morality'

The cynical Cecil Graham, asked by Lord Windermere in Act III of Oscar Wilde's 1892 play *Lady Windermere's Fan* what the difference is between scandal and gossip, replies:

> Oh! gossip is charming! History is merely gossip. But scandal is gossip made tedious by morality. Now, I never moralise. A man who moralises is usually a hypocrite, and a woman who moralises is invariably plain.

Although fictional characters are not usually a mouthpiece for their authors, Oscar Wilde's voice can be heard in his characters' words more often than in the case of most writers; and these lines suggest that Wilde might have found the title of our book – to use terms he often used – vulgar or childish.

In his next play, Wilde returned to the theme in even more pertinent terms. In Act I of *An Ideal Husband* – written two years or so before Wilde's ruin – Mrs Cheveley lectures Sir Robert Chiltern at some length:

> Remember to what a point your Puritanism in England has brought you. In old days nobody pretended to be a bit better than his neighbours. In fact, to be a bit better than one's neighbour was considered excessively vulgar and middle-class. Nowadays, with our modern mania for morality, every one has to pose as a paragon of purity, incorruptibility, and all the other seven deadly

virtues – and what is the result? You all go over like ninepins – one after the other. Not a year passes in England without somebody disappearing. Scandals used to lend charm, or at least interest, to a man – now they crush him. And yours is a very nasty scandal. You couldn't survive it ... Sir Robert, you know what your English newspapers are like. Suppose that when I leave this house I drive down to some newspaper office, and give them this scandal and the proofs of it! Think of their loathsome joy, of the delight they would have in dragging you down, of the mud and mire they would plunge you in. Think of the hypocrite with his greasy smile penning his leading article, and arranging the foulness of the public placard.

Although this passage is heavy with dramatic irony for us that know how the Oscar Wilde story ended, Wilde himself – already embroiled in the homosexual liaisons that were to bring him down – almost certainly wrote these lines knowingly, well aware that circumstances could easily arise where they would apply to his own situation. He was getting in his retaliation in advance.

Wilde also considered the question of scandal – in equally ironic and prescient terms – in his 1891 essay 'The Soul of Man under Socialism':

There are possibly some journalists who take a real pleasure in publishing horrible things, or who, being poor, look to scandals as forming a sort of permanent basis for an income. But there are other journalists, I feel certain, men of education and cultivation, who really dislike publishing these things, who know that it is wrong to do so, and only do it because the unhealthy conditions under which their occupation is carried on oblige them to supply the public with what the public wants, and to compete with other journalists in making that supply as full and satisfying to the gross popular appetite as possible. It is a very degrading position for any body of educated men to be placed in, and I have no doubt that most of them feel it acutely.

We are therefore rebuked from beyond the grave before our book even begins – although it is fair to point out that those that feast with panthers (to use the famous expression Wilde later used of his sexual adventures in the first half of the 1890s) do so in the knowledge of the consequences that will follow if the world comes to hear of it. Indeed, those whose conduct exposes them to the risk of scandal are often those that are most vociferous in denouncing its malignity.

The summer of 1894 was not Wilde's only scandalous summer. Indeed, most of the last dozen or so summers of his life were scandalous in one way or another, apart, of course, from those he spent in prison. Just as scandalous as the Worthing summer, for example, was the Goring-on-Thames summer of the previous year, which is briefly described in the first chapter of this book. The summers of exile after Wilde left prison are outside the remit of this book, but in some respects they were the most scandalous of all, since in France and Italy he was able to indulge his taste for teenage boys without hindrance. However no public scandal arose from this.

There are several reasons for focusing detailed attention on the Worthing holiday. First, the period has up till now been dealt with only fleetingly. Richard Ellmann's magisterial 1987 biography of Wilde, for instance, devotes just five sentences to it. Secondly, although on the one hand it was a unique and self-contained episode, it was also in many respects a microcosm of Wilde's life during the crucial period between his becoming involved with Lord Alfred Douglas and his downfall. All the elements were there: Douglas's presence, alternately life-enhancing and infuriating; Constance Wilde's unhappiness; Wilde's sexual relations with a teenage boy; Douglas's father, the Marquess of Queensberry, seething in the background, waiting to pounce; and considerable literary achievement in the face of these distractions – for it was during the Worthing holiday that Wilde wrote *The Importance of Being Earnest*, the most-performed and best-loved comedy in the English language outside the works of Shakespeare.

The chapters of this book that focus on the Worthing holiday derive from a sequence of articles published in *The Wildean* between January 2010 and July 2013, although much of the material has been comprehensively reorganised and rewritten. The first and the last chapters – in effect a prologue and an epilogue – cover more familiar ground to those that have studied Wilde's life, but with, I hope, some fresh perspectives.

The fascination exerted by the life of Oscar Wilde never palls. Those that read this book and wish to know the full compelling story have no shortage of books to consult. Richard Ellman's biography is unlikely ever to be surpassed for the depth of its research and the perceptiveness of its insights. At the time he was writing, however, neither the accurate transcript of the libel trial nor the witness statements the boys gave Queensberry's solicitors were available. Important companion books, therefore, are Neil McKenna's *The Secret Life of Oscar Wilde*, which gives a detailed picture of Wilde's sexual history; and Merlin Holland's *Irish Peacock & Scarlet Marquess*, where we hear Wilde's exact words, recorded verbatim by the court stenographers during the Queensberry libel trial.

Even today, Oscar Wilde is judged and re-judged; but judgements about long-ago events are often based on an inadequate knowledge of the facts. In the case of Wilde, this works both ways. Wilde is often spoken of as a victim of Victorian injustice and hypocrisy, but, as we shall see, English justice was fair to him; and, while the attitudes of the time were not free of double standards, we can be sure that, *mutatis mutandis*, he would have been similarly pilloried today. These issues, particularly as they relate to Worthing, are discussed at the end of the final chapter.

1

'Three is company and two is none': A Disruptive Friendship

'You don't seem to realise that in married life three is company and two is none.'

The Importance of Being Earnest, Act I

When Oscar Wilde married Constance Lloyd on 29 May 1884, he was a few months short of his thirtieth birthday, and Constance was twenty-five. Although Wilde was well known as a wit and a lecturer – and for his colourful and flamboyant personality – his writings had not yet made much impact. He had written two plays, *Vera, or the Nihilists* in 1880 and *The Duchess of Padua* in 1883, but these melodramatic tragedies had attracted little interest. *Vera* ran for one week in New York in 1882 and *The Duchess of Padua* was not staged until 1891, when it had a three-week run, again in New York. Wilde had also been writing poetry since he was an undergraduate at Trinity College Dublin, and in 1881 he had published a collection of his verse. But literary fame still lay several years ahead.

Although it was more than a marriage of convenience, there were practical reasons for Wilde to marry, including the increasing amount of gossip about his sexuality. In addition, Wilde's finances were in poor shape. In the Victorian age, the financial situation of a potential bride was rarely irrelevant in upper-class families, and Constance had a decent income. She was also attractive and intelligent, and Wilde seems to have been genuinely in love with her – or thought he was, which comes to much the same thing. But he was not suited to fidelity, or indeed to the institution of marriage; and in the event the love of his life was to be not a woman but a young man.

There are differences of opinion about when Wilde first had sex with another male. Certainly there were some intense emotional entanglements with young men as far back as his student days, but there is no proof that these became physical. Both Wilde and Robert Ross[1] – the most loyal of Wilde's friends, and later his literary executor – said that Wilde's earliest homosexual experience was the occasion when he first had sex with Ross, then aged seventeen, in 1886. As far as sexual relations with women are concerned, Wilde does not seem to have had sex with a young woman of his own class prior to his marriage, although he had undoubtedly used the services of female prostitutes.

Wilde may have posed as a number of things, but he was not a poser when it came to his love of beauty. Indeed, his sensibilities in this regard were one of the reasons that his marriage to Constance so quickly failed. Although he later came to see beauty – as far as the erotic was concerned – exclusively in the form of boys and young men, when he first knew Constance she was a very beautiful woman. Had she, like Wilde's character Dorian Gray, possessed the miraculous gift of never ageing, the marriage might have worked for longer. But, fastidious as he was about beauty – more fastidious in the case of women than of young men – he quickly found Constance physically repellent, as he told Frank Harris many years later:

> When I married, my wife was a beautiful girl, white and slim as a lily, with dancing eyes and gay rippling laughter like music. In a year or so the flower-like grace had all vanished; she became heavy, shapeless, deformed: she dragged herself around the house in uncouth misery with drawn blotched face and hideous body, sick at heart because of our love. It was dreadful. I tried to be kind to her; forced myself to touch and kiss her; but she was sick always, and – oh! I cannot recall it, it is all loathsome. ... Oh, nature is disgusting; it takes beauty and defiles: it defaces the ivory-white body we have adored, with the vile cicatrices of maternity: it befouls the altar of the soul.[2]

(What, it might be asked, did Wilde's mirror by this time tell him about himself?)

This terrible account, although doubtless embellished by Harris – his memoirs of Wilde include improbable quantities of direct speech – rings largely true. It should, however, be noted that Wilde was speaking in exile during the last few years of his life, when his view of Constance was coloured by the bitterness of estrangement and by disputes about money. He was therefore being extreme and unfair, just as he was in his account of Lord Alfred Douglas in the long letter known as 'De Profundis', written in Reading gaol at a time when he wrongly believed that Bosie had abandoned him.

There are two pieces of evidence which confirm that the sexual side of the Wildes' marriage was brief. The first is the comment, years later, of Constance's brother Otho that around 1886 there had been a 'virtual divorce' between his sister and Wilde, an expression that indicated the end of sexual relations.[3] The second is that in June 1897, after the poet Ernest Dowson had persuaded Wilde to avail himself of the services of a female prostitute in Dieppe, Wilde told Dowson that it had been his first experience of sex with a woman 'these ten years'.[4]

Thus, although Wilde was still able to perform in the marriage bed after his elder son Cyril's birth – his second son Vyvyan was conceived in the spring of 1886 – there seem to have been no sexual relations between Oscar and Constance after Vyvyan's birth on 3 November 1886. Indeed, allowing for the period when Constance was pregnant with Vyvyan – Wilde would not have engaged in marital relations once pregnancy became evident – we may assume that the Wildes' marriage functioned sexually for less than two years.

Therefore, while there are various ways in which Lord Alfred Douglas could be argued to have stolen Oscar from Constance, he was certainly not responsible for Wilde's abandonment of the marital bed, which had happened some five years before they met. In any case, as we shall see in a moment, the sexual side of Bosie's and Oscar's relationship was itself brief. What in due course became hurtful and humiliating to Constance was to see Bosie usurp other important parts of her marriage, such as intellectual companionship and emotional support.

Indeed, in spite of her suddenly falling in love in the summer of 1894 with the bookseller and part-time publisher Arthur Humphreys, as we shall see in Chapter 6, nothing that we know of Constance suggests that the cessation of sexual relations would itself have been particularly upsetting to her.

But the fault lines within the marriage were not just to do with Wilde's having quickly found his wife sexually unattractive; it is hard to see that the marriage would anyway have flourished indefinitely. Being married to a self-absorbed genius is never easy, and Wilde and his wife were in many ways not well matched. Constance's nature was more serious than that of her husband. Her younger son Vyvyan later wrote of her, 'She may not have had much sense of humour, but then she did not have very much to laugh about.'[5] In addition, Constance became increasingly religious as the years passed, and close proximity to someone with an earnest and all-consuming faith is irksome for those that take a sceptical approach to religion, as Wilde did:

> Religion does not help me. The faith that others give to what is unseen, I give to what one can touch, and look at. ... When I think about Religion at all, I feel as if I would like to found an order for those who cannot believe: the Confraternity of the Fatherless one might call it.[6]

*

During the early years of the marriage, however, Wilde and Constance were happy. They had shared pleasures, including the creation of the interior of their 'house beautiful' at 16 Tite Street in Chelsea. And Wilde began to find literary success. In 1888 he published a book of stories for children, *The Happy Prince and Other Tales*, followed in 1890 by his only novel, *The Picture of Dorian Gray*, which attracted a great deal of attention, much of it hostile, on account of its unmissable homoerotic subtext. The year 1891 saw the publication of two collections of short stories for adults, *Lord Arthur Savile's Crime and Other Stories* and *The House of Pomegranates*, and Wilde's three most famous essays, 'The Soul of Man under Socialism', 'The Decay of Lying' and 'The Critic as Artist', the last two in a collection entitled *Intentions*.

In 1891 Wilde also wrote again for the stage, the result being the one-act tragedy *Salome*, written in French. It was not produced until 1896, in Paris, by which time Wilde was in prison.

It was during the productive year of 1891 that Wilde first met Lord Alfred Douglas, always known as Bosie, his nickname in the family as a child. They were introduced by Douglas's slightly older cousin, the poet Lionel Johnson, who was himself in love with Wilde. Johnson had lent Bosie his copy of *The Picture of Dorian Gray*, which Bosie read numerous times and which made a great impact on him. It was one afternoon in late June or early July 1891 that Johnson took Bosie to tea at the Wildes' house in Tite Street. According to Bosie, there was nothing exceptional about this first meeting:

> What really happened, of course, at that interview was just the ordinary exchange of courtesies. Wilde was very agreeable and talked a great deal. I was very much impressed, and before I left Wilde had asked me to lunch or dinner at his club, and I had accepted his invitation.[7]

However, Bosie says that at their second meeting a few days later Wilde made sexual advances. There is little reason to doubt Bosie's claim. By this time Wilde rarely delayed when he found a young man attractive, and even before they met he would have been aware from Lionel Johnson, also homosexual, that Bosie's sexual nature was similar to theirs – too similar, in fact, since Bosie's own preference for youth and beauty meant that that he did not find Wilde attractive.

In spite of this early attempt on Bosie, Wilde's and Bosie's friendship did not develop its special intensity for almost a year, although they saw each other a few times over the intervening period. In the meantime Wilde had his first stage success, *Lady Windermere's Fan*, first performed on 22 February 1892. The play had two West End runs and also toured the provinces, and in the first year Wilde earned something like £1,600 from it (about £160,000 today).[8]

By now Wilde had entirely given in to his homosexual orientation. Between February and May 1892 he had a relationship with an eighteen-year-old youth called Edward Shelley, who worked as a clerk at the offices of his publishers, Elkin Mathews and John Lane. Shelley came from humble stock and had left school at the age of thirteen, but he was intelligent and had intellectual aspirations, and was delighted to be the object of Wilde's attention.[9] Later Shelley was to be accusatory and self-exculpatory about their affair, but his evidence was so contradictory that the jury in the second criminal trial found Wilde not guilty of the charges in respect of him.

The event that brought Wilde and Bosie together – a foretaste of problems to come – was Bosie's being blackmailed in the spring of 1892 by a youth in Oxford over an indiscreet letter Bosie had sent him. Bosie wrote to Wilde asking for help. Wilde travelled down to Oxford and spent the weekend at Bosie's lodgings in the High Street. Back in London, he went to see his solicitor, George Lewis, who resolved the matter by arranging for the blackmailer to be paid £100 (about £10,000 today). Recourse to the law was not an option. If similar good sense had prevailed two years later, Wilde's downfall, if not necessarily averted, would at least have been postponed.

It was soon after this that Bosie gave in to Wilde's importunity – probably in May 1892. In a letter of 7 April 1897 from Reading Gaol to his friend More Adey, Wilde wrote, 'I never remember on any one occasion from May 1892 to April 1895 that A. D. [Alfred Douglas] had any money from either his father or his mother. He came to me for everything.'[10] April 1895 was the momentous month of Wilde's fall, and the fact that May 1892 is the other month he specifies suggests this was lodged in his mind as the equally momentous month when his relationship with Bosie began in earnest.[11]

The physical side of their relationship, however, was brief, as Bosie later told Frank Harris in explicit terms:

When I first met Wilde he started laying siege to me and I resisted him; not because at that time I had any moral objection to that sort of thing, but simply because with a man older than myself it did not appeal to me. At school and at Oxford I had been neither better nor worse than my contemporaries. What is euphemistically called 'the schoolboy nonsense' that goes on among boys at school and at college was perfectly familiar to me and I had

> participated in it freely ... It was not till I had known him for at least six months ... that I gave in to him. I did with him and allowed him to do just what was done among boys at Winchester and Oxford [that is, mutual masturbation] ... Sodomy never took place between us [though] he added what was new to me and was not (as far as I know) known or practised among my contemporaries: he 'sucked' me ... Much as I was fascinated by Wilde and much as I really in the long run adored and was 'crazy' about him, I never liked this part of the business. It was dead against my sexual instincts which were all for youth and beauty and softness. After a time he tumbled to the fact that I didn't like it at all and only consented to it to oblige him, and he very soon 'cut it out' altogether.[12]

Nonetheless each man fell in love with the other, in different ways and for different reasons. Douglas was a powerful cocktail. He was young, slim, and good looking. He was amusing and intelligent, though lazy. Inspired by Wilde, he started writing poetry, and soon became an accomplished sonneteer. He was the son of a marquess, and Wilde, in spite of his 1891 essay about socialism, was more of a snob than he was a socialist. There was also the happy coincidence that Bosie was an undergraduate at the college of which Wilde had been a member – Magdalen, the most beautiful and the most 'aesthetic' of Oxford's colleges.

Bosie, for his part, was captivated by Wilde's wit and charm, and doubtless by his celebrity; and of course it is always beguiling to be loved 'wildly, passionately, devotedly, hopelessly', as Algernon was later to claim to love Cecily in *The Importance of Being Earnest*. But there was a darker and more complex side to the relationship. Being adored gives power to the object of adoration, and Douglas misused the power he had over Oscar. Wilde put this succinctly in 'De Profundis': 'The basis of character is will-power, and my will-power became absolutely subject to yours.'[13]

According to Wilde, this darker side manifested itself in Bosie's attitude to money. As we saw earlier, Wilde claimed that between 1892 and 1895 Bosie relied entirely on Wilde for money. This, however, cannot be true. Initially, Bosie received an allowance from his father of £250 a year (£25,000 today) – an adequate sum for a man with no responsibilities, if he was not extravagant – although Queensberry withdrew this after Bosie refused to give up his friendship with Wilde.

Nonetheless, Wilde certainly spent a great deal of money on Bosie. But the issue was not just the outlay itself, which Wilde claimed was the principal factor in the financial difficulties in which he found himself by 1894. It was also Bosie's unattractive attitude to Wilde's financial support. In 'De Profundis', Wilde says that early in their friendship Bosie's mother, Lady Queensberry, had warned Oscar that Bosie's two chief faults were vanity and being 'all wrong about money'. Wilde says it did not take him long to see what Bosie's mother had meant:

> Your insistence on a life of reckless profusion: your incessant demands for money: your claim that all your pleasures should be paid for by me whether I was with you or not: brought me after some time into serious monetary difficulties ... You demanded without grace and received without thanks. ... But it was no pleasure to me to have to pay every single thing for you from your morning shave to your midnight hansom. It was a horrible bore ... your living on me was a matter in which my wishes were not consulted for a moment. It was simply a peculiar, and to me personally most distressing, form that your devotion to me took.[14]

In his 1914 book *Oscar Wilde and Myself*, Bosie furiously rejected these accusations:

> Even in those early days I spent a great deal more money on Wilde than he spent on me ... so far as my money was concerned, we had a common purse. It never occurred to me to refuse him anything ... It is grotesquely untrue that he wasted any appreciable part of his substance on me.[15]

As often, neither Wilde nor Bosie can be fully believed. 'De Profundis' was written when the balance of Wilde's mind was disturbed, and he demonised Bosie. *Oscar Wilde and Myself* was a furious and venomous riposte to 'De Profundis', by someone whose balance of mind was arguably always disturbed. And, while

Wilde was often guilty of exaggeration in 'De Profundis', Bosie was sometimes guilty of outrageous lies.

The most preposterous of these is the claim he made in *Oscar Wilde and Myself* that, when Wilde was charged, 'he assured me that the suggestions and accusations against him were quite false and without foundation. I had not the smallest reason to believe that he was lying to me.' It was, wrote Bosie, only when he visited Wilde when he was in Holloway prison on remand that Wilde told him that 'in a way' the charges against him were true: 'I was shocked at what he told me.' Also, in one of the most breathtaking displays of hypocrisy in literary history, Douglas – more promiscuous with boys even than Wilde – says that Wilde was charged 'for having made a low, squalid and abominable brute of himself'.[16]

As we have seen, the sexual side of Wilde's and Bosie's relationship seems to have been over within a matter of months. It might at first sight seem puzzling that the end of sexual relations, and indeed after so short a time, did not – as is usually the case when two people are in their sexual prime – mean the end of love. But the bonds that tied them were complex ones, and Bosie's being sexually accommodating was not essential to their affair. In any case, Wilde was a man for whom the period of wooing – which, in his case, rarely lasted long – was as important as the conquest. Once a boy had succumbed, Wilde usually lost interest after a while:

> Desire, at the end, was a malady, or a madness, or both. I grew careless of the lives of others. I took pleasure where it pleased me and passed on.[17]

However Wilde never lost interest in Bosie, and perhaps, in some paradoxical way, the ending of sexual relations brought them even closer together. They had shared a bed on a few occasions, and consummation did not need to be reinforced by repetition. But then Bosie was in every way a special case, because Bosie was adored. Among all the boys and young men with whom Wilde had sexual relations, only in the case of Bosie was there an element of the type of love that Socrates and Plato might have recognised.

In any case their relationship still had a sexual component, albeit a vicarious one. They were linked erotically in their pursuit of boys, some of whom they shared, including Alfred Wood, a seventeen-year-old male prostitute who Bosie passed on to Wilde in February 1893 and who was to feature extensively in the trials; and a schoolboy called Claude Dansey and a servant called Walter Grainger, about both of whom we shall learn more in a moment. Pursuing youths was one of their shared pleasures, and there were also constant conversations about sex, although Wilde later claimed that he eventually found these tedious:

> The trivial in thought and action is charming ... But the froth and folly of our life grew often very wearisome to me: it was only in the mire that we met [Wilde means that 'the mire' was the only common ground they had]: and fascinating, terribly fascinating though the one topic round which your talk invariably centred was, still at the end it became quite monotonous to me. I was often bored to death by it.[18]

Although Bosie was a closer intellectual match for Wilde than Constance was, he was not Wilde's equal. Few were. Behind the pose of everything coming easily to him, Wilde was a hard worker, a reader and a thinker – a genuine 'intellectual'. Bosie was not. Although clever, he was lazy and lightweight.

In some perverse way, it may have amused and pleased Oscar to indulge Bosie's lowbrow tastes – for example, Bosie loved going to the music hall. Wilde's attitude to young men had something of the Lady Bracknell about it: 'I do not approve of anything that tampers with natural ignorance. Ignorance is like a delicate exotic fruit; touch it and the bloom is gone.'

Later, however, from the reflective isolation of Reading Gaol, Wilde failed to see any charm in this aspect of Bosie's character, and claimed that at the time he was not even aware of it: 'It did not occur to me then that you could have the supreme vice, shallowness.'[19] It is difficult to see what took him so long.

He went on to maintain that the friendship had laid waste to his own intellect:

> I blame myself for allowing an unintellectual friendship, a friendship whose primary aim was not the creation and

contemplation of beautiful things, to entirely dominate my life. From the very first there was too wide a gap between us. You had been idle at your school, worse than idle at your university ... [Your friendship] was intellectually degrading to me.[20]

*

In the winter of 1892–93, Oscar and Constance leased Babbacombe Cliff, Lady Mount Temple's house in Devon.[21] As was to be the case twenty-one months later in Worthing, Constance arrived first, in mid-November, to make the house ready, and Oscar joined her there later, at the start of December.[22] Wilde began work on *An Ideal Husband*. By the beginning of February Constance was in Italy, and Bosie came to Babbacombe, but left at the end of the month after he and Oscar had one of their violent quarrels. Wilde was back in London at the start of March 1893, and he and Bosie spent that month at the Savoy, engaging in indiscreet sexual liaisons with a number of boys whom they brought to their suite. It was a period that was to feature prominently in the three trials two years later.

On 19 April 1893, Wilde's second successful play, *A Woman of No Importance*, opened at the Haymarket Theatre. One of the characters, Lord Alfred Rufford, a lazy young nobleman constantly in debt, was, as his name suggests, clearly partly inspired by Douglas. Meanwhile, the real Lord Alfred was due to take his final exams at Oxford in June 1893, but claimed ill health and did not turn up. Wilde congratulated him on his decision to remain a permanent undergraduate. It is ironic that in 1893 Wilde was flattering Bosie over his idleness and anti-intellectualism, and four years later was complaining about these characteristics at great length.

Wilde and Bosie spent the summer of 1893 at a rented house at Goring-on-Thames called the Cottage. Constance, Cyril and Vyvyan were there for a while, but in due course Constance took her sons to Dinard in France for a seaside holiday.

The Goring summer was in some ways a parallel event to the Worthing holiday of 1894. Indeed, since some of Wilde's penultimate play was written at Goring, it could be described as the scandalous summer of *An Ideal Husband*, just as 1894 was to be the scandalous summer of *Earnest*. In 1893, Constance, however, was even more fully excluded from her husband's life than she was to be in Worthing, where, although she saw little of him, at least she was the joint head of the household. In Goring, that role was in effect filled by Bosie. Again there were rows between Oscar and Bosie, and, when Oscar went to Dinard for a fortnight, Bosie was furious that he was left behind.

In Goring, as in Worthing the following summer, there was a boy who was to feature prominently in the Queensberry libel trial. This was Bosie's Oxford servant Walter Grainger, who seems to have been brought to the Cottage for the specific purpose of providing Wilde with sexual recreation. Grainger, whose official and grandiose title was 'under-butler' – under Wilde, one might lubriciously comment – was allocated the next-door bedroom to Oscar, and Oscar's sexual encounters with him are documented in the statement that Walter gave Queensberry's solicitors in the spring of 1895.[23]

Wilde had on the whole continued to treat Constance with affection and respect even after their 'virtual divorce' in 1886, but during the time she was in Goring she was comprehensively usurped by Bosie, and this was reflected in Wilde's treatment of her, as she told her friend Lady Mount Temple: 'I cannot make out whether it is my fault or Oscar's that he is so cold to me and so nice to others ... His butler knows his other plans and I know nothing. Darling, what am I to do?'[24]

In addition, the household at Goring was a more ill-ordered household than the household at the Haven the following year, presided over as it was by two men who were, in their different ways, both Lords of Misrule. Even the servants, taking their cue from their employers, behaved badly.

*

We do not know how much Constance by this time knew or guessed about her husband's sexual inclinations and practices. According to Otho, writing nearly twenty years later, Constance suspected nothing until she made an unexpected return to 16 Tite Street one day in 1895.[25] But even if this was the first time that evidence was directly presented to her eyes, it would stretch credibility to suggest that Constance had no suspicions at all.

It is true that, until Wilde's downfall, people in the mainstream of all classes of Victorian society would have had little knowledge of homosexuality, something located beyond their experience and on the outer edges of human depravity. It would therefore not have been easy for Constance to accept that her husband's interest in Greek love might have been finding a physical expression. In addition, although Oscar had long abandoned conjugal intimacy, he had functioned satisfactorily in the marital bed during the first two years or so of their marriage; and the concept of a bisexual orientation might have been particularly puzzling to a woman of that era.

Nevertheless, there had over the past few years been no shortage of clues, not least in Wilde's own writings, and of gossip and innuendo – to say nothing of her husband's quasi-uxurious relationship with a good-looking and slightly effete young man who clearly had little interest in girls. Perhaps Constance convinced herself, to use a word that was soon to haunt them, that her husband was merely 'posing'. However it is difficult to avoid the conclusion that for much of her marriage she simply turned her eyes away from a possibility too terrible to contemplate.

Wilde himself, in a letter to Robert Ross from Reading prison in April 1897, touched on this in the context of the possibility that Constance would sue for divorce. He tells Ross that he had hoped to defend the divorce case on the basis that she had condoned his activities, but that he had discovered that such a defence would not be sustainable:

> I now learn that no condonation is of any value where more than one offence may be charged. My wife has simply to say that she condoned X, but knew nothing of Y, and would not hear of condoning Z.[26]

This suggests that Constance knew something, but far from everything.

*

The summer of 1893 also brought an episode that came perilously close to bringing Robert Ross and Bosie, and perhaps Wilde too, to the attention of the police.

Five years earlier, Ross had become friends with Biscoe Hale Wortham, an Anglican clergyman who ran a boarding school for boys in Bruges. In the spring of 1893, Ross, then almost twenty-four – he was a year and a half older than Bosie – spent a week with the Worthams, and befriended one of the pupils at the school. This was Claude Dansey, son of a retired Army officer, later described by Biscoe as 'a nice-looking, well-mannered rather attractive boy a little over sixteen, of no particular strength of character'.

Robbie became besotted with Claude, and during the summer holiday of 1893, when the boy was in London, the relationship became sexual. Ross unwisely wrote to Bosie to tell him about the affair, whereupon Bosie rushed up to London, snatched Claude away from Ross, and took him back to Goring. Oscar Browning, Wortham's brother-in-law, who had himself been dismissed from his post at Eton eighteen years earlier for inappropriate relationships with boys, provided a summary of the hectic three days that followed:

> On Saturday the boy slept with Douglas, on Sunday he slept with Oscar. On Monday he slept with a woman at Douglas's expense. On Tuesday he returned to Bruges three days late.

Claude's adventures – which would have provided compelling material for the standard schoolboy essay 'What I Did in the Summer Holidays' – came to light immediately on his arrival back at Wortham's school, when he was questioned by his headmaster about the reasons for his lateness. The 'no particular strength of character' that had made him so susceptible to seduction was again in evidence, and Claude told his headmaster the whole story. Wortham's suspicions about Ross's friendship with his own teenage son were now aroused, and he discovered that Ross had had sexual relations with him too. Wortham was, of course, appalled, writing to Oscar Browning:

> Ross is simply one of a gang of the most absolutely brutal ruffians who spend their time in seducing and prostituting boys and all the time presenting a decent appearance to the world. Two other persons beside himself are implicated in the business.

Although Oscar Browning – who heard the story from Ross as well, and clearly revelled in every detail – knew that one of these 'persons' was Wilde, it appears that Claude Dansey did not give his headmaster the name of the man he had slept with on the Monday. It may be that he never knew it. Furious though he was, Wortham took a pragmatic approach, doubtless partly because of the damage that would be done to his school's reputation if the scandal came to court. But Colonel Dansey was, as Wortham told Browning, 'by no means easy to manage'. In the end, however, Dansey was advised that, while Ross and Bosie would receive two-year prison sentences, his own son would get six months; and he reluctantly decided not to prosecute.

In spite of this close brush with disaster, Wilde and Douglas continued to believe that they were somehow immune to the law, a belief that was soon to have fatal consequences. There was, however, now a pause in the downhill rush towards ruin. A couple of months after the Dansey scandal, Wilde wrote to Bosie's mother, Lady Queensberry, telling her that Bosie seemed to him to be in a 'very bad state of health ... sleepless, nervous, and rather hysterical ... He does absolutely nothing. And is quite astray in life ... His life seems to me aimless, unhappy and absurd.' Wilde suggested to Lady Queensberry that she might arrange for Bosie to go to Egypt to stay with her friends Lord and Lady Cromer in Cairo, where Cromer was British Consul-General. Lady Queensberry followed Wilde's suggestion, and Bosie was in Egypt at the start of December 1893.

Initially Wilde was relieved by separation from Bosie, and indeed determined to make it permanent:

> In the meantime you are writing to me by every post from Egypt. I took not the smallest notice of any of your communications. I read them, and tore them up. I had quite settled to have no more to do with you. My mind was made up.[27]

Bosie left Egypt early in February 1894, and went to Athens, where he persuaded his mother to write to Wilde, pleading for the friendship to be restored. But Wilde held firm. Bosie then sent a telegram to Constance asking her to use her influence to get Wilde to write to him; which she did. Wilde wrote in reply that he had no intention of seeing Bosie 'for many months to come'.

Bosie now proceeded to Paris, where he sent Wilde a long telegram that appeared to end with the threat that he might commit suicide. At this Wilde relented, and he was reunited with Bosie at the end of February or start of March amid much holding of hands, and floods of tears on Bosie's part. Bosie then took it into his head to resume his studies at Oxford, but he did not remain there long. Early in April he was staying in rooms that Wilde rented in St James's Place between October 1893 and April 1894, ostensibly to write in peace, but also as a convenient location for sexual liaisons. In mid-April Bosie went to Florence, where Oscar joined him early the next month, and they rented a flat for a few weeks. By the middle of June they were back in London.

On 30 June, Bosie's father, the Marquess of Queensberry, who for a long time had had strong objections to Wilde's friendship with his son, rightly suspecting that it was homosexual in character, called on Wilde at his house in Tite Street, and there was a terrible scene. During July, Wilde and Bosie met intermittently. Then, in the second week of August, Wilde went down to Worthing for a family holiday and to write a new play. Four days later, Bosie was there too.

2

'Anything is better than London': The Haven in Worthing

'The house, I hear, is very small, and I have no writing-room. However, anything is better than London.'
    Oscar Wilde to Lord Alfred Douglas, 9 August 1894

The Wildes' decision to spend their summer holiday in Worthing seems to have been sudden. On 30 July 1894, only eight days before she was to set off for Sussex, Constance Wilde wrote to her friend Georgina Mount Temple,[1] 'We are very likely going to take the boys to Worthing for a month if we can get a house there.' Within five days the arrangements were in place, and Constance was writing to Georgina, 'On Tuesday [7 August] we go off to Worthing for 4 or 5 weeks.'

The house she had found was called the Haven. It was a four-storey end-of-terrace house, part of a development of four terraced and four semi-detached houses called the Esplanade, just off the seafront on the edge of the town. In 1894 these were the final buildings at the eastern end of Worthing.

There is nothing surprising about the choice of Worthing for the Wildes' holiday. A resort within reasonably easy reach of London was desirable, and indeed Wilde and Constance each made one or two day trips to the capital during August and September. Wilde was familiar with Brighton, and had stayed there a number of times, but the smaller and quieter resort ten miles or so to the west would have been better for young children. Although there had been a serious typhoid epidemic in Worthing the previous year, extensive measures had been put in place to prevent a recurrence, so only the timorous would have stayed away in 1894.

Worthing would also have been cheaper than Brighton, and the unhappy state of Wilde's finances is a recurring theme in his letters that summer. Only a few weeks before the Worthing holiday, Wilde had had to decline an invitation to accompany some friends to Paris, explaining to Bosie, 'I have no money, as usual, and can't go.'[2] At about the same time, Wilde sent the actor-manager George Alexander a brief outline of the play that was to become *The Importance of Being Earnest*, asking him for £150 (about £15,000 in today's money) in return for first refusal, and rather optimistically assuring Alexander that he would return the money if the play was not in the end suitable. 'I am so pressed for money, that I don't know what to do,' he said. He admitted that his own extravagance was partly to blame, but added that he had to pay for his mother's household as well as his own.[3] Alexander did, in due course, oblige.

In a letter Wilde wrote to Bosie the day before he went down to Worthing, Wilde returns to the question of his financial difficulties:

> I am overdrawn £41 [about £4,100 today] at the bank: it really is intolerable the want of money. I have not a penny. I can't stand it any longer, but don't know what to do ... Ernesto has written to me begging for money – a very nice letter – but I really have nothing just now.[4]

It was vital that Wilde quickly earn some money. *An Ideal Husband* was finished and was scheduled for production, but – while the likely proceeds from one play would be a help – Wilde's desperate financial situation meant that he felt he needed the earnings from two.

Giving the children a holiday and finding somewhere relatively quiet to concentrate on writing a new play were not, however, the only reasons for leaving the capital. In his letter to Bosie, Wilde commented that 'anything' was better than London, followed by a brief paragraph explaining why:

Your father is on the rampage again – been to Café Royal to enquire for us, with threats etc. I think now it would have been better for me to have had him bound over to keep the peace, but what a scandal! Still, it is intolerable to be dogged by a maniac.[5]

Worthing would, among other things, provide temporary respite from Queensberry, since even he would hesitate to intrude upon a family holiday.

The aptly named Haven was owned by a woman called Miss Lord. During the Queensberry libel trial, Wilde said that the house was rented from 'a friend of my wife's'. It has been suggested that this was an acquaintance of the Wildes called Henrietta Lord, an early translator of Ibsen's plays,[6] but there is no evidence for this. Indeed Constance's letter of 30 July makes clear that she was actively seeking out accommodation in Worthing, with no suggestion that it might be provided by a friend. In addition, Constance learnt the reason for Miss Lord's having vacated the Haven only when she arrived at the house and heard 'bad accounts of Miss Lord's health' from one of the servants there: 'She seems to be at Matlock crippled with rheumatic gout.' If Miss Lord had been a friend, Constance would surely have already known of this.

Although the typhoid epidemic had devastated Worthing's holiday trade the previous summer, the town was, according to the *Worthing Gazette* of 8 August, doing excellent business in 1894:

> Evidences of restored confidence in the absolutely secure sanitary condition of the town have been accumulating during the past few weeks, until we have arrived at a time when the visiting public are with us in numbers fully equal to those of the corresponding period in any past year.

The paper reported that on 6 August – Bank Holiday Monday, which at that time was at the start of the month – a record 3,526 people passed through the pier turnstiles. The previous year, during the typhoid epidemic, the number had been 924. On 7 August, the chairman of the sanitary committee told the town council that the death-rate for the past three months had been 'of an even more satisfactory character' than that for the previous quarter.

The exact figure – which had not been available to the sanitary committee's chairman, but was obtained by the *Gazette* – was 8.6 per thousand, 'being splendid testimony to the extreme healthiness of the borough'. Importantly, there had been 'no death from any notifiable disease', such as typhoid.

Constance arrived at the Haven on Tuesday 7 August. The main reason that she preceded Oscar to Worthing was probably to ensure that the household was running smoothly by the time he arrived. Organising a new household was, however, a task that she herself dreaded, as she made clear to Georgina Mount Temple on 4 August, three days before she left for Worthing:

> I have today signed the agreement with Miss Lord [in the Wilde household, this was evidently woman's work], and as I have to take down linen, plate, & cutlery you can imagine how busy I am, and busy with the things that I most <u>detest</u> [underlined twice]. I wish that things would settle themselves in some sort of convenient way. I shall have to keep house for 5 weeks with strange servants, and my heart sinks at the prospect!

Once she arrived in Worthing, Constance's anxieties seem largely to have subsided, for she immediately reports to Georgina Mount Temple, 'I like Miss Lord's dear little house and Miss Walker has made us most comfortable.' (Miss Walker was presumably one of Miss Lord's servants.) The weather, however, was 'terribly windy'.

The wind continued for several days. The Watermen's Regatta, scheduled for Wednesday 8 August, had to be postponed by a day, and the conditions were still far from ideal, as the *Worthing Gazette* reported:

> Even on Thursday the atmospheric conditions, though sufficiently favourable to enable the programme to be carried out, were far from satisfying the conditions which such an occasion demands. It was bright and clear overhead, but a powerful westerly wind was blowing, and while the sailing boats in speeding over the course were materially assisted in their progress, the oarsmen found their task a very laborious one ... Owing to the difficulties encountered, the labour of getting through the programme was

a most formidable one, and the patience of the onlookers was sorely taxed by the slowness of the proceedings.[7]

Wilde arrived in Worthing a few days later. During the Queensberry libel trial, he was asked by Sir Edward Clarke, 'When was it you went down to Worthing?', and, according to the court transcript, replied, 'I think the 1st of August I went there.'[8] However this date is over a week adrift, contradicted as it is by irrefutable evidence in Constance's letters.

As we have seen, on 4 August Constance had written to tell Georgina Mount Temple that she and the boys were going to Worthing in three days' time. On 7 August, she duly wrote from the Haven, 'Here am I settled with my two dear boys and Oscar comes, I believe, on Friday [10 August].' In view of Constance's 'I believe', we cannot be certain that Oscar arrived on the projected day, but it is reasonable to assume that he did. Certainly he cannot have arrived any later, since – as we shall see in Chapter 6 – Arthur Humphreys visited the Wildes in Worthing on the Saturday.[9]

There are two possible reasons for the erroneous date Wilde gave in court. The first is that his memory was adrift – he had, after all, had much on his mind over the previous few months. The second is that his reply was incorrectly transcribed from the shorthand notes taken at the trial.[10] Errors were often introduced during the transcription process, and mis-transcribing '10 August' as '1 August' would have been an easy mistake to make.

*

In a letter to her brother Otho on 31 August, Constance provides a list of the occupants of the Haven: 'Our expenses are 10 guineas a week [about £1,050 today],[11] that is for Oscar & myself, Cyril and Vivian, Arthur Fenn,[12] cook & housemaid here, & the cook's little boy.'

The 'horrid, ugly Swiss governess' mentioned by Wilde in a letter he wrote Bosie as soon as he arrived in Worthing (see Appendix B) is absent from Constance's list. Unless this was a slip by Constance, which seems unlikely, the governess must – by 31 August, and perhaps well before – have been found to be surplus to requirements at the holiday house, not least because one of the roles of Constance's 'page-boy' Arthur Fenn was to look after Cyril and Vyvyan. Gubernatorial supervision during the family's summer holiday was thus unnecessary, and indeed almost certainly unwelcome to the children. In view of the fact that Oscar found *la Suisse* so little to his liking, perhaps she was given leave of absence, or sent back to her homeland. Either way, the Haven was presumably a more relaxed place for her departure.

Arthur Fenn is an interesting minor figure in the Wilde story and, since he has elsewhere received no more than a passing mention, a brief digression may be of interest.

Biographers of Wilde refer to Constance's 'page-boy' variously as a butler, footman, valet and factotum. Little is known about him beyond the fact that he was the servant present when the Marquess of Queensberry called at 16 Tite Street on 30 June 1894, and that he was seventeen at the time;[13] that during the Worthing holiday he 'twice made a chaos of' the manuscript of *The Importance of Being Earnest* by 'tidying up';[14] and that on 5 May 1895, the day of Wilde's arrest, he helped Robbie Ross break into two locked rooms at 16 Tite Street so that they could collect some clothing for Wilde and remove some of his papers.[15]

Arthur was probably the servant known as 'Ginger' whom seventeen-year-old Alfred Wood saw at least once during several visits that he made to Wilde's house at Tite Street early in 1893 while Constance was staying at Babbacombe with Lady Mount Temple.[16] During the Queensberry libel trial, Edward Carson questioned Wilde about a ginger-haired male servant that Wood claimed to have encountered, initially referring to this servant as a 'butler', and then as a 'boy'. Since Wilde emphatically denied that Wood had ever been to the house, he had also to deny the existence of the ginger-haired servant, as otherwise Wood's story would be substantiated. Wilde therefore claimed he had no manservant at the time; that he had never had a servant called Ginger; and that he had never called any boy by that name.[17]

Whatever his precise job specification, this junior Jeeves stayed on at the Haven after Constance and the children left. We know this because, since he was the only one of the Wildes' London servants who went with them to Sussex, he must have been the servant referred to in a letter Constance wrote to Lady Mount Temple from 16 Tite Street on 15 September: 'I am expecting the

Duncan family to lunch and as one of my servants and nearly all my silver are at Worthing, I am rather in difficulties! However I daresay we shall manage with kitchen spoons.'

Although Arthur remained in Worthing to look after Oscar, perhaps he was given the evening off on those occasions when Alphonse Conway, a boy only a year or so younger than himself, was entertained to dinner at the Haven; but not necessarily so. Miss Lord's cook presumably prepared the meal, so Wilde may not have bothered to empty the house of the other servants. Wilde was extraordinarily incautious about members of the servant classes, appearing to think that they had neither eyes nor ears.

Arthur himself must anyway have had some idea about the unconventionality of his employer's personal arrangements since, as we have seen, he seems to have encountered Alfred Wood at 16 Tite Street. Also, when Lord Queensberry called at Tite Street on 30 June 1894, it was to Arthur that Wilde said, 'This is the Marquess of Queensberry, the most infamous brute in London. You are never to allow him to enter my house again.'[18] If Arthur saw Alphonse at the Haven, therefore, he probably guessed what was going on between him and Wilde.

There is, however, another possibility with regard to Arthur Fenn's role in the Wilde household. Prurient suspicion may be an unworthy trait, but in the case of Oscar Wilde it is often justified; and it is difficult for posterity not to raise an eyebrow at the fact that the most famous ephebophile of the nineteenth century should have had a teenage valet. Seducing servants was certainly far from unknown in Victorian households, and indeed, as we saw in Chapter 1, Bosie's Oxford servant, Walter Grainger, a boy of the same age as Arthur Fenn, was seemingly brought to the Cottage at Goring-on-Thames in the summer of 1893 for the specific purpose of providing sexual recreation for Wilde.[19]

By this time Wilde seems to have taken the view that most working-class youths were willing to oblige gentlemen with charismatic, forceful personalities and open wallets – a belief supported by his experience of the louche sexual underworld in which he increasingly moved. Wilde's appetite for boys was by now voracious, so it is difficult to believe that he would not, albeit cautiously at first, have tested out a teenage boy who lived under his own roof. Indeed, if Arthur knew about Wilde's sexual tastes, as in all likelihood he did, he would probably have been surprised not to be the subject of attention. Had Arthur made it clear that he was not amenable, Wilde would doubtless have been gracious in rejection, and tipped the boy a few pounds to compensate him for the embarrassment caused. But if Arthur Fenn did indeed sometimes serve Wilde in an additional respect, he remained scrupulously discreet and loyal, since the historical record knows nothing of it.

*

The stay in Worthing was a family seaside holiday, and Wilde enjoyed spending time with his sons, of whom he was very fond. Many years later, Vyvyan wrote:

> Perhaps my father was at his best with us at the seaside. He was a powerful swimmer; he also thoroughly enjoyed sailing and fishing and would take us out with him when it was not too breezy. I do not think we took to it very much; personally I was much too concerned for the plight of the fish flapping about on the floor boards. I preferred helping my father to build sand castles, an art in which he excelled; long, rambling castles they were, with moats and tunnels and towers and battlements ... He was an exceptionally strong swimmer and has been described to me as ploughing through the waves in a rough sea at Worthing like a shark, in a way that struck awe into the onlookers.[20]

As one would expect, Constance's Worthing letters include affectionate references to Cyril and Vyvyan (whose name she always spells 'Vivian'). On 11 August, she writes to Georgina Mount Temple:

> The boys are very happy here, collecting crabs for their aquariums,[21] and looking radiant, especially Cyril whom I have never seen looking so handsome as he is just now. Flannels are so very becoming to him. School has improved both the boys enormously, and they are both of them very happy at school, but still loving their home most. I have my page-boy Arthur down here to take them out on the sands and in boats on the sea, so I am not much troubled about them.

And on 31 August she tells Otho:

> There are wonderful sands here, and Cyril generally bathes twice a day, and is becoming a famous little swimmer. There is a small lake at Bedales [Cyril's school at that time], and the boys learn to swim there but – he does not yet read with any pleasure!

Although Vyvyan is not mentioned or referred to in this brief account for Otho – only Cyril was at Bedales – Constance writes in similar terms to Georgina on 3 September, and this time Vyvyan is included:

> Cyril is marvellously well here, and bathes in the sea generally twice a day. He is as brown as a berry. Vivian does not look as well as I should like him to look, and is pale, though he is always in excellent spirits.

It would appear from even these brief comments that Cyril was the favourite son: Vyvyan is mentioned less than Cyril, and the sense of disappointment at his being less 'radiant' than his elder brother is palpable. Indeed, Vyvyan was himself aware of being the less favoured child, writing sixty years later in his autobiography:

> I was always conscious of the fact that both my father and my mother really preferred my brother to myself ... I was more sensitive than Cyril, who was a tough little animal with higher spirits than I possessed.[22]

Wilde's surviving letters from Worthing never mention Vyvyan. Cyril appears once, when Wilde records that his elder son accompanied him to a concert at the Assembly Rooms, an event described in the next chapter.

*

The family component of Wilde's Worthing holiday lasted five weeks. Although Constance had initially intended to return to London on Tuesday 4 September, it was on Wednesday 12 September that she and her sons left Worthing.[23] On 25 August, Constance had written to Georgina Mount Temple, 'We leave here on the 4th, and Oscar has written a play here, so I <u>love</u> this place now!' By the end of August, however, the proposed date has changed, for on 31 August she is writing to Otho, 'We shall [be] here till the 12th.' And on 3 September she writes to Georgina, 'Lady Wilde is very weak and will, I fear, be disappointed at our not going back to-morrow as she expected us to do.' No reason is given for the change of plan. Then, on 11 September, Constance writes, in her final letter from Worthing, 'I am going home to-morrow to see after boys [*sic*] clothes and things.'

Constance's departure date of Wednesday 12 September helps to explain the sudden flurry of correspondence between Wilde and Bosie on Saturday 8, Sunday 9 and Monday 10 September (see Chapter 4 and Appendix B).[24] Once Constance and the children had left Worthing, family obligations would at last be at an end, and Oscar was keen to put in place amusing arrangements for immediately after they had gone. Indeed, not a day was to be wasted, because in a letter to Bosie written on 8 September,[25] Wilde suggests that he and Bosie spend a few days in Dieppe, leaving on the Saturday, with Bosie perhaps coming to Worthing first, 'say on Thursday' – the day after the departure of Constance and the children. Clearly Oscar was much missing Bosie, and impatient for his return.

3

'The beauty and grace of everything': Oscar Wilde and the Worthing Festivals

'I have been much struck at the regatta, at the lifeboat demonstration, and other festivals, with the beauty and grace of everything I have seen.'
Oscar Wilde, speaking in Worthing on 13 September 1894

Oscar Wilde attended several events that took place in Worthing in the summer of 1894. We know this from a comment he made in a speech he delivered on 13 September after the Venetian Fete, at which he gave away the prizes: 'I have been much struck at the Regatta, at the Lifeboat Demonstration, and other festivals, with the beauty and grace of everything I have seen.' This remark indicates that Wilde was present not just at three major aquatic events in August and September 1894, but also at other 'festivals'.

As with any seaside resort of the time, most of the summer entertainments available in Worthing – including musical ones – were out of doors; but we will first address those that were not.

Worthing did not have a dedicated theatre in 1894, but plays and concerts were held at the Assembly Rooms in Bath Place (see illustration 27), the entrance to which was almost opposite the front door of 1 Bath Place, where Alphonse Conway's mother lived with her son and kept her small lodging house.

The Assembly Rooms had opened ten years before, in 1884. Soon after Wilde's visit, the auditorium was remodelled – in

1896–97 – and the venue renamed the New Theatre Royal.[1] A red American marble stone was laid in June 1897 by Captain A. B. S. Fraser, by then the mayor – an individual who, as we shall see, was a recurring supervisory or organisational presence at the Worthing festivals during the summer of 1894.

It is not fanciful to see Captain Alexander Bruce Siddons Fraser – to give him his full name – as a counterpoint to Wilde that summer in Worthing, indeed as the antithesis of Wilde, each man being everything that the other was not. Captain is not a very elevated military rank, equating to lieutenant in the Navy, so perhaps it was to compensate for a modest military career that Captain Fraser strutted his stuff on the small stage that was Worthing in the 1890s. Later he set his sights on a grander target, and from 1907 till 1910 this relentless municipalist was mayor of Hove. Captain Fraser may have had his reservations about Oscar when they met at the Venetian Fete in September 1894, and any doubts he had would have been amply confirmed by the events of the spring of 1895 – at which point the Captain Frasers of Britain turned against Wilde to a man.

Captain Fraser's family history is sufficiently interesting to justify a brief digression, not least because it reminds us that potential for scandal can lurk below the surface of the most apparently respectable of families. Alexander Fraser and his younger brother Campbell – also active in Worthing in 1894 – were both born in India, the two legitimate children of General Alexander Fraser and his wife Caroline. General Fraser had a long and distinguished career as a civil engineer, building railways, lighthouses, wharves and docks across India and Burma. By 1867 the marriage had broken down, and Mrs Fraser returned to London with her two sons and began writing novels under the pen-name 'Mrs Alexander'. The first, *Not While She Lives*, a novel about bigamy, was published in 1870, and a further twenty-two followed over the next quarter of a century, the last, *A Mayfair Tragedy*, being published in 1894. By 1891, Mrs Fraser and her extended family had arrived in Worthing, where the multi-generational household consisted of Mrs Fraser, her mother, her two middle-aged sons, and her younger son's wife and their four-year-old daughter, together with a butler, cook, parlour maid and nurse. Seventeen of Mrs Fraser's twenty-three novels were in three volumes. Their titles – which include *Her Plighted Troth*, *False Hearts and True* and *Purple and Fine Linen* – suggest that, like Miss Prism's three-volume novel in *The Importance of Being Earnest*, they may have been 'of more than usually revolting sentimentality'. Perhaps Captain Fraser discussed his mother's literary achievements with Worthing's distinguished visitor when they met at the Venetian Fete.

General Alexander retired in 1886 and returned to England, where he set up house with a young woman nearly forty years younger than himself called Charlotte Smith, who had two illegitimate children by him. The elder, Cecil Fraser, became a lieutenant-colonel in the Army. The younger, Bruce Fraser, became Admiral of the Fleet, First Sea Lord and Chief of the Naval Staff – the highest position in the Royal Navy – and was created Baron Fraser of North Cape. Admiral Fraser died unmarried, as did his half-brother Captain A. B. S. Fraser. When Captain Fraser was mayor of Worthing in 1896–98, his younger brother's wife served as his lady mayoress.[2]

It appears from a meeting of the town council reported in the *Worthing Gazette* on 5 September that Captain Fraser was a combative character. Alderman Cortis, chairman of the sanitary committee – who in 1890–91 had been the first mayor of Worthing – moved that nine houses in Cook's Row (see illustrations 39 and 40) be condemned and demolished. There was immediate approval from those present, followed by a spat between Alderman Cortis and Councillor Captain Fraser (the report in the *Gazette* uses indirect speech, which is here rendered as direct speech):

SEVERAL MEMBERS: Good! Hear, hear!
Alderman Cortis starts to read extracts from the Act.
COUNCILLOR FRASER *(interrupting him)*: I will second the proposition.
ALDERMAN CORTIS: I know you can be very rude.
COUNCILLOR FRASER: So can you!
THE MAYOR *(to Alderman Cortis)*: Please proceed.
ALDERMAN CORTIS: I think that is rude. I don't know what you think.

THE MAYOR: I think it is, rather.
ALDERMAN CORTIS: I was simply giving information for the benefit of those who are not so well informed.
COUNCILLOR FRASER: I seconded it so that it might be put to the vote.
ALDERMAN CORTIS: I know Councillor Captain Fraser is ready to vote at any moment.
COUNCILLOR FRASER *(warmly)*: Not for you!
ALDERMAN CORTIS: But you were ready to second it!
Councillor Fraser afterwards declined to second the motion, and Alderman Linfield undertook that duty. The motion was carried.

After that glimpse of Captain A. B. S. Fraser in petulant action, we return to the Assembly Rooms in Bath Place, where Wilde certainly attended one event, for he described the occasion briefly in a letter he wrote Bosie on 8 September.[3] This was the concert given on 7 September by the Olympian Quartet, whom Oscar refers to as 'the vagabond singers of the sands'. The *Worthing Gazette* of 12 September gives this short account:

> The four vocalists who have given performances on the sea-front during the season, and who style themselves the Olympian Quartet, had a farewell benefit concert at the Assembly Rooms on Friday evening. They had secured the patronage of the Mayor (Alderman R. Piper), Lord William [*sic*] Douglas, and Mr Oscar Wilde, and a large audience was present. Various performers assisted them, an ample and interesting programme being presented.

Bosie had left Worthing by then, so Oscar took Cyril to the concert. In his letter, Oscar told Bosie that there was applause as they entered and that the audience thought Cyril was Bosie.

There is something rather mysterious about the vagabond singers of the sands. Their activities had recently been discussed by the general purposes committee of the town council – indeed earlier in the same meeting at which Captain Fraser and Alderman Cortis sparred. The 5 September edition of the *Gazette* carried a report under the headline 'Singers on the Sea-Front'. There is a lack of clarity as to dates, but the issue seems first to have been discussed on 13 August, with the further discussion taking place after the minutes were read at a subsequent meeting.

A certain Mr J. E. Nash had written to the council to complain about the singers:

> My brother has been sent by his medical attendant to the sea-side, and is now lying seriously ill at 38, Marine Parade [this house was in the centre of Cambridge Terrace, just west of the pier – see illustration 51], and he complains most painfully of the abominable nuisance occasioned from morning to night by the itinerant street singers on the sea-front opposite his residence.

The minutes recorded that the committee had passed the following resolutions: first, 'that the Town Clerk inform Mr Nash that steps will be taken to remove the singers to other parts of the beach'; and, second, 'that the inspector be instructed not to permit any singing on the beach or Parade, between the east side of the pier and the band stand'.

After the minutes were read, there were some exchanges about these 'itinerant street singers' (the *Gazette*'s report uses indirect speech, again rendered here as direct speech):

> ALDERMAN GREEN *(laughingly)*: I suggest the substitution of the word 'country' for 'beach' in the first resolution, which would thus read: 'That the Town Clerk inform Mr Nash that steps will be taken to remove the singers to other parts of the country.' *(Laughter.)*
>
> COUNCILLOR HINE: I am sorry to hear Alderman Green speak like that, as the singers are the only attraction the beach has had. People enjoy their performances a great deal more than they do those of the Socialists on Sundays, Salvationists, and so on.
>
> ALDERMAN CORTIS: It was only a bit of pleasantry on Alderman Green's part. We must cater for all sorts. *(Hear, hear.)*
>
> COUNCILLOR FRASER: I agree with you for once. *(Laughter.)*
>
> ALDERMAN LINFIELD: The singers have been found to be very

ready to move in a case of illness. It would be very unwise to try to prevent them singing there, as a lot of people are glad to stand and listen to them, and all classes must be catered for. Councillor Haywood has suggested that the singers should use the Band Stand, but it might be better to have the Cabmen's Shelter there for them. *(Laughter.)*

This discussion increases rather than diminishes the mystery of the vagabond singers of the sands, who call to mind the decadent-looking group of singers and instrumentalists that serenaded Gustav von Aschenbach and Tadzio on the hotel terrace in Visconti's film of *Death in Venice*. However, in view of the fact that Wilde and Bosie took so much interest in the Olympian Quartet that they sponsored their concert, perhaps the Worthing singers were young and, as their name implied, 'Hellenic' – to use the word Wilde chose for Percy, the handsome boy Bosie favoured that summer.[4] Or perhaps the vagabond singers appealed to Oscar and Bosie simply because they were free spirits. Either way, it is surprising that the mayor should have wanted to co-sponsor a concert featuring this unusual and controversial group of *al fresco* singers.[5]

The Assembly Rooms also intermittently hosted touring theatrical productions. Just before the Wildes arrived, for example, the D'Oyly Carte Opera Company performed Gilbert and Sullivan's *Utopia Ltd* for two nights (3 and 4 August), while at the end of his stay – when Bosie was in town – *Charley's Aunt* occupied the theatre for three nights (1–3 October).

We do not know whether Wilde and his family went to any plays while he was in Worthing. If they did, the most likely candidate is perhaps a popular farce of the time called *The New Boy*, which was performed on 24 and 25 August. The *Worthing Gazette* of 15 August printed a preview of the event, including brief extracts from several reviews of the London production. The *Daily Telegraph* had described *The New Boy* as a 'rattling good farce' and reported that 'the audience laughed incessantly for two good hours', while the *Financial Times* said that it was 'as funny as anything London has ever seen, and everybody should see it'.

The 29 August issue of the *Gazette* carried a brief report of the production that came to Worthing:

This successful farcical comedy, the work of Mr Arthur Law,[6] was given at the Assembly Rooms on Friday and Saturday, there being also a special matinee on the latter day. The company by which it was presented had been selected and rehearsed by Mr Weedon Grossmith,[7] the original 'New Boy', and all the available merriment was successfully extracted by the performers from a play which depicts the droll adventures of a little man forced by stress of circumstances to become a boy again and go through the torments of school life.

The 'available merriment' might not have been enough to amuse Wilde, a playwright of a different character, but might have delighted Cyril and Vyvyan – or indeed Alphonse Conway, his special friend that summer, since Wilde said that he gave the boy tickets for the theatre on two occasions.[8] Regardless of which – if any – of them went to see *The New Boy*, there would have been posters advertising the play everywhere in the town,[9] and the irony of the title would not have been lost on Wilde, since the play was performed just a few days after he had met – and a few days before he seduced – a new boy of his own; and indeed a boy who lived only a few feet from the Assembly Rooms.

In the main, however, as already indicated, the entertainments on offer in Worthing in the summer of 1894 were in the open air. Three illuminated promenade concerts were held that year in the grounds of Warwick House, once the finest house in Worthing but now unoccupied and due to be demolished two years later. These concerts took place on 1, 14 and 29 August, so the second and third of them were during the time the Wildes were in Worthing.

The *Worthing Gazette* of 8 August was lukewarm about the first of the concerts. The paper thought the admittance fee of a shilling (about £5 today) was too high, and suggested that on future occasions sixpence should be charged. The Band of the Royal Marine Artillery was described as 'a skilled body of musicians, whose efforts were regarded as generally acceptable', but 'exception was taken in some quarters to the composition of the programme, which, it was declared, was not altogether suited to the occasion'. Refreshments were provided by the Aerated Bread Company.[10]

The second concert was held on 14 August, the day Bosie arrived in Worthing at the start of his first visit. The bandstand, which was situated at the eastern end of the grounds of Warwick House (see illustrations 25 and 37), was only a quarter of a mile from the Haven, so, even if none of the Wilde party paid for admission or wandered along Brighton Road to listen from the street, they would have heard the Band of the Royal Marine Artillery playing in the distance.

The next day's *Worthing Gazette* carried a detailed and evocative account that is worth reproducing in its entirety, including the list of mostly forgotten music by mostly forgotten composers. Those that subscribe to the pathetic fallacy will note that Bosie's arrival in Worthing coincided with exceptionally high and troublesome winds. However, although the weather caused problems for the organisers of the concert, English improvisation ensured that the evening was a success:

> Some six hundred people were present in the grounds of Warwick House last night, at the second of this season's illuminated promenade concerts. A powerful wind prevailed all the afternoon, threatening to prevent the holding of the event in the open air, in which case the promoters would have had recourse to the Assembly Rooms. This undesirable eventuality was, however, fortunately avoided, for the Committee pluckily persevered with their preparations, and were enabled by dint of much exertion to bring the fixture to a fairly successful issue. A catastrophe was narrowly averted, for about seven o'clock, when the several thousand lamps and lanterns were properly arranged, and were ready to be lighted, a tremendous gust of wind swept across the grounds, causing havoc in the paddock. Had the lamps been actually lighted at the time, the damage must have been very great, but in the circumstances the stock practically escaped uninjured. A hasty re-arrangement of the display had to be made, the band stand being hurriedly dismantled and removed to a more sheltered position on the lawn. It was capitally constructed in its new quarters, the busy workers being fully rewarded for their diligence by the attractive show they were enabled to present when the time arrived for the opening of the proceedings. Thus the Committee involuntarily redeemed their promise to

furnish 'new designs'. The rustic bridge in its shortened splendour was but a shadow of its former self; and, from the cause already mentioned, there was little illumination in the eastern part of the grounds, if we except the appropriate device, formed of coloured bucket lamps: 'Welcome to our Visitors!' But in the western section of the grounds the display was an exceedingly pretty one, a new feature being a brilliant search-light flashed by Mr. E. B. Blaker from the small balcony at the top of the house. The splendid band of the Royal Marine Artillery [the reporter seems to have forgotten that a week earlier he had described its efforts as no more than 'acceptable'], under the conductorship of Mr. A. Williams, Mus. Bac., Oxon., was again in attendance, its popular programme comprising the following items:

March – 'Habus à Ideè' – Neidhart
Overture – 'Zampa' – Herold
Valse – 'Gruss au Hannover' – Labitsky
Selection – 'Morocco Bound' – Carr
Selection – 'Utopia, Ltd' – Sullivan
Cornet Aria – 'I'll Follow Thee' – Farmer
Mr Huddle
Selection of Bishop's Songs – Hartmann
Polko – 'Laughing' – Conradi
Reminiscences of Ireland – Godfrey
Nautical fantasia – 'Voyage in a Troopship' – G. Miller
Galop – 'Post Horn' – Koenig

The centrally positioned Mr Huddle was presumably a cornet soloist, who played not only 'I'll Follow Thee' but also – for the composer John Hartmann specialised in arranging music for the cornet – the selection of Sir Henry Bishop's songs. These probably included Bishop's most famous composition, 'Home! Sweet Home!'.

The account in the *Gazette* ends with a repetition of the complaint about the high cost of admission, which meant that many listened from the street:

> In addition to the hundreds who entered the grounds, there were hundreds more who remained in the roadway, satisfied with an imperfect view of the feast of lanterns within, and of [*sic*] the

strains of music borne to them on the breeze. So large a crowd outside was an embodiment of the dissatisfaction which continues to exist in consequence of the unwillingness of the Committee to reduce the charge for admission to the popular figure of sixpence. Refreshments were supplied on the ground by the Aerated Bread Company.

The *Gazette*'s report of the final concert, held on 29 August, is brief, but says that the event was a 'great success' and that the 'attractive programme' was this time played by the Band of the 1st Battalion Connaught Rangers.

Music was everywhere in Worthing that summer. As we shall see from the account of various outdoor events, there were always bands present – in the case of the Lifeboat Demonstration and the Venetian Fete, no fewer than three. The Town Band itself, however, which played in a humble bandstand 250 yards to the west of the pier (see illustration 55), was apparently inferior to those elsewhere in Sussex. The first letter in the correspondence column in the 22 August issue of the *Worthing Gazette* was from one W. Hurran of 110 Beresford Road, Harringay Park, London N. Under the heading 'A Well-Intentioned Grumble', W. Hurran starts by complaining about the charges levied to stroll along the pier and listen to music in the pier pavilion – those at Hastings being lower. He then turns his attention to the Town Band:

> Then again, the Town Band. Good music, in my opinion, is more seductive in inducing people to visit a place than anything else. I would not for a moment attempt to throw cold water on the efforts of those now engaged, but there is not half enough of them; besides, a string band, without it is of very great strength, is not suitable for outdoor performances. Here, again, a leaf might well be taken out of Hastings' book, which supports a strong military band by a grant from the town and voluntary subscriptions.

Another entertainment offered in Worthing in the first half of August which may have attracted a visit from Wilde and his family was the circus. Two of the most famous circuses in Britain at that time were Lord George Sanger's and Lord John Sanger's circuses – the Sanger brothers had been in partnership until 1884 but thereafter ran competing operations – and both circuses visited Worthing in August 1894.[11]

The *Worthing Gazette* of 8 August carried a brief report on the visit of Lord George Sanger's Circus on Friday 3 August. Since this was a week before the Wildes' arrival, the family would have missed the 'ample programme, the principal feature of which was an exciting military spectacle, illustrating the war in the Soudan, [which] was capitally planned and carried out'.

However, Lord John Sanger's Circus was in town ten days later, on 13 August, and, since this was the day before the distracting Bosie arrived in Worthing, perhaps Oscar took his sons to see it. The *Worthing Gazette* of 8 August featured an advertisement for the event, announcing that 'Lord John Sanger and Son's Royal Circus, Hippodrome and Menagerie' had a 'special enormous production for the tour of 1894'. This was 'A Grand Military Spectacle: The War in Matabeleland', featuring over 300 men and horses, and 'introducing several striking and sensational incidents of the recent campaign'. In more general terms, the circus claimed to have 'the greatest Company of Riders, Acrobats, Gymnasts, Equilibrists, Fancy Skaters, Bicycle Riders, Variety Artistes, Campanologists, ever amalgamated', together with a 'the Herd of Elephants, the Team of Camels, the Flock of Llamas, Brahmin Bulls, Tapirs, Leopards, Panthers, and the Group of Forest-Bred Lions, the whole forming one of the Grandest Entertainments ever witnessed, and as presented to Her Majesty the Queen at Windsor Castle (by special command) on July 13th, 1892'.

If Oscar Wilde saw the re-creation of the war in Matabeleland, he left no record of it. The only three outdoor festivals that we know for certain he attended in Worthing that summer were three aquatic events; and it is on these that we will now concentrate.

The first of these was the Lifeboat Demonstration on Wednesday 22 August, which belatedly attracted the attention of the author of the 'Small Talk' pages in the London *Sketch* on 5 September (from which illustration 26 is taken). At the beginning and end of his paragraph the reporter refers obliquely to the previous year's typhoid epidemic in the town, when there had been about 1,500 cases and 188 people had died:

Worthing is once more basking in the sunshine of prosperity, I am glad to say. The heart of the local boarding-house keeper is rejoicing at the arrival of luggage-laden cabs. Materfamilias is again to be seen surrounded by her active young family on the beach, enjoying negro melodies. No fewer than twenty-five thousand people[12] lined the seafront at the splendid lifeboat demonstration which took place at Worthing a few days ago. Many leading townsmen worked hard for the success of the day, and their efforts were rewarded by an extremely effective *fete*. After noon the shops were closed, and the streets were crowded, hundreds of excursionists coming from Brighton by the steamboat Princess May. The Mayor of Worthing, Alderman Piper, entertained about eighty gentlemen to luncheon at the Royal Hotel, and in returning thanks for the toast of his health gracefully alluded to the efforts of Alderman Patching and Mr. H. Hargood in connection with the day's arrangements. The procession, led by coastguardsmen, comprised various fire brigades, bands, and the lifeboats from Brighton, Shoreham, Littlehampton, and Worthing. The latter executed various manoeuvres, amid great applause from the multitudes of onlookers. The coxswain of the Worthing boat was Charles Lee, who has saved no less than thirty-seven lives. A capital nautical concert took place in the evening in the presence of a large company, and fireworks completed the festivities. The secretaries, Mr Walter Paine and Mr George Piggott, have every reason to congratulate themselves on the final consummation of their onerous exertions, which have done so much to put Worthing on its feet again.

The Lifeboat Demonstration was the most important of the festivals in Worthing that summer. Not only did it interest the national press, but the *Worthing Gazette* covered the event in exceptional detail, devoting two and a half long broadsheet columns to it in the edition published on the evening of the event itself. The paper stated that no event of the kind had previously taken place on this part of the coast, hence the fact that 'Mr Hargood [the principal organiser] rightly conceived that the day might be made one of an essentially red letter character'.

The event had been planned by a 'somewhat numerous'

general committee. Fifty people are named, divided among four sub-committees – the life-boat and procession committee, the reception committee (one of whose members was Councillor A. B. S. Fraser), the finance and advertising committee, and the collecting committee.

One section of the long report is of particular interest, not only because it gives a vivid account of part of the event but also because it includes a reference to Wilde:

THE LAUNCH

The procession having arrived in South-street, the sailors and soldiers marched on to reserve an enclosure for the lifeboats, and the firemen having dismounted from their engines they also proceeded to assist in that duty. Shortly after three o'clock, the four boats [these were the Worthing, Shoreham, Littlehampton and Brighton lifeboats] having been drawn on to the beach to the east of the Pier, and the massed bands having played a verse of the National Anthem, the signal was given for the launch, and the lifeboats glided simultaneously into the water to the loud hurrahs of the spectators and the strains of 'Rule Britannia' played by the bands. At this time, the Parade between Bath-place and Bedford-Row and the shore half of the Pier was filled with one vast concourse of people. The placid sea was dotted with small rowing and sailing craft; and eastward a particularly clear view of Brighton was obtainable, the *Princess May* being seen in the distance approaching. It was a very pretty sight as the four red, white, and blue boats, with their blue and white oars, and the crews, in their cork jackets and their caps of a vivid scarlet, made their way seawards. Both on sea and land the sight was a most picturesque one; among those who viewed it was Mr Oscar Wilde, who is now on a visit to Worthing, and was one of the occupants of a small rowing boat busily flitting about.

Since Bosie was in Worthing at that point, he was almost certainly one of the occupants of the 'small rowing boat', as very likely were Constance, Cyril and Vyvyan. Alphonse's memory at the time of the statement he gave Queensberry's solicitors in March 1895 was that he had met Wilde around 20 August. If that date was correct

– or if the date was earlier – then it is possible that Alphonse was in the rowing boat too, if it was not too small to contain six or seven people. Indeed, even if the word 'occupant' did not itself suggest passivity, the busily flitting nature of the boat's progress suggests that someone other than Oscar – or indeed Bosie – was at the oars. During the Queensberry libel trial, Wilde said that Constance saw Alphonse 'constantly'. If this was true, then it appears that Wilde integrated Alphonse fairly fully into the family holiday.

The launch of the lifeboats was followed by two lifeboat races. The first was a rowing race, and the second was meant to be a sailing race, but 'in the absence of the necessary breeze, the oars had to be resorted to after a part of the course had been completed'. The Worthing lifeboat won the first race 'by a good two lengths', and in the second race it 'had an easy win'. In both races Shoreham came second, Littlehampton third and Brighton last. After 'the events on the sea-front had been brought to a close' there was 'a new source of diversion' in South Street, where 'a large body of local and visiting firemen … went through a most interesting series of drills'.

The bands that played during the afternoon were the Band of HMS *Vincent*, on the Pier Head; the Band of the H Company of Volunteers, on the Parade opposite the Steyne Hotel; and the Band of the Brighton Volunteer Fire Brigade, which played on the lawn of the Royal Hotel, before moving to a position opposite the town hall for the Fire Brigade drills.

The final paragraph of the *Gazette*'s report summarises the rest of the day's events:

> At half-past five o'clock the prizes were presented in the Pier Pavilion by the Mayoress (Mrs Piper), this event having been preceded by a nautical concert, those who contributed to the programme including The Pier Band, Miss Edith Chaplin, Mr Armstrong, and thirty young sailors (boys from the Richmond-road School) who in their smart naval attire attracted much attention as they passed through the streets, a few minutes earlier, under the direction of the Head Master, Mr A. W. Woolgar. As a fitting conclusion of an eventful day, a grand illumination of the Pier by Brock and Co of the Crystal Palace,[13] is promised this evening.

[This 'illumination of the pier' was the firework display referred to by *The Sketch*.]

The second of the aquatic festivals that Wilde attended was the Worthing Annual Regatta, which was held on Wednesday 5 September. As we shall see in the next chapter, Bosie left Worthing at some point very early in September, and probably before this event took place, but again perhaps Alphonse Conway joined the Wilde family on this occasion, either as part of the crowd on the beach or on one of the small boats viewing the event from the sea.

The weather for the Annual Regatta was perfect, according to the report published in the *Worthing Gazette* the same evening:

> Under exceptionally favourable conditions Worthing Annual Regatta was held this afternoon. The morning opened brightly, and although about midday some ominous clouds made their appearance, the danger which their presence betokened speedily disappeared, and the patrons of the fixture found themselves favoured with an afternoon of perfect brilliancy. To spectators of the scene the genial surroundings afforded unalloyed delight, while to those who took a more than passive part in the proceedings the conditions were equally favourable. There was, when the races commenced, scarcely a ripple upon the surface of the sea, and for the rowing contests the state of the water was perfection itself. For the sailing matches, however, the state of affairs was not peculiarly well adapted, for there was at first scarcely a breath of wind, and the progress of the boats over the course was a very slow matter, from their point of view though, a considerable alteration for the better set in a little later on. The scene on the front possessed all the elements of picturesqueness. Promenaders found their way to the Pier; there was the customary large crowd on the beach, east and west of the structure, and on the sea was an unusually large number of rowing boats and small sailing craft.

There were two bands in attendance at the regatta – the Rhine Band, 'which played upon the Pier'; and Mr G. Wright's Brass Band, 'which was stationed on the Parade, opposite the Marine Hotel'. The ubiquitous Captain A. B. S. Fraser was on the regatta's executive committee and was the judge of rowing, and Captain C. E. Fraser was also on the executive committee.

The third aquatic event that Wilde attended was the lamp-lit water carnival – the Venetian Fete – held on Thursday 13 September, at the end of which he gave away the prizes. The fete took place on the day Oscar had suggested for Bosie's return to Worthing prior to the trip to Dieppe,[14] so it may well be that Bosie attended the event and was present in the pavilion at the sea end of the pier (see illustrations 28 and 48) – which had a 'pretty miniature stage and a comfortable auditorium capable of accommodating an audience of 500'[15] – to hear Wilde's speech. Perhaps Alphonse was in the audience too, quietly proud of his friendship with Worthing's famous visitor.

The account of the Venetian Fete that appeared in the *Worthing Gazette* of 19 September is worth reproducing almost in its entirety – only a few lists of names being omitted – not only because it vividly evokes this enchanting occasion but also because it gives us a delightful glimpse of Oscar during the last largely carefree summer of his life (the report makes use of subheadings in a way that looks peculiar to modern eyes):

WATER CARNIVAL AT WORTHING

Whatever form next season's attractions may assume, a Venetian fete will of a certainty find a place in Worthing's list of fixtures. A spectacle of this description was provided on Thursday evening, and within its too narrow limits it proved such an emphatic success that its repetition in future years is assured. It was undertaken at short notice by a Committee consisting of Councillor Captain Fraser [and thirteen others]; with Captain C. E. Fraser, G. R. Etherton, and T. E. Hetherington as a Sub-Committee. The whole length of the pier was brilliantly illuminated with Japanese lanterns and bucket lamps, and at the entrance to the structure, over the gateway, was the device, in coloured lights: 'Go it, Worthing!' Among those who gave useful assistance in illuminating the Pier were [nine names are given]. At the Royal Hotel, the Pier Hotel, Stanhoe Hall, and other establishments on the front, there were effective illuminations, and there is little doubt that, had more extended notice been given, the movement would

have been more generally supported, and a really brilliant display presented. The chief feature of the evening's entertainment was a
PROCESSION OF ILLUMINATED BOATS
nearly twenty having entered for the prizes offered by the Committee. These comprised [a full list of the boats and their owners follows]. The promoters were favoured with a beautiful night, and the pretty spectacle was witnessed by some thousands of people on the Parade and beach; while on the Pier, where the ordinary tolls were suspended and a charge of sixpence made for admission, 1,330 people had congregated. The competing boats assembled opposite Warwick-buildings, and a rocket was fired from the Pier-head as a signal for the start. The sight, as the boats proceeded in a line in a westward direction, was an exceedingly pretty one. Some novel designs were displayed in the illumination of the boats, and coloured fire was burnt and discharged on the journey, while from Mr Ralli's boat a powerful electric search-light was flashed. The marshals of the procession were Mr Lang, Chief Officer of Coastguards at Worthing; Mr R. J. Billett, his predecessor in that post; and Mr William Paine, Captain of the Britannia Rowing Club. Voting cards were issued to the public with the request that each voter might give his or her opinion as to which were the three best boats, and announcing that the prizes would be awarded accordingly. By this means
THE PUBLIC BECAME THE JUDGES
and increased interest was taken in the result. A very large number of tickets were filled up in the manner required, collected at a specified time, and counted by the Committee, the result being as follows:

> Mr C. R. Ramsay   1
> Mr G. A. Ralli   2
> Mr Marshall   3

At the head of the procession was a steam launch containing Mr G. F. Wright's Band; in the Pavilion the Pier Band played a selection of music; and about halfway down the Pier Mr H. Binstead's Band was stationed.
MR OSCAR WILDE DILATES ON WORTHING'S CHARMS
At the close of the spectacle a concert was given in the Pier Pavilion, and the prizes were distributed by Mr Oscar Wilde,

who has been on a visit to Worthing for some weeks past. In afterwards proposing a vote of thanks to the Committee, he congratulated Worthing on the extremely beautiful scene of that evening. Worthing, he said, had already arranged some extremely pretty shows. He had been much struck at the Regatta, at the Lifeboat Demonstration, and other festivals, with the beauty and grace of everything he had seen. He thought, however, there was one thing that marred the Regatta. There was a sailing boat, not belonging to Worthing, but coming from some wicked, tasteless spot, bearing a huge advertisement of a patent pill. He hoped that boat would never be allowed to enter Worthing again (much laughter). He could not help feeling the change that had taken place this year in the town, and expressing the great pleasure it gave visitors to return. He considered that such a charming town would become one of the first watering places on the South Coast. It had beautiful surroundings and lovely long walks, which he recommended to other people, but did not take himself (laughter). Alluding to the

EXCELLENT WATER SUPPLY,

he said he was told that the total abstainers who visited Worthing were so struck with the purity and excellence of the water[16] that they wished everybody to drink nothing else (laughter). Above all things he was delighted to observe in Worthing one of the most important things, having regard to the fashion of the age – the faculty of offering pleasure. To his mind few things were as important as a capacity for being amused, feeling pleasure, and giving it to others. He held that whenever a person was happy he was good, although, perhaps, when he was good he was not always happy (laughter). There was no excuse for anyone not being happy in such surroundings. This was his first visit, but it would certainly not be his last (applause).

Captain A. B. S. Fraser acknowledged the vote of thanks on behalf of the Committee, and also proposed a similar compliment to Mr Wilde for his kindness in presenting the prizes, the proceedings then coming to an end.

Wilde's speech at the Venetian Fete was of sufficient interest also to attract a commentary in the 'Local Notes' column on another page of the same issue of the *Gazette*. The writer of these notes begins by repeating much of the information already given in the report of Wilde's speech, to which he adds brief comments of his own. He writes that 'our distinguished visitor has perceived beauty in all that the community has been privileged to put before his gaze', before noting Wilde's remark about the sailing boat advertising the patent pill and the fact that it provoked much laughter – 'thereby, we fear, increasing the agony already endured by Mr Wilde'. (This is a non sequitur, since Wilde was obviously making a joke.) He adds that 'it is certain that a tremendous outrage was perpetrated upon that gentleman's aesthetic instincts by the shameless spectacle here alluded to'. He then repeats Wilde's comments about Worthing's having lovely long walks and the 'faculty of offering pleasure' and adds pointlessly – but perhaps facetiously – 'Praise from Mr Oscar Wilde is praise indeed.'

In his final paragraph, the writer enters fresh territory:

Time was when Mr Oscar Wilde and his movements occupied no inconsiderable space in the public journals; but less attention has of late been given to him and his utterances. There are, however, frequent references to him in the prints of the day, showing that he is still held in remembrance as furnishing readable copy. Thus the *Globe* [a London evening newspaper] of Friday evening: 'Oscar's very latest role is that of patron of aquatic enterprise. At Worthing, last evening, he presented the prizes for the best decorated boat in a Venetian fete, and made the highly original observation that anything so pretty he had never seen before. It was not brilliant, but then no-one expects the great wit to say brilliant things in the provinces.'

Captious criticism, this. The writer should rather have given Mr Wilde praise for his good nature and credited him with his epigrammatic utterance: 'He held that whenever a person was happy, he was good; although, perhaps, when he was good he was not always happy.'

Although the writer is careful to be civil, the tone is somewhat arch; and it would appear from some of his asides – including the contradictory passage in which he suggests that people were losing interest in Oscar – that he may not have been entirely enamoured of Worthing's famous visitor. He does not make this explicit; but then in those days, as now, local journalists were more guarded in expressing their views than their national counterparts.

The Venetian Fete was the last major aquatic event of that summer, but a similarly decorative festival of a land-based nature was held the following week, on Wednesday 26 September. Wilde must have been aware of it and may well have been present, perhaps with Alphonse Conway – unless that was the night the two of them stayed at the Albion Hotel in Brighton, which, according to Queensberry's Plea of Justification, was 'on or about the twenty-seventh day of September'. Certainly, if Wilde did attend this event it was not with Constance and the children, who had left Worthing by then. Nor was Bosie in Worthing at that point – as we shall see, he returned to Sussex on 30 September.

This event in question was an Illuminated Cycle Procession, 'carried out in connection with the Excelsior Cycling Club'. Prizes were 'offered by the President of the Club, Councillor Captain A. B. S. Fraser'. The procession was led by Mr G. F. Wright's band, which had also played at the Annual Regatta and the Venetian Fete. This time it 'rode in Mr Town's brake, Harkaway'. The report in the *Worthing Gazette* of 3 October notes that 'considerable ingenuity was displayed in the decoration of the machines', with a sailing boat being a favourite design. 'The New Woman was in evidence' – her newness presumably being demonstrated by her being bold enough to ride a bicycle in a public procession – and some of the riders wore fancy dress: there was a Yankee millionaire, a Nabob, Tommy Atkins, sailors and a Chinaman. Some of the bicycles and tricycles had placards with mottos on them such as 'Go it, Worthing!', 'Good luck to Worthing!' and 'Advance, Worthing!'

The procession went through the western part of the town and ended up by the pier, where the judging took place and the prizes were awarded in two categories: tricycles and bicycles. The judge of the tricycles was Mr G. A. Ralli – whose boat had won second prize at the Venetian Fete – while Captain C. E. Fraser judged the bicycles. The tricycles, which, being more stable, afforded more opportunity for creativity, were the more ambitious. Mr E. Laker won the first prize in the tricycle category, 'his machine representing a yacht, no fewer than 160 lanterns being employed'. The second prize went to Mr A. Hewer, who 'had designed a torpedo boat, carrying 93 lanterns'; while Mr William Paine's entry, which won third prize, was 'a gondola bearing 72 lights'. After the judging, the procession made its way through the eastern part of the town – passing within 150 yards of the Haven when it turned right into Brighton Road out of Farncombe Road – before ending up again at the pier, where the National Anthem was played, after which the crowd dispersed. The *Gazette* summarised the event as follows: 'Bucket lamps were found almost impossible to manipulate, but a brilliant show of lanterns was made, and the beautiful spectacle was greatly admired by the thousands of people who went forth to see it.'

The Illuminated Cycle Procession was the last event in Worthing that summer that could be described as a festival. Indeed, by then the season was almost over, and most of the holidaymakers were gone.

As we shall see in the next chapter, Bosie returned to Worthing on 30 September, but was soon bored and restless. Worthing in October would have seemed very quiet and provincial, and with the onset of autumn there would have been few ephebic attractions on the beach. So Oscar came under pressure to take Bosie to Brighton.

Bosie's final, brief visit coincided with the Worthing Poultry Show, which was held on 3 and 4 October under the aegis of the Worthing Fanciers' Association. The *Worthing Gazette* of 3 October carried a report of the first day. There were 884 exhibits in five categories: poultry, pigeons, rabbits, cavies (guinea pigs) and cage birds. Before the show opened, there was a luncheon for the committee and officials, held at the headquarters of the association in Paragon Street. Even at the chilly end of the Worthing summer, Councillor Captain A. B. S. Fraser was not found wanting. He was one of the vice-presidents of the Worthing Fanciers' Association, and he took the chair at the luncheon.

Sadly, 'De Profundis', though informative on a few other matters relating to Worthing, is silent on the subject of the Worthing Poultry Show. Indeed, perhaps the presence in the town of so prosaic and quasi-agricultural an event, so different from the lamp-lit charm of the Venetian Fete – and held, to add insult to injury, at the Literary Institution in Montague Street – affronted Oscar's sensibilities as much as the sailing boat that polluted the regatta with its advertisement for the patent pill.

Whether or not the poultry show was the final straw, it was on its second day that Oscar Wilde and Lord Alfred Douglas packed their bags and decamped to Brighton. The time for festivals was over.

4

'You will come, won't you?': Bosie

'But you will come, won't you? At any rate for a short time – till you are bored.'
>> Oscar Wilde to Lord Alfred Douglas, 9 August 1894

Lord Alfred Douglas visited Worthing three times during the summer of 1894. We know this because, in reference to Bosie's final visit, Wilde writes in 'De Profundis': 'the two [other] visits you had paid to me had ended'.[1]

Information from the diaries and letters of Wilfrid Scawen Blunt and from the two longest surviving letters that Oscar wrote to Bosie from Worthing (see Appendix B) – together with some material from elsewhere and a little informed conjecture – allow us to piece together the dates of Bosie's three stays in Worthing.[2]

The day before Oscar left London for Worthing – thus, almost certainly on 9 August[3] – Oscar wrote to Bosie strongly urging him to join him in the town:

> I go down to Worthing tomorrow ... When you come to Worthing, of course all things will be done for your honour and joy, but I fear you may find the meals, etc., tedious. But you will come, won't you? at any rate for a short time – till you are bored.

As soon as Wilde arrived in Sussex he wrote in haste to contradict his earlier suggestion.[4]

The reason for the change of heart was that when he got to Worthing he was exposed to the full horror of a conventional family seaside holiday – not only were his own children 'tedious' at meals but, to make matters worse, the household included an omnipresent 'horrid, ugly Swiss governess' who was 'quite impossible'. The thought of Bosie, 'the gilt and graceful boy', trapped in such a hellish manifestation of domesticity appalled him. 'Don't come here,' he told Bosie. 'I will come to you.'

Nonetheless, Bosie arrived in Worthing only four days after Wilde.

Bosie's movements between 5 and 13 August 1894 are documented in the diary and letters of the poet and traveller Wilfrid Scawen Blunt. Blunt, who was much older than Bosie – he was nearly fifty-four – refers to Bosie as his cousin, but he was a distant one, the first cousin of Bosie's mother's uncle.

On Sunday 5 August, Bosie was one of several guests at Crabbet Park, Blunt's house near Crawley in West Sussex; and the next day Bosie and Blunt set off on an expedition to Shakespeare's grave:

> This was followed by a pilgrimage to Stratford-on-Avon, which I had long intended, and which I now accomplished, going by road with my four horses, and taking my cousin Alfred Douglas with me, stopping at several friends' houses on our way, Lady Hayter's at South Hill, and Dr Watney's at Buckholt, and Mr Harvey's at Woodstock. Then across the Wolds by Chipping Norton, to Stanway, where we were amongst relations, and so on, two days later, to Stratford [where they arrived on 13 August] ... Here Alfred left me in a hurry to return to London, while I stayed on fulfilling the object of my pilgrimage by reading the Sonnets at the poet's tomb.[5]

Blunt alters the facts in one respect, since Bosie's own later account makes clear that he was present while Blunt knelt by Shakespeare's tomb for an hour and read some of the sonnets 'to himself'; and that, 'being at the time ... a typical undergraduate', he was 'impudent enough' to tell Blunt that he was making an exhibition of himself. Blunt 'squashed' him, and Bosie later apologised and felt ashamed of himself.[6]

The date evidence from Blunt's diary is confirmed in two letters Blunt wrote during this trip – a trip that involved camping and associated rigours to which Bosie was not accustomed. Indeed, the effete young poet and the veteran of much travel in North Africa and the Middle East were an ill-assorted pair, and on Saturday 11 August Blunt wrote to his daughter Judith:

> Alfred is a simple travelling companion, all things being new to him, from getting up in the morning to going to bed without dinner at night. He is surprised when it rains and surprised when drops fall on his pillow and surprised when the sun rises in the East at 4 o'clock ... Alfred shows signs of distress but I feel full of going – so do the mares.[7]

On Wednesday 15 August, Blunt wrote to his wife:

> I left Stanway on Monday morning [13 August] and drove with all speed to Stratford where we sat on Shakespeare's tomb. I read his sonnets as an appropriate form of prayer and then I went on alone to Shipston on Stour, he [Douglas] being tired of the journey and having an engagement to stay with Oscar Wilde at Worthing.[8]

Back in London on 14 August, Bosie wrote a notorious postcard to his father that was later to be read out during the libel trial. It was addressed to Carter's Hotel, but Queensberry was in Scotland by then, so it did not reach him for several days. There are various intermediate postmarks, but the original postmark is 14 August.[9] Like most of the correspondence between them at this period it was childish and undignified, but it upped the stakes in mentioning for the first time the possibility of Wilde suing for libel. Bosie also threatened to shoot his father:

> If OW has to prosecute you for libel in the criminal courts you would get several years' penal servitude for your outrageous libels ... If you try to assault me I shall defend myself with a loaded revolver which I always carry, and if I shoot you or he shoots you, we should be completely justified as we should be acting in

self-defence against a violent and dangerous rough, and I think if you were dead not many people would miss you. A.D.

It might have saved a great deal of trouble if the quarrel between Douglas and his father had indeed ended in a shoot-out, preferably to the death.

Queensberry replied on 21 August, calling his son a 'reptile' and claiming not to have read the postcard, which was, indeed, barely legible. Bosie replied by telegram, whereupon Queensberry, on 28 August, told Bosie that he had asked Carter's not to forward any more communications from his son, but to tear them up. He refers to Wilde as 'a horrible brute' and says his son's behaviour suggests that he (Bosie) 'must be demented', which, amusingly, Queensberry attributes to there being 'madness on your mother's side'.[10] (Bosie was in Worthing at the time these letters were posted, but Queensberry may not have known this, and perhaps both sides of the correspondence were being forwarded.)

Wilde was also in London on 14 August, to sign the contract for *Oscariana*, and, since Bosie was a witness,[11] he and Wilde almost certainly travelled down to Worthing together later that day.

The fact that Bosie was in Worthing only four days after Oscar had told him not to come indicates that there was further discussion in correspondence that has not survived. This seems to have included their arriving at a solution that would mitigate the worst aspects of the family holiday – namely that Bosie stay at a hotel, and so be partially separated from the routines of the Wilde household.

In the letter he wrote just before he left London, Oscar had warned Bosie that the house in Worthing was 'very small', with no writing room. This information must have come to Wilde in a letter written to him by Constance as soon as she arrived. Although by our standards the Haven was a decent size, it evidently had less accommodation than Wilde was used to at 16 Tite Street.

Bosie, writing in 1940, asserted that Wilde 'wrote the whole of *The Importance of Being Earnest* at a house in Worthing where I stayed with him, and most of it while I was sitting in the same room with him'.[12] However, Bosie is not stating unequivocally that during his visits to Worthing he always stayed at the Haven, but merely that at some point he stayed there – which he certainly did on his second and third visits.

Vyvyan, Wilde's younger son, told Rupert Croft-Cooke many years later that Bosie had 'stayed with the family in Worthing' and played with him and his brother.[13] However, Vyvyan said he could remember very little about the Worthing holiday – he had been seven at the time – and in his own autobiography, published in 1954, there is no direct reference to Worthing, although the general paragraph (quoted in Chapter 2) about his father being 'at his best with us at the sea-side' must refer partly to the summer of 1894.[14] Bosie would often have been at the Haven in the daytime during his first visit, and in Vyvyan's hazy memory of events sixty years later this may have translated into the belief that he had slept there also.

Either way, there is conclusive evidence that Bosie stayed at a hotel during at least part of the first visit.

In the 'storm letter', written on 10 September,[15] soon after Bosie's first stay in Worthing ended, Wilde describes how, drenched to the skin after they finally got back safely to Worthing pier, he, Alphonse and Stephen 'flew to the hotel for hot brandy and water'. He says he found there a letter for Bosie 'from dear Henry',[16] which the hotel had forgotten to forward and which he now enclosed. Henry's letter would not have been addressed to the hotel unless Bosie had been staying there – and indeed for a period long enough for him to be using it as an address for correspondence. Therefore, during some or all of his first visit, Bosie must have stayed at whichever hotel it was that provided the brandy on the night of 9 September.

The hotel in question was probably the Marine (see illustration 29), since we know from evidence Wilde gave at the Queensberry trial that Bosie, Alphonse and one of the other boys lunched there on the second day of their acquaintance – and Wilde's use of the definite article in the 'storm letter' suggests that the hotel to which they went that night was one that Wilde and Bosie regularly used. In addition, Wilde makes it clear that it was to Worthing pier that they returned in their sailing boat that night, and the Marine Hotel's situation just opposite the pier was ideally located for 'shipwrecked mariners' in need of hot brandy.

Constance refers only once to Bosie in her letters of the Worthing period. Writing to Lady Mount Temple on 17 August, three days after Bosie arrived for his first visit, she confines herself to seven words: 'Lord Alfred Douglas is staying with Oscar.' The lack of any supplementary comment tells its own story; and indeed Constance's saying that Bosie is 'staying with Oscar' rather than 'staying with us' distances her from the role of co-host. Constance was, however, also addressing the facts of the matter. Even if not actually 'staying with Oscar', he was certainly not staying with Constance.

A literal interpretation of Constance's curious phrase would have Wilde absenting himself from the Haven and taking a room in the same hotel as Bosie. Comparable arrangements were far from unprecedented. There was, as we saw in Chapter 1, the notorious month of March 1893, when Wilde stayed with Bosie at the Savoy, and Constance saw her husband only when she brought his mail to the hotel; and the Albemarle Hotel is a recurring presence in Wilde's story during the first half of the nineties.

In a small town like Worthing, however, abandonment of the marital household in favour of a hotel would have been more conspicuous than in London, and indeed more humiliating for Constance; and there are also the Wilde children to consider. It is true that Oscar never cared much about appearances and, by this stage of their marriage, often not about his wife's feelings either. Nonetheless, this interpretation of Constance's remarks must be regarded as improbable.

Although it is likely that Bosie stayed at a hotel throughout his first visit, it is just possible that initially he was accommodated at the Haven, but that relationships in the house became so uncomfortable that Oscar relocated him to the Marine Hotel.

Even if Oscar continued to sleep at the Haven, he might just as well not have been there for all the benefit Constance had of his company. The relationship between Constance and Bosie was by now not a comfortable one. Bosie himself referred to this in the context of this particular holiday: 'I had great fun [in Worthing], though the last few days the strain of being a bone of contention between Oscar and Mrs Oscar began to make itself felt.'[17] Wilde later expressed similar views, in a general rather than a Worthing context: 'Our friendship had always been a source of distress to her: not merely because she had never liked you personally, but because she saw how your continual companionship altered me, and not for the better.' However, he added that Constance had always been 'most gracious and hospitable' towards Bosie.[18]

*

Most of what we know about Bosie's first visit comes from the 'storm letter', in which Wilde describes being caught in a storm the previous day (a Sunday) when he, Alphonse Conway and Alphonse's friend Stephen were returning from Littlehampton in a sailing boat. The letter allows us to calculate fairly accurately when Bosie's first visit ended, since Wilde refers to Percy's having left the day after Bosie.[19] Clearly this was a recent event, so Bosie must himself have left fairly soon before the letter was written on 10 September – thus sometime in early September. Bosie's first stay in Worthing was therefore of about three weeks' duration.

Other evidence suggests that the most likely date for Bosie's departure was 3 or 4 September. On 3 September, as we shall see in Chapter 6, Constance wrote to tell Georgina Mount Temple that she was lonely and depressed, which suggests that Bosie was still in Worthing. Then, on 4 September, Constance's clergyman friend Leslie Lilley came to stay, and it is reasonable to assume that the coast was clear of Bosie in time for Lilley's visit.

During Bosie's first stay he and Wilde regularly went out in a sailing boat – sometimes with Cyril and then, after 20 August, often with Alphonse, Stephen and Percy also. Percy is of interest, because after Bosie left Worthing, Alphonse referred to him as 'the Lord's favourite'. By the time he made this remark, Alphonse was involved sexually with Wilde, and probably had no illusions about Bosie's sexual preferences. Nonetheless, there is nothing in Alphonse's innocent, everyday comment to suggest that Bosie had seduced Percy. Percy was clearly a good-looking boy – the fact that Wilde uses the word 'Hellenic' of him in the 'storm letter' suggests as much – and Bosie evidently took a special liking to him; but the probability is that he left Worthing with his virtue intact.

We know about Bosie's second visit mainly in the context of the three- or four-day trip to Dieppe that he and Wilde took in mid-September. There is no doubt that the trip proposed by Wilde in the letter he wrote Bosie on 8 September[20] actually took place, because, when asked during the Queensberry trial whether he was 'continuously' in Worthing during August and September 1894, Wilde replied, 'I went once to Dieppe, that was for four days.'[21] In the letter of 8 September, Wilde indicated that the trip to Dieppe – a town he advertised to Bosie as 'very amusing and bright' – could be for only three days, because he was so busy.

As we have seen, Wilde suggested that Bosie either meet him on Saturday 15 September in Newhaven – which then, as now, was the port for ferries to Dieppe – or come to Worthing for a couple of days first so that they could go on to Newhaven together.

If Bosie followed Oscar's suggestion, then he probably arrived in Worthing on 13 September; and if Wilde and Bosie indeed took the ferry from Newhaven on 15 September, then the three days of Wilde's original suggestion and the four days he referred to in court can reasonably be conflated into a stay of three nights / four days – in which case they returned to England on Tuesday 18 September. It is reasonable to assume that Bosie then stayed on in Worthing for a while. This time Bosie – for reasons of both economy and convenience – would certainly have stayed at the Haven. Constance and the boys had left, so the Haven would have become a more relaxing and spacious environment. Perhaps Bosie stayed on in Worthing almost until Oscar took Alphonse away to Brighton for the night, which, according to Queensberry's Plea of Justification, was on or around 27 September.

The dates of Bosie's third and final visit to Worthing can be given with precision, since it is clear from 'De Profundis' that he arrived – unexpectedly – on a Sunday in late September.[22] Wilde does not specify the length of this final stay,[23] but the Sunday Bosie arrived can only have been 30 September; and we know that it was on 4 October that Oscar and Bosie themselves left Worthing for Brighton, where they initially stayed at the Metropole (see illustration 31).[24]

Although Bosie again stayed at the Haven during this brief final visit, this – for a specific reason – did not apply on the first night. Bosie's second visit to Worthing seems to have lodged in his mind the idea that the Haven, now occupied only by Wilde, Arthur the 'page-boy' and Miss Lord's servants, would be a convenient location for illicit pleasures. As a result, when he 'suddenly' appeared for a third visit, it was with a 'companion' who he proposed should stay with him in the house. Wilde, however, was adamant that he should not. When he reminds Bosie of the occasion in 'De Profundis', he says, 'I (you must admit now quite properly) absolutely declined.'[25]

It is unlikely that this was simply because Bosie's companion was embarrassingly young and from a different social class – though he was almost certainly both – since Oscar and Bosie had always taken a relaxed approach to introducing lower-class youths and young men into all sorts of establishments, from the Savoy Hotel downwards. Indeed, in Wilde's case this had included his own house at 16 Tite Street.

However, Wilde had a particular reason not to want to attract attention to dubious goings-on at the Haven, for, as we shall see in the next chapter, it was at this period – with Constance and the children gone – that he several times entertained the sixteen-year-old Alphonse Conway to dinner and sexual intimacy. Indeed, the odd eyebrow may already have been raised at Alphonse's visits, and perhaps not only by Miss Lord's servants at the Haven. In 1894 the houses in the Esplanade terrace faced onto open ground, and the comings and goings of visitors would not have been private. If a second and very possibly younger boy was seen visiting Wilde's house – in the company of a slender young man with a 'flowerlike sort of beauty'[26] – the neighbours might reasonably have concluded that the Haven was a nest of pederasts.

Although he was not prepared to entertain Bosie and his companion at the Esplanade, Wilde records that, having 'no option in the matter', he did entertain the two of them 'elsewhere, and not in my own home'; and Bosie and his friend must then have spent the night at a hotel in the town. The next day, a Monday – thus, 1 October – Bosie's companion 'returned to the duties of his profession'; which, we may assume, was not an exalted one.[27] Bosie then stayed three nights at the Haven, before Oscar succumbed to the pressure to take him to Brighton.

As we shall see in Chapter 7, Bosie's third visit to Worthing was unwelcome to Oscar, who wanted to devote his attention to *The Importance of Being Earnest*. Alphonse Conway was a less demanding holiday companion, since presumably he turned up when invited, but did not bother Wilde otherwise.

By the start of the autumn, however, the town of Worthing had served its purpose. After 4 October 1894, when he and Bosie left for Brighton, Wilde never set foot there again. Other very different destinations lay ahead.

*

In his mid-sixties, Lord Alfred Douglas returned to Sussex. Between 1935 and 1944 he lived in Hove, and he spent the last three months of his life staying with Edward and Sheila Colman at Old Monk's Farm, Lancing,[28] where he died on 30 March 1945. In view of the fact that Bosie's conversion to Roman Catholicism in 1911 was a factor in the repudiation of his homosexual past – and that his atheist father, Queensberry, and Wilde himself, albeit in ambivalent circumstances, had both been received into the faith just before their deaths – it is ironic that a Catholic church now stands in the former garden of Old Monk's Farm and that its priest lives in the house where Bosie died – a house just four miles from the Esplanade in Worthing, where Bosie had stayed with Oscar Wilde half a century before.

5

'A happy, good-humoured companion': Alphonse

'He had been a very pleasant, happy, good-humoured companion to myself and my children.'
     Oscar Wilde under cross-examination on 3 April 1895

The lower-class boys with whom Wilde was involved during the first half of the 1890s have generally not been thought deserving of sympathetic attention, and have often been treated as if they were little more than corrupt sexual fodder for Wilde. H. Montgomery Hyde, for example, writes, 'So far as is known, [Wilde] never debauched any innocent young men. All his accomplices ... were already steeped in vice before Wilde met them.'[1] Richard Ellmann says, 'Except for Shelley, they were prostitutes, to be bought and sold.'[2]

Alphonse Conway, however, does not deserve to be memorialised in such terms, and this chapter will give an account of a relationship that was very different from any other in Wilde's life.

When Edward Carson, at the Queensberry libel trial, asked Wilde how old Alphonse was, Wilde replied, 'About eighteen.' This was disingenuous. A document has recently become available that gives Alphonse's date of birth. This is the record at St Andrew's church, Worthing of the boy's baptism on 28 March 1891,[3] which records his date of birth as 10 July 1878. He was thus twelve years old when he was belatedly baptised, and about six weeks past his sixteenth birthday when he met Wilde. On the baptism record Alphonse's mother's first names are shown as Julia Sarah. His father's name was Alphonse also, and he is shown as 'deceased'.

There is confirmation of Alphonse's age in another source, the April 1891 census, the only census in which there is any trace of either Alphonse or his mother. Sarah Conway is the head of the household at 2 Warman Terrace, Teville Road, Worthing. She is a widow, forty-two years old. She was born in Petworth, twenty miles from Worthing. She is listed as 'of independent means', a phrase that indicated merely that she was not in formal employment. Her son, 'Alphus', is a 'scholar' – that is, a schoolboy – and is twelve years old. He had been born in Bognor, eighteen miles west of Worthing. 'Alphus' was presumably the guess that the census enumerator made when confronted with the semi-legible schedule that Sarah had completed.

As we shall see in a moment, Conway was almost certainly Sarah's maiden name rather than a married name. If so, her father was probably John Conway, who was living in New Street, Petworth at the time of the 1841 census. He is shown as a general dealer aged thirty-seven, and thus would have been born around 1804. He does not feature in the 1851 census – nor does Sarah – but a John Conway of Petworth died some time during the first three months of 1859.[4] If Sarah was indeed his daughter, she was left fatherless at the age of about ten.

In books about Wilde, Conway's first name appears in three versions: Alphonse, Alphonso and Alfonso, but the fact that both his and his father's name appear as Alphonse on the baptismal record indicates that Alphonse is correct.

It cannot be a coincidence that Alphonse's baptism occurred just eight days before the official date for the 1891 census. Then, as now, there were penalties for entering incorrect information on the census records, and Sarah's sudden decision to get her son baptised at the age of twelve was almost certainly because she hoped that his baptismal record – however recent and belated – would give semi-official status to the surname which her son was using, and which she was about to enter on the census.

When Alphonse was baptised, 'Alphonse' was, as we have seen, entered as the father's first name in the parish register. The widowed status that Sarah declared would lead to the assumption that the father's surname was Conway, like hers. In reality, however, Sarah was almost certainly never married to Alphonse's father. Not only is there no trace of an Alphonse Conway senior in any of the historical records; it is in any case unlikely that any such person existed.

Alphonse is not an English name. Almost every Alphonse recorded in nineteenth-century censuses had a French surname and had been born in France, Belgium or the Channel Islands; there is also the occasional Alphonse from Germany or Italy. The existence of two generations of Alphonse Conways would posit that there was an original Alphonse in the family in a previous generation – an entirely foreign individual with a foreign surname, who had been the brother or the father of the Worthing boy's paternal grandmother – and that the foreign first name 'Alphonse' was improbably carried down to two generations of Conways.

So Alphonse was almost certainly illegitimate; and his true surname was not Conway.

During the Queensberry libel trial, Wilde said that Conway's father had died young. However he was already absent from Sarah's life when she first appeared in Worthing – which, as we shall see in a moment, was only four years or so after her son's birth – so they probably never cohabited.

At the libel trial, Wilde also said that the boy had told him that his father had been an electrical engineer and, if this was not an invention of Alphonse's – or of his mother's – it seems curious that a boy born into a respectable lower-middle-class family in 1878 was not baptised at birth. There would, however, have been good reason for this omission if embarrassing details indicative of illegitimacy would have had to be entered onto the church register. In addition it is possible (see Appendix G) that Alphonse's father was a convicted criminal. With the passage of time, however – and in a town at a safe distance from that of the boy's birth – it would have been easy to enter on the records a father now conveniently deceased.

The first Worthing directory in which Sarah's name appears is that of 1884.[5] Mrs J. Conway – as we have seen, Julia was Sarah's first name – is listed at 2 Western Terrace, West Street in the Worthing Directories of 1884, 1885, 1886 and 1887. No other Conways appear in Worthing directories of the period: it was not a Worthing name.

Frustratingly, the relevant page in the copy of the 1883 directory at Worthing Library is missing, so we do not know if she was listed in that year. She does not appear in the 1882 edition.

Since directory information generally related to the situation that applied in the previous year, Sarah Conway probably arrived in the town in 1883 or – since we do not know whether or not she featured in the 1882 directory – perhaps in 1882. However, the directories list only householders, so if Sarah and her son were initially in lodgings, they may have arrived earlier – possibly soon after the boy's birth.

2 Western Terrace still stands, although much altered. It has been incorporated into the house next door and no longer has a front door onto the street. West Street is a narrow street of no great distinction, and in the Conways' time it was one of the poorest parts of the town, the occupants of the other houses being labourers, hire carriers, bricklayers and so on. Here, as later, Sarah Conway kept a lodging house, but this one had an unappealing location next door to Amoore's slaughterhouse, so Sarah's lodgers were probably labourers or slaughtermen rather than holidaymakers. The Rambler Inn, a rough pub once notorious as the haunt of smugglers, was located a little further along the street on the other side.

Although the street where Alphonse Conway spent his early childhood was insalubrious, at least the house he shared with his mother was just a few yards from the seashore, a circumstance that doubtless helped to nurture the love of the sea to which Oscar Wilde referred during the Queensberry libel trial: 'One thing he cared about was the sea.'[6]

Sarah Conway does not appear in the Worthing directories for the years 1888–90. Perhaps she and Alphonse left the town for a couple of years. More likely, they were themselves in lodgings. In 1891–92 they were at 2 Warman Terrace, Teville Road, a decent though modest house in a respectable part of the town, and conveniently located for lodging house purposes near the railway station. Warman Terrace still stands, although it no longer bears that name. By the time the 1893 directory was being prepared, Alphonse's mother had moved to 1 Bath Place, just off the seafront,[7] and she and her son remained there until they left Worthing in the spring of 1895 when the Oscar Wilde scandal broke.

Alphonse turned fourteen in July 1892, and that may have been the year he left school. At that time children were required to attend school only till the age of ten, but the census record tells us that Alphonse was still a 'scholar' in April 1891, two months short of his thirteenth birthday. If Alphonse had been at school in the Teville Road area of Worthing, then the end of his education would have been a convenient time for Sarah to move to a more central and profitable location for the running of a small lodging house. Wilde said she 'had' her own house, but this probably meant occupation rather than ownership. Even so, Sarah's ability to rent a four-storey Georgian town house just off the seafront and almost opposite the pier suggests that she was adequately well off – although Wilde told the libel trial said that she had 'very little money' and had only one lodger.

Sarah Conway and her son do not appear in any records after 1895, either in Worthing or elsewhere. After the shame and embarrassment that Alphonse's involvement with Oscar Wilde brought on the family, it is unsurprising that he and his mother did not remain in Worthing, and, as we shall see, it would seem that they were living in Shoreham in the spring of 1895. A possible reason for their subsequent disappearance from the historical record is that they changed their names.

*

The facts about Wilde's association with Alphonse Conway come to us primarily from the answers Wilde gave during the libel trial held on 3–5 April 1895, the complete transcript of which came to light only in 2000.[8] (The full text of the sections relating to Alphonse Conway is printed in Appendix D.) There is other evidence about the friendship in the 'storm letter' to Bosie, written on 10 September 1894, and in the statement Alphonse made to Queensberry's solicitors in March 1895.[9]

We do not know what Alphonse looked like. Although in the 'storm letter' Wilde described Percy, Bosie's favourite, as 'Hellenic', he had no reason to comment on Alphonse's looks in his letters to Bosie – and, for obvious reasons, this was a subject to be avoided in court, as Wilde's terrible lapse in respect of Walter Grainger demonstrated (see pages 138–9) – so we do not know whether or not Alphonse was Hellenic also. However since, as we shall see, Wilde kissed him on the road to Lancing one evening in late August, Alphonse cannot have been unkissably ugly, like poor Walter.

In court, Wilde initially said that Alphonse had been his companion for six weeks. He then quickly retreated to 'a month' – but the original reply was correct.

As we have seen, Bosie paid three visits to Worthing during Oscar's time there, and he and Oscar used regularly to go out on the sea in a sailing boat. It was one afternoon around 20 August that they met Alphonse.[10] A boat they had hired was being dragged by the boatmen towards the water from high up the beach. Two boys, Alphonse and 'a younger boy in flannels', joined in to help – doubtless they used to earn a few tips in this way during the holiday season. The boy in flannels was called Stephen.[11]

When the boat was down by the sea, Oscar suggested to Bosie that they ask the boys to join them on their outing. The boys enjoyed themselves so much that the trip was repeated the next day, and afterwards Oscar took Bosie, Alphonse and Stephen to lunch at the Marine Hotel, situated opposite the pier. After that, Alphonse, Stephen and the third boy, Percy, came out sailing every day; and Oscar and Alphonse became, in Wilde's own phrase, 'great friends'. The party would bathe from the boat in the morning and fish in the afternoon.

Constance Wilde seems to have been acquainted with Alphonse. According to Wilde, she met him regularly and knew him 'quite well'. These meetings were sometimes on the beach when Wilde and his friends returned from sailing trips, but Alphonse apparently also went to 'a children's tea' at the Haven. Wilde claimed that Alphonse was a great friend of 'his son's'. Oscar referred several times to his 'son' or his 'son's friends', and this son would have been Cyril, who was not only the elder but also the more outgoing and robust of the two. Probably Vyvyan, still not yet eight and, as we saw in Chapter 1, less confident than Cyril, spent more of his holiday time with his mother.

There is little in Constance's letters from Worthing about her husband's holiday activities, and part of the reason for this was that she did not know much about them. Indeed, Wilde may during the libel trial have exaggerated the extent to which Alphonse was integrated into the family holiday. Although we are reliant on Wilde's answers in court for much of our information about the Worthing holiday, a certain amount of scepticism is appropriate. It was, for example, clearly in Wilde's interests to paint Alphonse as just as much Cyril's friend as his own, and as someone Constance knew reasonably well.

Equally, if Alphonse did indeed, as Wilde claimed, attend a 'children's tea' at the Haven 'while my wife was there', it must have been an odd occasion. Who else was present? Was it just Alphonse, Cyril and Vyvyan who were being fed, with the Wildes' young servant Arthur handing round the muffins and the fruit cake, and Constance on hand in case one of the boys got butter on his cuffs? Or was it a more extensive affair, with a guest list that included, on the one hand, the children of a few other upper-middle-class holidaymakers and, on the other, Alphonse and his somewhat rough-and-ready teenage friends, Stephen and Percy?

Edward Carson more than once asked Wilde whether he knew that Alphonse sold newspapers on the pier at Worthing, but Wilde said he did not. When Sir Edward Clarke, Wilde's counsel, returned to the subject the next day, asking Wilde if he had ever heard of Alphonse's being employed as a newspaper boy, Oscar had his quip ready: 'I never heard of it, nor had any idea that he had any connection with literature in any form.' While many of Wilde's responses under cross-examination were untrue or evasive, he seems genuinely not to have known about this occupation. He said that Alphonse had told him he had never had a job. Thus either Alphonse had kept this information to himself because he was embarrassed by it or – more likely – he acquired the newspaper-selling job only after Wilde left Worthing.

Carson then asked Wilde what Alphonse did, and Wilde replied that he enjoyed himself being idle. Carson used the disobliging term 'loafer' to describe the boy, but Wilde said he preferred to say that he had 'a happy, idle nature'. But Alphonse was not without aspiration – Wilde said that he was keen to go to sea as an apprentice in the Merchant Navy, although his mother (whom Oscar never met) had mixed feelings about this.

According to Alphonse's witness statement, it was just a few days after their first meeting that Oscar asked Alphonse to join him on the parade at about nine o'clock one evening. They walked out of the town towards Lancing, along what at that time was a quiet road between fields and the sea. Oscar kissed Alphonse, put his hand inside the boy's trousers, and masturbated him until he 'spent'. However, he did not ask Alphonse to 'do anything'. The event was repeated a night or two later. Alphonse also says in his statement that he had dinner at the Haven on two or three occasions and that after the meal Oscar would take him to his bedroom, where they would undress and get into bed.[12] This, of course, was in the second half of September, after Constance and the children returned to London.

In the 'storm letter' of 10 September, Wilde brings Bosie, back in London at that point, up to date with the boys' doings. Percy, whose seaside holiday had presumably ended, had left Worthing. Alphonse was 'still in favour' and remained his 'only companion, along with Stephen'. Oscar reported that Alphonse always referred to Bosie as 'the Lord' – he would observe, for example, that 'Percy was the Lord's favourite'.

In this letter Oscar describes a boat trip that had taken place the previous day, a Sunday. He, Alphonse and Stephen sailed the seven or so miles to Littlehampton in the morning, bathing on the way, but then got caught in a severe gale, and it took them five hours to get back, reaching Worthing pier only at eleven o'clock at night. Wilde calls this 'a dangerous adventure' and says that all the fishermen were waiting for them at the pier. After they returned, they went to 'the hotel' – this was probably again the Marine – where the proprietor had to give rather than sell them brandy because it was past ten o'clock on a Sunday night. Wilde reported that the absurdity of English licensing laws had, no doubt with encouragement from himself, turned Alphonse and Stephen into anarchists.

Wilde denied in court that he had given Alphonse money, but Carson's questioning suggests that there was information in Alphonse's witness statement that the boy had received a total of £15 (about £1,500 today) over the period of their acquaintance. Wilde's other presents to Alphonse included a cigarette case, inscribed 'Alphonso from his friend Oscar Wilde'; a photograph of himself, inscribed 'Oscar Wilde to Alphonso'; a book called *The Wreck of the Grosvenor*, inscribed 'Alphonso Conway from his friend Oscar Wilde. Worthing, September 21st 1894'; a copy of *Treasure Island*, inscribed 'Alphonso Conway from his friend Oscar Wilde. Worthing, Sept. 1894'; and a silver-mounted, crook-handled grape-vine walking-stick, which Wilde suggested cost about ten shillings. (Carson thought fifteen more likely – about £75 today.)

Wilde also gave Alphonse a blue serge suit and a straw hat with a red-and-blue ribbon. Wilde denied that the clothes had been bought for the trip that, as we shall see, they took to Brighton in late September. He said that they had been acquired for an earlier occasion, a regatta the boy had wanted to go to. This would have been either the Worthing Annual Regatta on 5 September or the Venetian Fete on 13 September. He said that Alphonse had wanted this new outfit because he was ashamed of his shabby clothes.

Oscar had promised Alphonse that before he left Worthing he would take him on a trip to a place of the boy's choice as a reward for being 'a very pleasant, happy, good-humoured companion' to him and his sons. Alphonse would have liked to go to Portsmouth, but Oscar felt that this was too far, and he was busy finishing *The Importance of Being Earnest*. The extra time to Portsmouth by train would in fact have been less than three-quarters of an hour, but perhaps part of the sea-loving Alphonse's treat was that they would go by boat – and a sea journey to Portsmouth would certainly have been more time consuming than the short trip by paddle steamer from the pier at Worthing to the West Pier at Brighton.[13] In addition, a visit to Brighton, a nearby town well known to Wilde, would have been simpler to organise than a visit to Portsmouth, which was more or less unknown territory. It would have been cheaper too, and Wilde was short of money.

However, Alphonse was apparently content with the idea of Brighton, partly because he wanted to go to the theatre. According to Queensberry's Plea of Justification, this trip took place on or around 27 September. Wilde did not accompany Alphonse to the play – perhaps he preferred to work on *Earnest* – but they dined together at a restaurant. They stayed the night in a three-room suite (a sitting room and two bedrooms) on the first floor of the Albion Hotel, and returned to Worthing the next day. According to Alphonse's witness statement, he spent two hours in Wilde's bed that night, and on this occasion Wilde 'used his mouth'.[14]

There were two Albion Hotels in Brighton in 1894.[15] One, at 35 Queen's Road, run by Thomas Gadd, was a terraced building of three storeys, an attic floor and a cellar, not unlike the house at 1 Bath Place in Worthing where Alphonse was living with his mother. In other words, it was little more than a lodging house. The other, the Royal Albion (see illustration 30), was a large but at that time somewhat decayed hotel on the seafront.[16] The Royal Albion had originally been called simply the Albion when it opened in 1826; a five-storey extension was added about twenty years later, and it was at that time that 'Royal' was added to its name.

Previous writers who have considered the location of the hotel where Wilde and Alphonse stayed have favoured the humbler establishment.[17] However it seems most unlikely that it was there that they spent the night, for several reasons. During the libel trial, Wilde said that he had often stayed at 'the Albion', including with Bosie, and it is improbable that Wilde would have been a regular patron of a downmarket establishment near Brighton railway station. In addition, people spending nights with unconventional companions usually opt for large, busy hotels, where they are less likely to be subjected to curious scrutiny. At the Albion in Queen's Road, the ill-assorted pair of Oscar and Alphonse would have been conspicuous, and the situation embarrassing for both. Furthermore, it is unlikely that the more modest of the two Albions would have run to a three-room suite of the type that Oscar and Alphonse shared.

In all probability neither Wilde or Carson would even have known of the existence of the Queen's Road establishment, and it is common in everyday parlance to shorten the names of locations or institutions – often, indeed, those with 'Royal' in them (the Haymarket Theatre, the Albert Hall, the Marines). It is likely that 'the Albion' was the way the Royal Albion Hotel was referred to in colloquial usage. Indeed the only situation in which clarification would have been needed in court would have been if the Albion being referred to had not been the well-known hotel on Brighton seafront.

Happily, there is a piece of evidence that settles the matter. There are four letters that Wilde wrote from the Royal Albion Hotel in late January and early February 1894.[18] During the Queensberry trial Wilde said that the hotel where he stayed with Alphonse was one where he had stayed 'often', including with Lord Alfred

Douglas – and these letters prove that the Albion that he patronised in Brighton was indeed the Royal Albion.

The trip to Brighton was Alphonse and Oscar's swansong. At the start of October, as we saw in Chapter 4, Bosie put in a final appearance in Worthing, which he now found boring – Percy was long gone – and he insisted on Wilde's taking him to Brighton. This time the hotel was the Metropole, where Oscar and Bosie checked in on 4 October.[19] However powerful Oscar had found Alphonse's charms – and perhaps their novelty was beginning to wear off – Bosie's claims on him were always stronger than anyone else's.

Oscar did not see Alphonse again between then and the time of the trials, although he wrote him one letter, probably in November 1894 – he had spoken to a ship-owning friend of his about the possibility of the boy becoming an apprentice in the Merchant Navy, and wrote to tell Alphonse what he had found out.

Then, in March 1895, Wilde's decision to sue Queensberry for libel sent Queensberry's detectives scouring London and elsewhere for boys who could confirm that Wilde was a 'somdomite'. Richard Ellmann cannot be right when he says that Conway's address was among those found at the former lodgings of Alfred Taylor, Wilde's co-defendant in the criminal trials,[20] because this incriminating evidence had lain there undisturbed since before Wilde's holiday in Worthing.

Therefore it is probable that Littlechild and Kearley, aware that Wilde had been in Worthing for a couple of months the previous summer, simply went on a fishing expedition to Sussex. The Haven was doubtless the detectives' first port of call when they arrived in the town, and the source that led them to Alphonse was probably the housemaid or the cook who had looked after the Wildes in August and September 1894. Servants were the detectives' most productive source of information about Wilde, with generous cash inducements available to encourage co-operation;[21] and the housemaid and cook were the servants of Miss Lord, the owner of the Haven, and therefore had no special debt of loyalty to Oscar or his family. These two servants would still have been in attendance after Constance and the children left Worthing on 12 September, and indeed it was presumably the cook who prepared the food when Alphonse dined at the Haven on two or three occasions in the second half of September.[22]

Once the detectives heard about the boy who had several times visited Wilde at the Haven, it would not have been difficult in a small town like Worthing to track Alphonse down, either to his mother's house in Bath Place or to the newspaper kiosk at the end of the pier (see illustration 47), where he seems to have been working by that time.

At some point between Alphonse Conway making his statement to Queensberry's solicitor[23] and the opening of the first criminal trial on 26 April, Alphonse – presumably with his mother – appears to have moved to Shoreham, five miles to the east. The evidence for this is that the words 'Conway, 5 Buckingham Road, Shoreham' appear on the back of the title page of the copy of *Treasure Island* which Wilde had inscribed to Alphonse, and which was found after the Second World War among the possessions of the late Detective-Inspector Brockwell.[24] This was not one of the exhibits produced at the libel trial, so it must have been a piece of evidence gathered subsequently while the criminal case against Wilde was being prepared. The words were probably written in a police hand to identify the location from which a piece of property had been taken.

5 Buckingham Road – which still stands, albeit somewhat altered – was a modest two-storey house just north of Shoreham railway station. Now part of a terrace, it may at that time have been semi-detached.[25] It was a significant step down from the house in Bath Place where Alphonse and his mother had been living until then – or even from 2 Warman Terrace, their previous Worthing address – and it is unlikely that Alphonse's mother was there long enough to attempt to use it as a lodging house.

Alphonse must have been in London for the libel trial, since, had the prosecution case not been abandoned, he would have been called upon to give evidence in the witness box. Wilde's friend George Ives asserted that the witnesses were 'terrified into giving evidence against him: they were even locked up and kept on bread and water'.[26] It should not be forgotten that – though less culpable than Wilde on account of their youth – they too could have been imprisoned for engaging in homosexual acts.

However, they seem also to have been well paid by Queensberry. There is evidence that the witnesses each received £5 a week (£500 today) during the period between Wilde's arrest and his conviction;

and that Edward Shelley was paid £20 (£2,000) to be present at the libel trial.[27] These payments run counter to Ives's 'bread and water' thesis, but the likelihood is that witness co-operation was secured by a combination of threats and bribes.

We do not know if Alphonse was in London for the first of the criminal trials, but he was certainly there for the second since on 24 May Sir Frank Lockwood, prosecuting Wilde, asked him when he had last seen Conway, and Wilde replied, 'Outside the court two days ago.'[28] What Alphonse was doing there is a matter for conjecture. He could not have been called to give evidence, since Wilde was not charged in respect of him – in those days offences that occurred in Worthing were dealt with at Lewes Crown Court. For similar reasons Wilde was not charged in respect of Walter Grainger, since Goring-on-Thames was also outside the remit of the London courts. Perhaps Alphonse's presence outside the Old Bailey was due to Queensberry's having brought to London various youths who were still on his payroll, in the hope of embarrassing and distressing Wilde and making a public display.

After this unhappy final encounter, Alphonse Conway disappears not only from the Oscar Wilde story, but also from the historical record.

*

By the time of the libel trial, the other young men available to Carson were none of them younger than eighteen. Alphonse, however, was still sixteen; and a sixteen-year-old in the 1890s would typically have looked younger and less mature than his counterpart today. Had the libel trial not been aborted, Alphonse would have appeared in the witness box, and his appearance and demeanour would have been unhelpful to Wilde. He would have come across as a simple, pleasant boy from a small seaside town – Worthing's population in 1891 was under 17,000 – and untainted by the whiff of darkened, scented rooms and metropolitan corruption that clung to many of the others.

Alphonse Conway's being only six weeks or so past his sixteenth birthday when he met Oscar puts him halfway in age between two of the others who were often on the boat trips – Cyril Wilde had turned nine on 5 June; Bosie would be twenty-four on 22 October. Alphonse was thus young enough to engage in boyish activities with Cyril, but old enough to relate to a young man like Bosie – and indeed he comes across as outgoing, friendly, cheerful and self-confident, relaxed in the company of both children and grown-ups. He was clearly an outdoors boy, practical and physical, at his happiest mucking around on the beach or spending time out on the sea, on which, as we have seen, he would have liked to make a career.

Alphonse stands out from the generality of Wilde's relationships in a number of ways. In the case of the boys who were in effect procured for Wilde by his co-defendant Alfred Taylor, the nature of the transaction was implicit from the start. Everything we know about Alphonse, however, suggests that he was a 'respectable' boy, whom Wilde and Bosie met and befriended in the relaxed atmosphere of a seaside town in August. Those were more innocent times, and neither Alphonse nor Stephen would have felt any initial need to be cautious about their impressive new friends. Alphonse was also presentable enough to be introduced to Constance, to be invited into the Wilde household at the Haven, and to play with Wilde's sons.

(Carson, in his speech for the defence on the third morning of the libel trial, professed horror at Wilde's assertion that Conway had met Constance and the children. He said he sincerely hoped that this was not true, adding that if Conway had indeed been 'in association with' Wilde's children it would be 'an extraordinary fact'.)

It is wrong to suppose that Wilde, relentless pursuer and accomplished seducer of boys though he was, was solely interested in sexual gratification. Even in the case of the young men he took to bed in London, the relationship consisted of more than a financial transaction and the act of sex. Wilde also enjoyed the wider context of the friendships: talking to the boys, dining with them, giving them presents. Silver cigarette cases, famously, were ubiquitous. During the second criminal trial, Wilde said that in 1892 and 1893 alone he probably gave cigarette cases to as many as seven or eight young men.[29] He even took a certain amount of interest in the boys' well-being – on behalf of Conway, as we have seen, he made enquiries of a friend about his prospects in the Merchant Navy.

This element of companionship was more than usually pronounced in the case of Alphonse, in part because of the relaxed circumstances of that summer in Worthing, but also because the boy was such pleasant company. Wilde's account of the boat trip to Littlehampton and the stormy return late at night to Worthing shows that affection, good fellowship and enjoyment of time spent in innocent pursuits were an important component of his association with Alphonse. Oscar was not in love with Alphonse – no one could compete with Bosie for his love – but the words Wilde used about him during his trials suggest that he was genuinely fond of him. Indeed, he used warmer terms about him than about any of the other boys about whom he was questioned.

Further evidence that Alphonse was different from Oscar's other conquests is the modest level of the sexual activities in which they engaged. Wilde pleasured him, but seemingly did not expect him to return the favour. This shows some delicacy on Oscar's part, and respect for the boy's youth and inexperience. But then, on this occasion – to use Montgomery Hyde's terms – Wilde indubitably did 'debauch' an innocent young man who was not 'already steeped in vice'.

Alphonse did not reject Oscar's advances in the summer of 1894, and we do not know to what extent, if any, he protested. However, it is often easier in such circumstances to yield than to resist. In any case, teenage boys, driven by powerful sexual urges, are often flexible about the routes they take to erotic gratification. Oscar was not physically attractive, but he had great charm and charisma. Alphonse would have been impressed and flattered by being wooed by so famous a man – and indeed one who had 'the Lord' as his best friend – and would have enjoyed being admired and made to feel special. Besides, Oscar was his friend.

Wilde's generosity to him was doubtless a factor too. This was unlikely to have been a direct *quid pro quo*, as it was for Wilde's London boys. However Alphonse – who had never earned any significant money in his life – would have revelled in the pampering he received from Wilde: the daily sailing trips, the meals, the unlimited cigarettes, the presents. It was a heady and corrupting mixture. Worthing in the winter of 1894–95 after Wilde left must have seemed very dull.

In his witness statement, Alphonse indicated that Wilde's advances were sudden – and therefore, by implication, unexpected. However, they may not have come as a complete surprise.

Although we do not know the exact date of the event on the road to Lancing, it appears to have been in the last week of August. By late August, sunset at Worthing is already before eight o'clock. Nine o'clock in the evening was a curious time for Oscar to suggest that he and Alphonse meet, since a twilight meeting could not have related to any of their normal activities. In addition, Alphonse must have become aware of Oscar's special interest in him even during the fairly short time they had known each other.

Perhaps, therefore, Alphonse had some inkling of Oscar's intentions in making the late evening arrangement. If so, he may have arrived at the assignation with some idea about what might take place, and have been a willing enough participant when it did. There were a number of further sexual episodes, so Alphonse can hardly have been appalled by what happened that evening; and indeed there does not seem to have been any adverse effect on their friendship as the result of its having become sexual – Alphonse would not have urged Oscar to take him on a trip that involved staying in a hotel if he was not by then comfortable with the inevitable intimacies.

Alphonse's presence outside the court on Wednesday 22 May 1895, the third day of the second criminal trial, is the last we hear of him. Perhaps he secured his ambition to go to sea. Perhaps, like Wilde's elder son Cyril, he was killed in the First World War – he would have been thirty-six when war broke out and thus subject to the two Military Service Acts of 1916, which prescribed the compulsory enlistment first of unmarried (and then of all) men between eighteen and forty-one. Or perhaps Alphonse and his mother simply went to another part of the country and started life again, and Alphonse, as already suggested, changed his name to one without a shameful history. If the deductions about her past are correct, then Sarah Conway already had some experience in moving from place to place and disguising aspects of her background. Appendix H offers evidence of another intriguing possibility.

*

Wilde's relationship with Alphonse was atypical. All the other boys who were cited in the trials had been previously seduced by Alfred Taylor or Bosie, or were part of an agreed contract, or were fully old enough to make up their own minds. Even the luckless

Walter Grainger, the young servant at Goring in 1893, had almost certainly had sexual relations with Bosie before being passed on to Oscar. In any case, Oscar was in no way a companion or friend to Walter. When he was not serving Wilde in bed, he was serving him at table.

Alphonse, however, was unique, and indeed a uniquely attractive figure in the Wilde story. Part of his appeal for Wilde was almost certainly that he was a proper 'boyish' boy. The pleasure derived from feasting with panthers was essentially a corrupt pleasure, but Wilde's relationship with Alphonse was rooted in everyday friendship. There was no boy or young man in Oscar's life – if we exclude the special case of Bosie – with whom the proportion of time spent on innocent pursuits was greater; and running through Wilde's answers in court about Alphonse there is an unmistakeable undercurrent of affection.

We can only speculate as to how Alphonse subsequently thought of Wilde. Boys like Alphonse are essentially heterosexual in nature, and their involvement with men like Wilde is usually a passing phase. If the trials had never occurred, Alphonse might, as the years passed, have retained nothing but pleasant memories of an interesting and enjoyable – if unconventional – summer.

But the events of March to May 1895 changed everything. After the Wilde trials, any association with the love that dare not speak its name would have been the cause of immense shame and embarrassment. Conway's involvement with Wilde had delivered him into the hands of severe and unsympathetic detectives and lawyers, and many of his experiences over those three months must have been upsetting and frightening. He almost certainly met the other witnesses, some of them coarse, cynical, criminal young men who would have opened his eyes to a seamy side of life about which until then he had known nothing. In addition, his and his mother's lives and their ability to earn a living were badly disrupted. We can be sure that whatever generous payments Queensberry may have made to Alphonse and the other boys before Wilde's conviction, there would have been none subsequently.

When Sarah Conway arrived in Worthing in 1883, a single woman with a five-year-old son, she could do no better than a small house next to a slaughterhouse in a narrow working-class street.

Over the years that followed, she worked herself up from humble West Street, via the modest respectability of Teville Road, to an attractive Georgian terraced house in a prime position close to the pier and almost opposite the entrance to the theatre. Alphonse's involvement with Wilde meant that in 1895 Sarah had to leave a town where she had become well established. In addition, such hopes as she may have had for the future of her charming but feckless son had been greatly compromised.

Inevitably, the focus of posterity has been on the effect of the Wilde scandal on the major actors in the drama of 1895 – Wilde, Bosie, Queensberry – and on those close to them. Posterity rarely pays much attention to minor lives damaged or destroyed by the tribulations of the great. But life after the Wilde trials was certainly never the same again for Sarah Conway or for Oscar Wilde's happy, good-humoured boy of 1894.

If Alphonse felt bitter towards Wilde after the spring of 1895, it was probably above all because he had discovered that he had been far from unique. He had learnt that he was but one of many boys whom Wilde had wooed and feted; that those other boys had, like him, been flattered, pampered, and showered with expensive presents, including the inevitable silver cigarette case; and that afterwards Wilde, as he always did, had lost interest and moved on. Alphonse was certainly Wilde's particular favourite for a time. After so many distressing facts came to his attention, however, Alphonse may have concluded that he had been used and manipulated.

But that sad ending was long ago. What is appropriate now is that Alphonse Conway be rehabilitated and given his merited place a little apart from Wilde's other boys. It is no small matter to have been the intimate companion of a man of genius at the time when he was writing one of the one of the best-loved plays in the world – and indeed to have been at the heart of his life during the final summer before it broke apart. Wilde's 'bright, happy boy'[30] of 1894 deserves an honourable footnote in the history of English literature.

6

'No-one to talk to': Constance

'I have had no-one to talk to, and I have been rather depressed.'
Constance Wilde to Georgina Mount Temple, 3 September 1894

As we have seen, Oscar Wilde's holiday in Worthing was, as far as Wilde himself was concerned, both productive and enjoyable. He wrote the play that came to be regarded as his masterpiece; he was not deprived of the company of the handsome but difficult young man who was the love of his life; and there were the pleasures of regular boat outings with Alphonse, Stephen and Percy, and of sexual intimacy with Alphonse.

Although Wilde paid proper attention to his sons, he was not attentive to his wife, who felt lonely and neglected. The previous two years had been the worst period of Constance's marriage, with Bosie usurping the place in Oscar's affections that had once been hers. Health problems, unhappiness, and the strain of Oscar's relationship with Bosie had taken their toll. Nonetheless, Constance was still a very beautiful woman at this time, as is shown by illustrations 7 and 8.

On the back of one of the photographs is an ornate 'credit sheet' for the photographer. The firm's name appears as 'Mr H. S. Mendelssohns Studios' (in stylised print, with no apostrophe), and the address as 14 Pembridge Crescent, Notting Hill Gate, W. There is a display of medals and awards and the description 'High Art Photographer to the Queen and Royal Family'.

These photographs can be dated exactly, for on 30 July 1894

Constance wrote to Georgina Mount Temple, 'This morning I am going to Mendelssohn to be photographed.' The planned visit to the studio clearly did take place, for on 3 September there is another reference to it in a letter to Lady Mount Temple: 'I have just been photographed by Mendelssohn and as Oscar likes the photos, I suppose that they are good.'[1]

Oscar Wilde was of course a prolific letter writer,[2] but he was not the only member of his family writing regular letters during August and September 1894. Constance Wilde too was a keen correspondent, and eleven of her letters from Worthing survive.[3] One is to her brother Otho;[4] one to Arthur Humphreys,[5] who was shortly to publish *Oscariana*, a collection of Wilde's epigrams;[6] and nine to Georgina Mount Temple.[7] A few letters to Lady Mount Temple either side of Constance's stay in Worthing also provide relevant information about this period.[8]

The letters to Georgina Mount Temple[9] are of much interest, not least because of their relaxed and intimate tone. By this time Constance and Georgina had been close friends for about five years – indeed from soon after the death of the latter's husband in 1888. Constance, whose own mother had been guilty of much emotional cruelty to her, particularly during her teenage years, had adopted Georgina as a kind of surrogate mother, and most of her letters from Worthing begin 'My Darling Mother' and end 'Your devoted Bambina [little girl]'. On one level this is affectionate and charming; on another, perhaps slightly troubling.

Georgina Mount Temple (1822–1901) was the youngest and apparently the most beautiful of the nine daughters of Vice-Admiral John Tollemache. In 1848 she married the recently widowed William Cowper-Temple (1811–88), the stepson – and probably the illegitimate 'full son'[10] – of Lord Palmerston, the Victorian statesman. Cowper-Temple was himself a politician of substance, holding a number of senior government posts, and was created Lord Mount Temple in 1880. The Mount Temples, who had no children of their own – they had an adopted daughter, Juliet – owned the Broadlands estate, near Romsey, which after Lord Mount Temple's death passed, by way of distant relations and then marriage, into the Mountbatten family. Babbacombe Cliff, the Mount Temples' lavishly and exquisitely decorated house near Torquay in Devon,[11] was in effect their holiday home – indeed the Wildes rented it during the winter of 1892/93 – but by 1894 Georgina was living there more or less permanently, making little use of her London house at 9 Cheyne Walk. The Mount Temples were close friends of John Ruskin,[12] and Lady Mount Temple was much interested in religious, ethical and psychological questions – including what would now be described as New Age spiritual beliefs – and had a passionate hatred of cruelty and injustice. She was a vegetarian[13] and in 1882 became one of the vice-presidents of the Vegetarian Society; and both she and her husband were actively involved with the Victoria Street Society, the forerunner of today's National Anti-Vivisection Society. After her death, friends and local people subscribed to the erection of a bronze statue of her on the northern end of Babbacombe Downs. She is depicted feeding an injured bird.[14]

Although Constance's letters from Worthing to Lady Mount Temple and others add little to our knowledge of how Oscar was spending his time, they provide much interesting information, as well as offering an insight into Constance's state of mind at the time of the 1894 holiday. As already indicated, the Wildes' marriage – which had gone through a brief benign patch at the start of the year while Bosie was away in Egypt – was again in a poor state; and there is little sense of *joie de vivre* in any of Constance's letters. Constance was, however, growing close to two other men, both of whom visited her in Worthing.

*

One of these men was Arthur Lee Humphreys, with whom Constance fell briefly in love.

Constance was thirty-five at the time of the Worthing holiday, and Arthur Humphreys, who was born in 1865, was five or six years younger. Humphreys must have been of relatively humble origin, since he had started in Hatchard's bookshop in 1881 as a junior assistant at £1 a week (less than £100 today). Ten years later he was a partner in the firm, from which he retired in 1924. He was a man about whom no one seems to have had anything but good to say, and at about the time of his death in 1946 he was referred to as 'Mr Arthur Humphreys, most admired – I may say, most adored – of booksellers'.[15]

On Saturday 11 August, Humphreys spent a day with the Wildes in Worthing, presumably primarily to discuss the publication of *Oscariana*. The original arrangement, referred to in Constance's 7 August letter to Georgina Mount Temple, had been that Humphreys should stay overnight. We do not know why the plan changed, but perhaps one of Oscar, Constance or Arthur decided that the inherent awkwardness of the situation – as we shall see, Oscar seems to have been aware of his wife's emotional attachment to Humphreys – was better confined to a daytime visit.[16]

Constance wrote two letters that Saturday. One was to Georgina, to whom she gave this brief account of Arthur's visit:

> We have had Mr Humphreys down here for the day, so we have walked about and enjoyed the air and the sea, and now this evening has turned very stormy and wet.

That is all we know about what Humphreys did in Worthing on 11 August, beyond the fact that, as we shall see in moment, he smoked a cigarette.

The second letter was to Humphreys himself. Since this letter is the most important clue to the nature of the relationship between Constance and the only man she was ever in love with other than her husband, its complete text needs to be examined closely – as does the context in which it was written, which until now has been overlooked. These are not trivial matters, because the letter has elsewhere been used as the basis for the – almost certainly erroneous – deduction that there was a love affair between Constance and Arthur.[17]

Like all the letters Constance wrote during the Worthing holiday, the 11 August letter to Humphreys was written on 16 Tite Street writing paper. On this occasion, however, she did not bother to cross out the Tite Street address and replace it with the Worthing one, as was her usual practice. For reasons that will become clear in a moment, the address was irrelevant. Also, she was writing in haste.

The letter is dated 'Aug: 11: 1894.' This is the complete text:

> My darling Arthur,
>   I am going to write you a line while you are smoking your cigarette to tell you how much I love you, and how dear and

delightful you have been to me to-day. I <u>have</u> been happy, and I <u>do</u> love you dear Arthur. Nothing in my life has ever made me so happy as this love of yours to me has done, and I trust you, and will trust you through every-thing. You have been a great dear all the time quite perfect to me, and dear to the children, and nice to Oscar too, and so I love you, and I love you just because you <u>are</u> [underlined twice], and because you have come into my life to fill it all with love and make it rich. Your love will make me good so that I shall know my-self to be good, as I certainly do not at present even with all your sweet flattery.

Now the line must stop for fear of interruptions; I shall try and give you this; and if I can't I shall post it. I shall come up on Thursday, so let me have a letter when I arrive <u>please</u> [underlined twice].

Your always devotedly loving
Constance.[18]

This letter was composed not only on the day of Arthur's visit to Worthing – that much is evident from her reference to how dear and delightful Arthur has been 'to-day' – but also, as is clear from the first and the second-last sentences, while Arthur was still at the Haven. As Constance is writing her letter, Humphreys is smoking a cigarette. Perhaps he is in the drawing room, or perhaps he has strolled out onto the foreshore. Either way he is almost certainly with Oscar, since if Oscar had not been present Constance would not have had to worry about the feasibility of passing the letter to Arthur – and it would in any case have been odd for Oscar to absent himself from the house before his guest had left. Constance has perhaps retreated to her bedroom to write her letter while the cigarette is being smoked, although – wherever she is – she knows that she is not safe from possible 'interruptions'.

Arthur's day in Worthing had been a pleasant but conventional occasion. However, his charm and his kindness to Constance and the children – and indeed his 'niceness' to Oscar, who may have been prickly – appears to have served as a catalyst, provoking Constance into declaring her affection for him in terms that were probably more uncompromising (and indeed compromising) than any she had previously used.

The word 'love' has many meanings, and many nuances within those meanings, so it should be interpreted with caution, especially when it appears in a letter written over a century ago. It is true that 'My darling' is the way that lovers start letters, and it is clear from the rest of the letter that Constance was in love with Arthur at that point. Nonetheless, if considered carefully in both its totality and its context, Constance's letter of 11 August does not look like the letter of a woman writing to a man with whom she is having – or hoping to have – an affair.

This is not just a matter of instinct and intuition, although these play a part in the analysis.[19] There is also evidence in the letter itself that suggests that there was no affair.

One piece of evidence is the way that Constance refers to Oscar. It does not ring true that she would have written of Arthur's being 'nice' to Oscar if she was talking about a cuckold and the man who was doing the cuckolding. Indeed, it is unlikely that the three of them could have happily 'walked about and enjoyed the air and the sea' – in Constance's words to Georgina – if Constance had been Arthur's mistress (regardless of whether or not Oscar knew). If Constance and Arthur had been having an affair, a trip to Worthing to see the Wildes together would have been something that Arthur, in particular, would have avoided at all costs. And it was certainly not essential that Arthur come to Worthing to discuss *Oscariana* with them jointly, since other *Oscariana* business was conducted on a one-to-one basis between Arthur and whichever of Oscar and Constance was more appropriate at any given point – as on 14 August when Oscar went to London to sign the contract,[20] and on 16 August when, as we shall see, Constance was in London to discuss the book's publication.

In addition there is one particular sentence in the 11 August letter to Arthur which makes it improbable that he and Constance were sexually involved: 'Your love will make me good so that I shall know my-self to be good, as I certainly do not at present even with all your sweet flattery.' A woman in the throes of – or intent upon – an affair would not use the word 'good' in this way. Indeed, she would hesitate to use the word at all. Constance was a deeply religious woman with a strong moral sense, who always set herself the very highest of standards. There may have been many reasons why she felt that she was not as good a person as she would like to be, and therefore unworthy of the compliments Arthur paid her (which she self-depreciatingly dismisses as 'flattery'). But how could Arthur's love make her 'good' if it were expressed in an adulterous relationship?

The way that Constance uses the word 'trust' is also of significance. It was obviously a word with a special resonance for her. It occurs too in the only earlier surviving letter to Arthur, written on 1 June – a letter that begins, formally and conventionally, 'Dear Mr Humphreys':[21]

> But if we are to be friends, as I hope we may be, you must trust me. Indeed I can be trusted, as I believe that you can be. I am the most truthful person in the world, also I am intuitive.

Although it is true that an over-close and over-loving friendship between them would need to be concealed from others, Constance is surely not here invoking the kind of trust that those in inappropriate relationships require in order to ensure discretion and prevent discovery. The trust in question is something much deeper – to do, among other things, with the risk inherent in sharing one's inner thoughts and most intimate feelings with another person, and the attendant danger of being hurt. For Constance, love and trust were co-equals, each feeding off the other. Trust involved emotional honesty and the knowledge that neither party would do anything unworthy. Indeed, the trust in question very likely included the implicit understanding that, however close she and Arthur grew to one another, the mark would never be overstepped.

There is a second passage in the letter of 1 June that runs counter to any likelihood that Constance and Arthur ever had an affair:

> I feel as though I must write you one line to emphatically repeat my remark that you are an ideal husband, indeed I think you are not far short of being an ideal man! ... Your marriage was made for the sake of good, was the result of your character, and so was ideal.[22]

These comments indicate that Constance admired and respected Arthur's marriage, and it is all but impossible to believe that she would have contemplated intruding upon it or damaging it. And indeed it is telling that the word 'good' – that other word so important to Constance – is used by her in the context of the marriage.

Constance's sentiments probably also carry the implication that, by contrast, she did not see herself as an ideal wife, or Oscar as an ideal husband. Perhaps she had complained to Arthur about her unsatisfactory marriage and afterwards felt disloyal to Oscar for having done so, and this was one of the reasons that Constance thought herself less 'good' than she would have liked. Elsewhere in the 1 June letter she apologises for having discussed her unhappy childhood with Arthur, so she evidently regarded it as poor form to talk too much about personal problems.

One other aspect of the letter Constance wrote in Worthing on 11 August merits comment – namely that she pleads for a reply when on the surface there is nothing for Arthur to reply to. No question is asked. No statement is made that requires a response.

However, this does not mean that a question was implicit – let alone that this unspoken question was whether Arthur shared her feelings and wished to embark upon an affair. It is entirely understandable that, having opened up her heart to Arthur in writing, Constance hopes that his response will also be in the form of a letter – even though the first opportunity she will have to receive his written reply will be when she next sees him in person. A letter has permanence, and can be kept and cherished; and things can be said in writing that are too personal to be easily spoken. Indeed, perhaps Constance felt that, however kind and affectionate he might be, Arthur would find it easier to express his feelings for her in a letter than face to face. Either way, although Constance refers to the compliments that Arthur has paid her as flattery, she – a woman much in need of love at this time – clearly longs for further sweet and loving sentiments.

Writing in great haste – her impulsive outpouring of affection must have taken less than five minutes to commit to paper – Constance may not have been fully aware of the effect of what she was saying. Ten years of marriage to Oscar Wilde would have given Constance a misleading impression of the emotional and sexual psychology of a typical male, and she was perhaps rather naïve in matters of the heart. An unscrupulous lothario in receipt of a letter such as hers of 11 August would have regarded the woman who wrote it as fruit ripe for plucking.

Whatever the nature of the reply that Constance hoped for, her request that Arthur give it to her in person the next time they met was above all practical. The response to such a letter could not be posted to the Haven, since if Oscar had caught sight of an envelope in Arthur's handwriting he would have assumed it contained a letter primarily about *Oscariana*, and would naturally have enquired about its contents. However, Constance may also have taken some pleasure in the necessary subterfuges – certainly her letter has something of the eager intensity of a schoolgirl in the grip of an illicit crush.

Constance tells Arthur that she will be coming up to London 'on Thursday'; and there is confirmation that she did indeed see him that Thursday – 16 August – in the letter that she wrote to Georgina Mount Temple on 17 August, in which Constance says, 'I went up to London yesterday to see Lady Wilde and also to see about the printing of *Oscariana*.' The uninformative brevity of Constance's account of her meeting with Arthur that day may just possibly smack of disappointment. Usually Constance mentions Arthur by name in her letters to Georgina, and in this context it would be more natural to refer to him than not to do so. Perhaps Arthur, sensing from Constance's letter that the situation was in danger of getting out of control, had decided to draw back a little from a relationship that, while not sexual, was nonetheless becoming over-emotional. Perhaps, indeed, instead of satisfying Constance's hope for a letter full of kind and loving thoughts, he had spoken seriously to her about their friendship, and counselled restraint.

But this can only be speculation. None of Arthur's own letters to Constance have survived, so we have no way of knowing whether his feelings for her were as strong as hers for him. Constance's phrase 'this love of yours to me' suggests that Arthur was very fond of her, but it is possible that Constance read more into his kind and affectionate attentions than was justified. Any man would have been delighted and flattered to learn that he was loved by so beautiful and intelligent a woman as Constance, and there would have been an added piquancy in the fact that she was the wife of one of the most brilliant men of the age. Arthur had perhaps let himself be drawn more closely into this highly charged situation than was wise. However, although he was certainly devoted to Constance, he was probably not in love with her in the way she was with him.

Also, however strongly Arthur may have been attracted to Constance, an affair with her would, if discovered, have had a destructive impact on his own 'ideal' marriage – and Arthur also had a daughter to think of.[23] (Any consequences for Constance would probably not have been so serious. In view of his own extensive extramarital adventures, Oscar was in no position to judge others, and would almost certainly have accepted the situation, however little he liked it. He would hardly have cast an errant wife into the street.)

We know from Constance's 11 August letter to Lady Mount Temple that Arthur, presumably with his wife, was leaving England for a European holiday two days after Constance's trip to London on 16 August: *Oscariana*, she says, 'has to be, if possible, in Mr Humphreys' hands before he goes abroad next Saturday'. So Arthur left for France on Saturday 18 August; and as soon as he arrived in Paris he wrote to Constance in Worthing, as we learn from Constance's letter of 20 August to Georgina:

> Mr Humphreys is abroad, and writes to me from Paris, where he has paid his first visit to the Louvre. Tomorrow he goes on to Switzerland, and from there I think, & hope, to Florence, where I shall cicerone him [serve as his expert guide] by letter tho' I cannot, alas! be there in person. I love Florence more than anything I have ever seen in my life, and I shall try and fire Mr Humphreys with my enthusiasm so that we may discuss it together when he gets back.

Since the letter from Paris was evidently addressed to the Haven, it must have been more neutral in tone than the hoped-for love letter. However it is a tribute to Arthur's affection for Constance, and possibly to his sensitivity to whatever had been the aftermath of her emotional letter – as well as to the speed of the seven-day-a-week postal service of those days – that Constance received a letter from him within two days of his leaving England. This time, Constance is relaxed about mentioning Arthur by name when she writes to

People and Places

The first sixteen pages of this block of illustrations consist of portraits of the main protagonists in the Oscar Wilde story; two pages from letters; and images of buildings, locations and events closely associated with the summer of 1894.

The buildings include the only four buildings in Worthing that we know Wilde spent time inside – the Haven; the Marine Hotel; the Assembly Rooms; and the pavilion at the sea end of the pier. None of these buildings survive.

1. This photograph shows Oscar Wilde and Lord Alfred Douglas at Magdalen College, Oxford, during a visit Wilde paid Bosie in May 1893. Wilde had himself been at Magdalen from 1874 to 1878 and had achieved a double first in Greats. Douglas, who also studied Greats, did not turn up for his final exams. (© National Portrait Gallery, London)

2. Oscar Wilde (1854–1900), photographed on 28 May 1889, five years after his marriage. (© National Portrait Gallery, London)

3. Oscar Wilde in 1892.

4. Lord Alfred Douglas (1870–1945), photographed in Egypt early in 1894.

5. The first page of the 'concert letter', written by Wilde to Douglas on 8 September 1894. The full text of the letter is printed in Appendix B.

6. Oscar, Constance and their elder son Cyril in 1892.

7. Constance Wilde (1859–1898), from the set taken at the studio of H. S. Mendelssohn at 14 Pembridge Crescent, Notting Hill Gate, on 30 July 1894, eight days before Constance travelled down to Worthing with her sons.

8. Another photograph of Constance Wilde from the set of 30 July 1894.

9. The second page of the letter Constance Wilde wrote to Georgina Mount Temple from Worthing on 3 September 1894, in which she complains of having 'no-one to talk to'.

10. The Wildes' elder son Cyril (1885–1915), photographed in Heidelberg in 1896. By then Constance and her sons were using the surname Holland.

11. Vyvyan Holland (1886–1967), the Wildes' younger son, also photographed in Heidelberg in 1896.

12 (*top left*). Lord Alfred Douglas's father, John Sholto Douglas, 8th Marquess of Queensberry (1844–1900).

13 (*top right*). The Marquess of Queensberry as a young man, in an 1877 'Spy' cartoon from *Vanity Fair*. Spy was the pseudonym of Leslie Ward (1851–1922).

14 (*right*). The Marquess of Queensberry, in a silhouette of 1889 by the *Punch* cartoonist Phil May (1864–1903). (© National Portrait Gallery, London)

15. Robert Ross (1869–1918), the most loyal of Wilde's friends and his literary executor, at the age of about twenty.

16. Frank Harris (1856–1931), another loyal friend, whose accounts of conversations with Wilde in exile provide much fascinating if not always reliable material about Wilde.

17. The poet and traveller Wilfrid Scawen Blunt (1840–1922), who took Lord Alfred Douglas on a 'pilgrimage' to Shakespeare's tomb at Stratford-upon-Avon early in August 1894. A champion of Irish Home Rule, Blunt was sentenced to two months in Galway prison in 1887 for sedition and resisting the police. Reviewing the collection of poems Blunt wrote in prison in the *Pall Mall Gazette* on 3 January 1889, Oscar Wilde wrote that prison had 'converted a clever rhymer into an earnest and deep-thinking poet', adding, 'An unjust imprisonment for a noble cause strengthens as well as deepens the nature.'

18. Lady Mount Temple (born 1821 or 1822, died 1901) and Lord Mount Temple (1811–88). For the last ten years or so of Constance Wilde's life, Georgina Mount Temple was her closest friend and her most regular correspondent.

19. Sir Edward Clarke (1841–1931), lead counsel for Oscar Wilde in all three trials in April and May 1895, photographed around 1897. (© National Portrait Gallery, London)

20. Edward Carson (1854–1935), lead counsel for the Marquess of Queensberry in the libel trial, photographed around 1900. (© National Portrait Gallery, London)

MAYOR AND COUNCIL OF THE BOROUGH.

COUNCILLOR W. H. B. FLETCHER
(Mayor).

ALD. A. CORTIS
(Mayor 1890-1).

ALD. R. PIPER
(Ex-Mayor).

ALD. E. C. PATCHING
Mayor 1891-2—1892-3).

ALD. E. T. COOKSEY

ALD. F. C. LINFIELD.

ALD. M. GREEN.

COUNCILLORS.

MR. G. SMITH
(Central Ward).

MR. L. W. PAYNTER
(Central Ward).

MR. J. HAYWOOD
(Central Ward).

MR. L. W. BURNAND
(Central Ward).

MR. W. BUTCHER
(Central Ward).

MAJOR CAMPBELL FRASER
(E. Ward).

MR. H. CHAPMAN
(E. Ward).

DR. G. B. COLLET
(N.E. Ward).

D. F. PARISH
(N.E. Ward).

MR. H. LEA
(N.E. Ward).

MR. G. BAKER
(N.W. Ward).

MR. T. J. LYNE.
(N.W. Ward).

MR. T. P. LUND
(N.W. Ward).

'APT. A. B. S. FRAZER
(W. Ward).

MR. H. B. BIRRELL
(W. Ward).

21. Worthing's mayor, aldermen and councillors in 1895, including several of the individuals mentioned in the third chapter of this book. The ubiquitous Captain A. B. S. Fraser is second from right in the bottom row. His brother, Campbell Fraser – left, second bottom row – has been promoted to the rank of major since the summer of 1894. Note the facial hair worn by everyone except Dr Collet.

22 (*left*). The Haven, the four-storey end-of-terrace house where Wilde and his family stayed in 1894 – Constance reported back to Oscar that the house was 'very small'. The photograph dates from around 1921.

23 (*right*). A snapshot of Lord Alfred Douglas outside the Haven, taken by the actor Donald Sinden when he and Bosie paid a visit to Worthing in the early 1940s.

24. A view of around 1905 of the Haven and Brighton Road. Selden Terrace, at left, no longer stands, but Cleveland Terrace, at centre-left, survives. The houses in the middle and far distance were built during the reign of Edward VII – in 1894 that section was an empty stretch of road, along which Wilde seduced Alphonse Conway one evening in late August.

25. The bandstand at the eastern end of the grounds of Warwick House, where three illuminated promenade concerts were held in the summer of 1894.

26. The most important festival held in Worthing in the summer of 1894 was the Lifeboat Demonstration on 22 August. The *Worthing Gazette* reported, 'Among those who viewed it was Mr Oscar Wilde, who is now on a visit to Worthing, and was one of the occupants of a small rowing boat busily flitting about.' The photograph reproduced here accompanied the report in the London *Sketch* on 5 September.

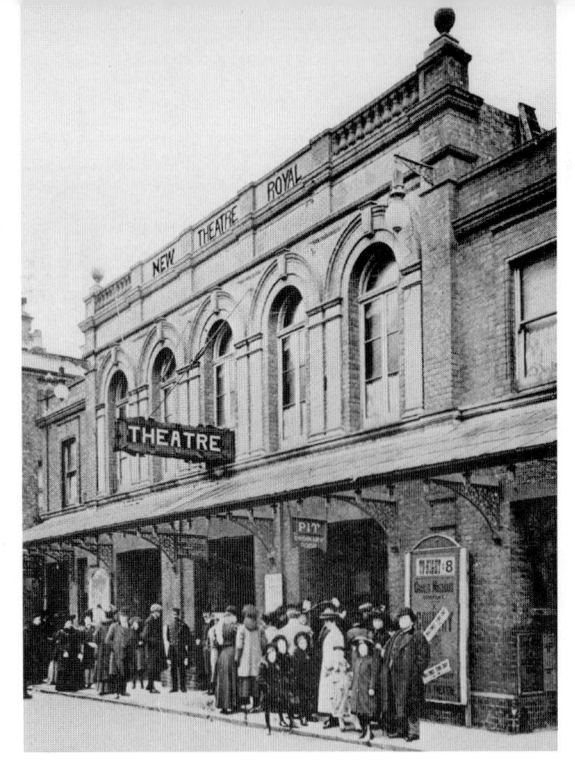

27. The New Theatre Royal in 1909. It was here that Wilde and his elder son Cyril attended a concert featuring the Olympian Quartet ('the vagabond singers of the sands') on 7 September 1894. At that time the building was known as the Assembly Rooms. The interior was restructured in 1897 and again in 1906, but the front, seen here, remained much the same, apart from the addition of the canopy.

28. It was inside this pavilion at the sea end of Worthing pier that Oscar Wilde delivered a speech when he gave away the prizes for the best-decorated boats after the Venetian Fete on 13 September. The pavilion, which had a capacity of 500, burnt down in 1933, only seven years after a pavilion in matching style replaced the kiosks at the land end of the pier. This photograph was taken from the paddle steamer *Princess May* on 16 August 1898.

29. A 1906 view of the Marine Hotel at the south-east end of South Street, just opposite the pier. It was here that Wilde entertained Bosie, Alphonse and Stephen to lunch the day after he and Bosie met the boys for the first time. This was probably also the hotel where Bosie stayed for some or all of his first visit to Worthing.

30. The Royal Albion Hotel, Brighton, where Wilde and Alphonse Conway spent the night on or around 27 September 1894. The photograph dates from 1890.

31. The Metropole Hotel, Brighton. This, and not the Grand – as Wilde misremembered when he wrote 'De Profundis' – was the hotel where Wilde and Bosie spent four nights after they left Worthing on 4 October. Note the use of French accents in 'Hôtel Métropole' and the term '*salle-à-manger*' for the dining room. This is a page from the *Illustrated London News* of 26 July 1890.

A Worthing Sequence

Most of the photographs in this section date from within a dozen years or so of Oscar Wilde's visit in 1894, and, except where noted, all show the town just as he knew it. The photographs are arranged in a strict geographical sequence, starting at the Esplanade at the eastern end of Worthing, and proceeding along Brighton Road and Warwick Street; down South Street to the pier; and then a few hundred yards west along the seafront.

The three maps of 1896 are reproduced to help readers of this book – especially those that visit modern Worthing – to identify the locations of Wilde's time.

32. The photograph above is a view of the Esplanade from the south-west in 1890. The Haven, where Oscar Wilde stayed, is the house in the centre of the picture, at the left-hand end of the terrace. (© The Francis Frith Collection)

33. This 1898 view of the Esplanade from the east shows, at right, the four south-facing semi-detached houses, Nos 1–4 (numbered from right to left); and, at left, the west-facing terrace, Nos 5–8 (also numbered from right to left). The Haven – No. 5 – is hidden behind the semi-detached houses.

34. In this view of around 1930 from the north-west, the Haven – by then renamed Esplanade House – is prominent on the left-hand side, between the two tall chimneys.

35. In 1894 this building was a boys' school called Worthing College, whose facilities included a skating rink, a kitchen garden and a room where pupils 'engaged in the mysterious art of amateur photography'. Worthing College closed in 1900 and the building, subsequently known as Beachfield, was occupied from 1901 to 1947 by the Catherine Marsh Convalescent Home. It was demolished in the 1960s. The photograph dates from around 1918.

36. The next house along Brighton Road after Worthing College was Beach House, which still stands, now divided into flats. This view of the south front dates from around 1910. From 1917 to 1923, Beach House was owned by another homosexual playwright, Edward Knoblock, the author of *Kismet*, filmed four times and later made into a musical.

37. A view of the south façade of Warwick House, which in the late eighteenth and early nineteenth centuries was the most important house in Worthing. By the time of Wilde's visit it had been unoccupied for several years, and it was demolished in 1896. This snapshot dates from 1894.

38. High Street, looking north from the junction with Warwick Street and Brighton Road in around 1890. The wall on the right marks the western boundary of the grounds of Warwick House.

39. This view of 1894 looks west up Cook's Row, which was the third street off the left side of High Street (and more or less on the line of modern-day Chatsworth Road). The decision to demolish the slum dwellings on the left and straight ahead was taken while Wilde was in Worthing, and they were gone by the time of the 1896 map. In 1894, Cook's Row jinked right and then left at the top of this picture, past the Cannon Brewery.

40. The Cannon Brewery, which stood on the northern side of Cook's Row, was demolished and replaced by a new building (the Cannon Inn) in 1894, probably at the same time as other parts of Cook's Row were cleared. Today the site is occupied by the offices of the *Worthing Herald*.

41. This view looking west along Warwick Street dates from 1889. The wall on the right is the southern boundary of the garden of Warwick House. The large sign above the wall probably advertises the fact that the house and its grounds were for sale.

42. Newington's, situated on the north-west corner of Warwick Street, was one of the leading tailors in Worthing in 1894, so it was perhaps here that Wilde bought Alphonse Conway the notorious blue serge suit and straw hat with a red-and-blue ribbon that featured prominently in the Queensberry libel trial the following year.

43. This view looking east along Warwick Street from the Town Hall dates from the late 1880s. The meetings of the town council, the monthly County Court sessions and the fortnightly petty sessions were held in the main chamber; below were a garage for the town's fire engine and cells for prisoners.

44. The clock tower of the Town Hall was removed in 1950 on safety grounds, and the rest of the building was demolished in 1966. This photograph dates from 1910.

45. In 1894, as now, South Street was Worthing's principal shipping street. This view, looking south from in front of the Town Hall, dates from around 1890. The Royal Hotel is visible at far right.

46. In this view of East Parade, taken from in front of the pier, the Marine Hotel is at far left and the Pier Hotel immediately to its right. The photograph dates from around 1905.

47. It was inside one of these kiosks at the northern end of Worthing pier, just across the road from the sea end of South Street, that Alphonse Conway was employed selling newspapers at some point after Wilde left Worthing. The kiosks were replaced by the current Pavilion Theatre in 1926–27. The photograph dates from 1906.

48. The pavilion and the landing stage at the sea end of Worthing pier had been built only in 1887–89. In 1894, the paddle steamers *Sea Breeze* and *Princess May* called here regularly. The photograph dates from around 1910.

49. The Royal Hotel, which in 1894 was Worthing's leading hotel, was destroyed by fire on 21 May 1901. The street to its right is South Street, and the entrance to the Marine Hotel is just visible at far right. The photograph dates from around 1900.

50. In this photograph of around 1895 the Royal Hotel is again prominent, with the Marine Hotel largely hidden by the group of people on the right of the picture. It was at the Royal that the mayor held a lunch for eighty male dignitaries before the Lifeboat Demonstration on 22 August 1894.

51. Cambridge Terrace, on the left in this photograph of around 1890, is one of the few buildings on the central section of Worthing seafront that survives from Wilde's time. In 1894, the building beyond, which was demolished in 1934, was a gentlemen's club called the County Club. Bath Place, where Alphonse Conway lived with his mother, is the street that runs between the two buildings.

52. This view of West Parade seen from the pier in 1910 shows, right to left: Cambridge Terrace, Montague Terrace (running north from the seafront), Montpelier Terrace, Nos. 48–49 Marine Parade, and Marlborough House.

53. The building on the left of this photograph of 6 July 1893 is Montpelier Terrace, demolished in 1975. In August 1894, Mr J. E. Nash's seriously ill brother, who was staying in a lodging house in Cambridge Terrace, centre-right, 'complained most painfully of the abominable nuisance occasioned from morning to night by the itinerant street singers on the seafront opposite his residence'. These were Wilde's 'vagabond singers of the sands'.

54. This scene is just west of the pier, whose kiosks are visible in the centre background. The photograph was taken on 20 April 1894.

55. Marlborough House, the handsome Regency building on the left of the picture, was demolished in 1940. In 1894, the bandstand in use on Worthing seafront was the modest structure seen here on the right. It was replaced in 1897 with an attractive 'birdcage' bandstand. The photograph dates from 1892.

56. At the right of this photograph of around 1895 is the western end of Augusta Terrace, a short terrace of four houses that stood between Prospect Place and Augusta Place, and a few yards west of Marlborough House.

Map 1: Marlborough House to Steyne Gardens

A. Cook's Row
B. Town Hall
C. Bath Place
D. Assembly Rooms
E. Marlborough House
F. Cambridge Terrace
G. County Club
H. Royal Hotel
I. Marine hotel
J. Pier Hotel
K. Great Terrace
L. Little Terrace
M. Clarendon House
N. Pier Kiosks

These maps were prepared for a sequence of photographs printed in *The Wildean* in January 2012. A more comprehensive photographic record of Worthing almost exactly as it was in Wilde's time appears in *Worthing: The Postcard Collection* (Amberley, 2013), which features 163 colour-tinted and monochrome photographs of the Edwardian town, with historical commentary.

Map 2: Bedford Row to Beach House

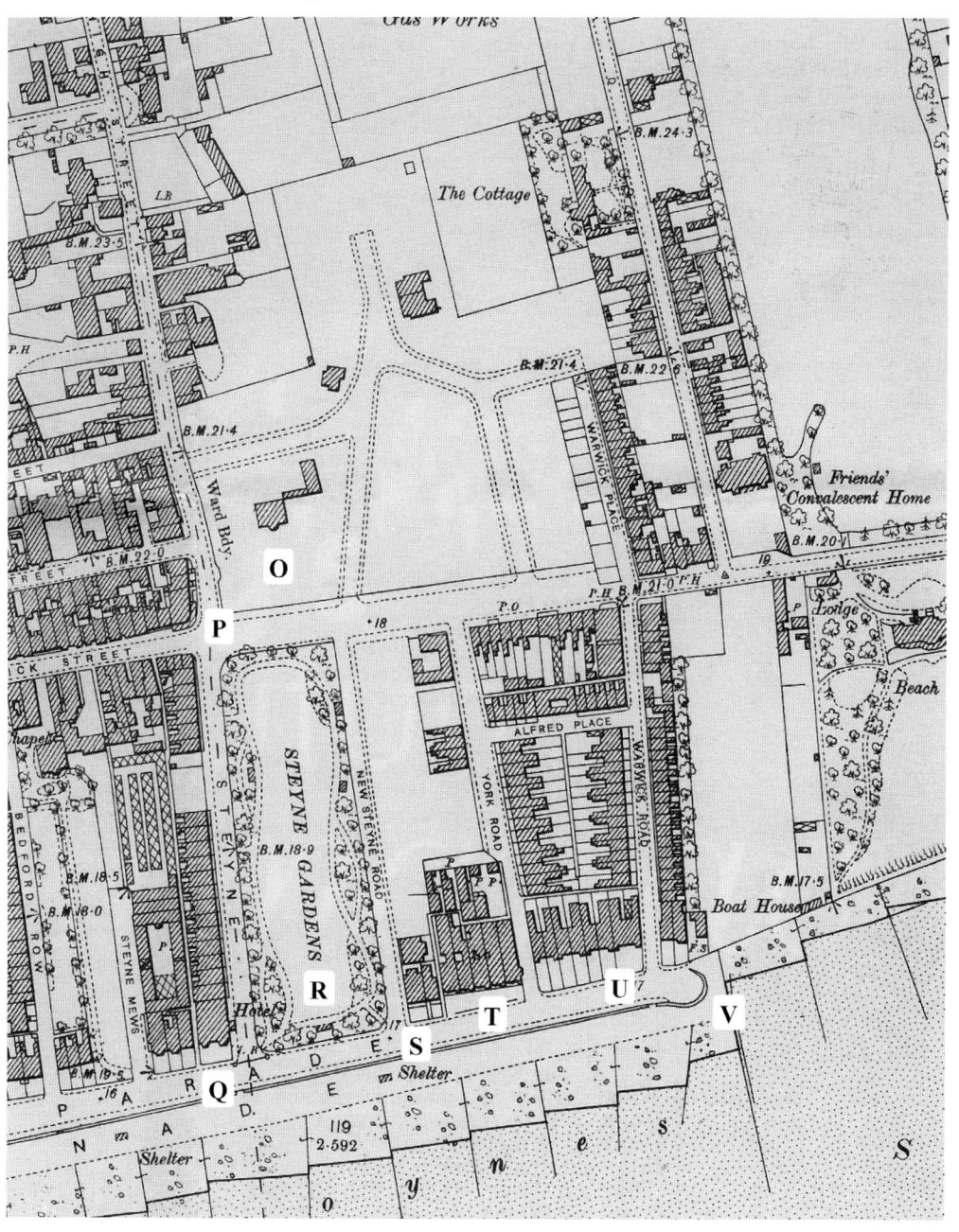

O. Warwick House
R. Steyne Gardens
U. Eardley House
P. The Colonnade
S. Steyne House
V. Splash Point
Q. Steyne Hotel
T. York Terrace

Between Wilde's visit in 1894 and the publication of this map in 1896, Warwick House and its grounds had been sold for redevelopment. The map shows the house already partly demolished, with the streets on which houses were to be built marked out on the grounds. This is the only important difference between Worthing as it was in 1894 and as depicted on these maps.

Map 3: Splash Point to the Esplanade

W. Beach House
Y. Merton Terrace
X. Worthing College
Z. The Haven

In 1894, the four terraced and four semi-detached houses of the Esplanade – and Cleveland Terrace, opposite them on the other side of Brighton Road – were the final buildings at the eastern end of Worthing. The Haven, at the north end of the Esplanade terrace, faced across forty yards of open ground, and also had a clear view along Brighton Road. The pier was a half-mile walk away along the seafront.

Georgina. Perhaps their relationship had indeed been subjected to some healthy adjustment the previous Thursday.

The trail then grows cold for two months. The third surviving letter from Constance to Arthur from this period was written on 22 October, and its tone is far from lover-like.[24] Gone are 'My darling Arthur' and 'Your always devotedly loving / Constance'. In their place are 'My dear Arthur' and 'Yours afftely [affectionately] / Constance Wilde'. It cannot be accidental that Constance now includes her surname in her signature.

The letter begins:

> The photographs have arrived & I think you might come and fetch yours. I shall have to come up to town to-morrow morning to get a book from the London Library, & I will come in & see you for a few minutes. But we must not talk of subjects that we do not agree upon. You have a very strong nature and perhaps it is natural that you should have no sympathy with the unfortunate of the world.

Constance goes on to describe a conversation she has recently had with a carpenter who has worked for her and Oscar for ten years – thus, their entire married life – who spoke to her 'with grief' of cases of 'thoroughly competent artizans' who could not get work and had to 'swell the rank of the unemployed' or work as labourers for sixpence an hour. 'But please do not let us speak of it again,' she reiterates; 'it is a subject that I feel most deeply on, and that is not serious [that is, of importance] to you.'

The letter ends with this functional paragraph:

> Are you coming to the P. R. S. meeting on Friday?[25] I shall try and go to it, because I want to see Mr Myers. I hope *Oscariana* is going on all right.

Although the cool tone of this letter was partly dictated by the fact that Constance had been upset by Arthur's lack of compassion for the unlucky poor, it is unlikely that this fact would have caused her to alter the way she began and ended her letter – or, indeed, to decide that she could spare only 'a few minutes' for the man whom, ten weeks earlier, she had told that nothing had ever made her so happy as his love. It is therefore clear that – whatever may have been the nature of their relationship in the summer – Constance and Arthur were by this time no more than conventional friends. Constance's fit of emotion had subsided. The impulsive letter that she had composed in Worthing on 11 August had, in all likelihood, been an isolated event, and indeed possibly one that had caused embarrassment to both.

Oscar Wilde seems to have been aware of the close and emotional friendship between his wife and Arthur at the time of the Worthing holiday. His letters to Humphreys about *Oscariana* – then and subsequently – appear brisk and frosty,[26] and it was while he was staying in Worthing that he sketched out for the actor-producer George Alexander the synopsis of a melodramatic play on the theme of marital infidelity.[27] The plot of the proposed play bears little resemblance to Oscar's own life – it ends with the husband committing suicide when his wife tells him she is pregnant by her lover – but the three main characters appear to approximate to Constance, Arthur and himself. Nonetheless, Wilde's idea for this play is not proof that he believed that Constance was having an affair. It is more likely that he was transmuting his feelings of jealousy at his wife's – unconsummated – love for another man into terms concrete and dramatic enough to work on the stage.[28]

Arthur Humphreys was a loyal friend to the Wildes and, in spite of the apparent awkwardness in his relations with Oscar at the time of the Worthing holiday, he stuck by him through his troubles and sent him books in prison. Letters from convicts were severely rationed, so Oscar had to ask his friend More Adey to pass on his thanks to Humphreys, which he did in a letter to Adey from Reading on 16 December 1896:

> Of the kindness of my good friend Arthur Humphreys, the publisher, I cannot trust myself to write. It is a very dear remembrance on his part of a pleasant literary friendship. Give him my warmest thanks. When I read Walter Pater I shall have two friends to think of.[29]

Then, early in June 1897, a few days after his release from prison,

Oscar was able to write personally to thank Humphreys, which he did in the most friendly and appreciative of terms.[30]

Sadly, a different note is struck in what was almost certainly the final letter that Constance Wilde wrote to Humphreys, on 27 February 1898, just over a month before her death:

> His [Oscar's] punishment has not done him much good since it has not taught him the lesson he most needed, namely that he is not the only person in the world.[31]

Although we cannot know for certain whether or not Constance and Arthur had an affair, the available evidence suggests that they did not. Almost everything hinges on the letter that Constance wrote in Worthing on 11 August 1894, its context and the way it is interpreted. It is true that Constance had long been neglected by her husband, both emotionally and sexually; that, as we saw in Chapter 1, they had had no physical relations since Vyvyan's birth almost eight years earlier; and that she was receiving ever-diminishing affection and respect from him. Nonetheless, her strong religious beliefs and moral sense, and her devotion to her sons, would almost certainly have made her draw back from embarking upon a sexual relationship with another man, especially a married man – while Arthur Humphreys, a decent and honourable man and 'an ideal husband', is unlikely to have been prepared to betray his wife and compromise his friendship with Oscar and Constance.

The strong probability therefore is that when Constance died less than four years later, at the age of just thirty-nine, Oscar Wilde was still the only man with whom she had ever shared her bed.

*

Arthur Humphreys is already known to us from the Oscar Wilde story, but the other man who seems to have been filling some of the empty emotional space in Constance's life at the time of the Worthing holiday is less familiar. This was a clergyman called Lilley. Until now little has been known of him other than that he was at this time one of Canon Richard Eyton's curates at Holy Trinity church in Sloane Street, the church that Constance attended; that, like Canon Eyton, he was much interested in radical politics; and that he married in January 1895.[32]

The key to unlocking Lilley's full identity comes in a letter Constance wrote to Georgina Mount Temple from 16 Tite Street on 3 October. Lilley's first name does not appear in Constance's letters,[33] but this letter gives his initials. Lilley had indicated to Constance that he would like to meet Georgina, and in her letter Constance expresses the hope that Georgina will arrange 'with Mr Hewitt for him to preach during the Octave'. (Father John Hewitt was the vicar of Lady Mount Temple's local church, All Saints' church, Babbacombe, and, like Lilley, an Anglo-Catholic.) Constance then gives Georgina Lilley's details – he is the Revd A. L. Lilley, and his address is 40 Sloane Square. Knowing Lilley's initials allows us to discover more about the man and his subsequent career.

His full name was Alfred Leslie Lilley. He was born in Clare, Co. Armagh in 1860 – so he was about the same age as Constance – and, like Wilde, he was educated at Trinity College Dublin. After two years as a curate in Ireland, he moved to London, first as a curate at Holy Trinity and then as vicar at St Mary's, Paddington. He became a canon of Hereford Cathedral in 1911 and Archdeacon of Ludlow in 1913, retired in 1936 and died in 1948. He was the author of a number of books, including *The Programme of Modernism: A Reply to the Encyclical of Pius X, Pascendi Dominici Gregis, with the Text of the Encyclical in an English Version* (1901) and *Sir Joshua Fitch: An Account of His Life and Work* (1906).[34]

The author G. K. Chesterton knew Lilley well, and this extract from Chesterton's autobiography suggests that, when Lilley acquired his own parish, it was run on somewhat unconventional lines:

> My old friend the Rev. A. L. Lilley, now a Canon of Hereford, was then the vicar of a parish in Paddington Green; and his large and genial sympathies expressed themselves in the marked eccentricity of his assistant clergy. For he was one of the two or three Broad Churchmen I have known who were actually broad. His curates were a group which we irreverently referred to at one time as a menagerie; one, I remember, was of gigantic stature with

fierce grey hair, eyebrows and moustaches very like Mark Twain. Another was a Syrian and actually, I believe, a runaway monk from some monastery in the desert. The third was Conrad Noel.[35] I have sometimes thought it must have been rather amusing to be a faithful parishioner of Paddington Green.[36]

Lilley's surname almost never appears in company with just one of his first names – his books were published under the name 'Alfred Leslie Lilley' – so it is not easy to be certain which first name was in everyday use. The name 'Alfred' appears in one record – on 5 April 1910, a man called William Evans was found guilty at the Old Bailey of 'breaking and entering St. Mary's Church, Paddington, and stealing therein two silver patens, one cup, and other articles, the goods of the Rev. Alfred Lilley, and one bunch of keys, one bottle of wine, and 3s in money, the goods and moneys of the churchwardens of the said church'.[37] However it is likely that 'Alfred' was the forename chosen by the court simply because it came first in the sequence, for on 29 May 1897 – as it happens, just eight days after Wilde's release from prison – 'the Rev. A. Leslie Lilley' officiated at a wedding at All Saints' church, Clifton; and in 1908, a book called *The Programme of Modernism* was published with an introduction by 'the Rev. A. Leslie Lilley'. We have therefore opted for 'Leslie'.

Although we know – from Constance's letters of 3 and 4 September to Georgina Mount Temple – that Leslie Lilley came to stay the night in Worthing with the Wildes on 4 September, he was obviously not as close to Constance as Arthur Humphreys. Nor was he as attentive a correspondent, for in the 20 August letter to Georgina in which she mentions Arthur's letter from Paris, Constance complains, 'Mr Lilley has not written to me since I came here a fortnight ago, so I don't know anything about him.'

It is not difficult to understand the appeal to Constance of this intelligent and charismatic clergyman with a social conscience. However, although Constance seems to have been strongly drawn to him, it was no more than a friendship, not least because, as we have seen, Lilley was at this time just a few months away from getting married. In any case it was their shared interests and Constance's strong faith that lay at the heart of the relationship.

Indeed it is striking how much of Constance's correspondence with Georgina Mount Temple from Worthing has a religious theme, partly, of course, because of Georgina's own religious beliefs and interest in spiritual matters.

On 4 August, for example, Constance, still in London, announces that she is going to 'early tryst' the next day, but that 'the other services will be dull, and I shall be very busy packing so probably this is all I shall do. I am afraid that I shall miss Mr Lilley altogether for a month'. On 7 August, now in Worthing, she tells Georgina what her devotional arrangements on that Sunday had actually been. Inspired by Lilley's return from an absence, she seems to have attended more than just the early service: 'Mr Lillie [sic] has returned as delightful as ever, and he celebrated at 8.30 on Sunday morning, preached at 11.30 and came to see me for an hour at 5.30. He brought me a photograph of the Luini crucifixion at Lugano.'[38] On 11 August, Constance tells Georgina that she has not yet been to any of the Worthing churches: 'I have not had courage to try the churches here. I never like strange churches and we have had Mr Humphreys down for the day.' (Constance evidently did not confine her worship to Sundays, since this letter was written on her first Saturday in Worthing.[39]) And on 2 September, Constance sends Georgina, who had been too ill to go to church – she had described herself as 'excommunicated' – a nine-side 'service', consisting of extracts laboriously copied from the scriptures and from religious authors such as Thomas à Kempis.

*

During the early part of the Worthing holiday Constance was spending much of her time choosing and putting together the material for *Oscariana*. Indeed, on 11 August – albeit only four days since her previous letter – she is apologising for having neglected Georgina Mount Temple: 'I have been so busy with collecting passages from Oscar's works for *Oscariana* that I have been obliged to neglect everything else including you my darling, and this to my sorrow.'

One way or another, Constance was doing a great deal of reading in Worthing. On 4 August she tells Georgina that she is 'going to take the *Ascent of Man* to read at Worthing, & hope I shall get some good out of it'.[40] The book is not mentioned again, so perhaps it proved less beneficial than Constance had hoped. The Worthing reading list Constance proposed on 4 August also included the works of Walter Pater,[41] who had died five days earlier, on 30 July: 'We are all so sad over the death of Mr Pater, and I feel that I have lost a real friend. I think that I shall take all his work down also to study.'

On 7 August, the day of her arrival in Worthing, Constance is pleased to find a copy of *Middlemarch* at the Haven and 'having forgotten it' is 'already deep in it again' by the time she writes to Georgina Mount Temple that evening – indeed she intends 'retiring to bed with it'. By 17 August she has finished *Middlemarch*, and has also read some 'light literature suited to the seaside' such as Anthony Hope's *The Prisoner of Zenda* and Israel Zangwill's humorous novel *King of the Schnorrers*.[42] However, in spite of her determination to read Pater during the Worthing holiday, his writings seem not yet to have engaged her attention, for there is a fresh statement of intent: 'But now that I have finished the first labour of *Oscariana*, I am going to devote myself to studying Pater.'

However, Pater continued to prove daunting, for seventeen days later, on 3 September, he had apparently still not been attempted: 'When I go back to London, I am going to read all my dear Walter Pater's books.' Although she has had difficulty with Pater, Constance has been finding solace in the philosophical writings of Marcus Aurelius.[43] She has also 'read heaps of odds and ends', including more books by Anthony Hope; a second, more serious novel by Israel Zangwill, *Children of the Ghetto*, set in London's East End Jewish community; and Frances Hodgson Burnett's *That Lass o' Lowrie's*, about the lives of Yorkshire mining folk.[44] She also notes that she has been reading 'all Oscar's books for *Oscariana*'.

We do not know if Oscar, whose holiday was so much more busy than Constance's, was finding time for any significant reading, since the only book mentioned in connection with him in any of Constance's Worthing letters is 'a little book called *I Woke*', which Constance recommends to Georgina Mount Temple on 25 August. Constance had apparently read it herself and passed it on to Oscar, who was '<u>much</u> interested in it'. It has not been possible to identify the book, but – in view of its title, Wilde's own well-documented interest in the paranormal,[45] and the fact that Constance recommended it to Georgina – it perhaps had to do with spiritualism.

In truth, Constance seems to have spent rather more of her summer holiday in the company of books than might be regarded as entirely healthy. While at least she did turn her attention now and then to 'light literature suited to the seaside', there is no evidence in her letters of her having indulged in any light activities suited to the seaside. She has almost nothing to say about Worthing itself in her letters, beyond telling Otho on 31 August, 'The Parade is about a mile long, there is a very handsome pier, and there [are] about 12 churches.' (Churches seem never to have been far from Constance's mind.) Conspicuous by its absence from Constance's correspondence, in particular to Lady Mount Temple, is any reference to anything that could be described as fun. Although this may partly have been because she thought Georgina would be more interested in serious-minded matters, it is difficult to avoid the conclusion that there was little gaiety in Constance's life in the summer of 1894.

It is a sad but telling reflection on the state of her marriage that on 3 September – sharing a holiday with a man who was not only her husband, but also the best conversationalist in Europe – Constance is writing to Georgina:

> I have had no very delightful thoughts lately, but tomorrow Mr Lilley comes to stay with us and I hope that he will give me some. I have had no-one to talk to, and I have been rather depressed; the reading I have enjoyed most has been Marcus Aurelius, who always makes me feel calm and happy at least <u>while</u> I am reading him.

*

Although Oscar claimed in court that Constance saw Alphonse Conway 'constantly' and knew him 'quite well',[46] Alphonse, perhaps not surprisingly, is not mentioned, at least by name, in any of her letters. Indeed, the one-sentence account of her husband's holiday routine that she gives Otho in her letter of 31 August invites speculation as to how much Constance actually knew about the way he was spending his time:

Your picture of Worthing is hopelessly inaccurate [perhaps Otho had assumed that it was an elegant watering-place where Oscar and Constance were socialising with others of their class], and Oscar asks me to tell you that he bathes twice a day goes out in a boat twice a day, and talks to no-one but fishermen.

In fact, Oscar was mainly talking to teenage boys who enjoyed going out on fishing trips – not the same thing. Even if Wilde's answers during the Queensberry libel trial about Constance's acquaintance with Alphonse were accurate, she perhaps preferred to save face by giving Otho a sanitised version of the truth – the introductory formula 'Oscar asks me to tell you' relieves her from responsibility for the veracity of the information. A reluctance on Constance's part to share with her brother and Lady Mount Temple whatever knowledge she had of Oscar's holiday companions would have been understandable, not least because her correspondents might have drawn their own conclusions.

But we return to Constance's few references to Oscar's holiday activities, the last of which comes in the 31 August letter to Otho:

Cyril went out with his father in a boat this afternoon, and this evening a man brought 150 prawns & 2 lobsters that had been caught, and I innocently said that I should like to go prawning with him one afternoon. After he had gone, Oscar explained to me the costume that the fishermen wear when they go prawning which is indeed like the Emperor's new clothes! So I think differently now about going!

It would appear from the phrase 'that had been caught' that the prawns and lobsters were the catch from Oscar's and Cyril's outing that afternoon. Oscar claimed during the Queensberry trial that Alphonse Conway was often on boat trips with him and Cyril, so it is just possible that the 'man' who brought the prawns and lobsters to the Haven in the evening was Alphonse. If so – since Alphonse had turned sixteen less than two months before and could not have looked much like a man – the choice of word would fit in with a pattern of evasion on Constance's part. Whether or not 'the man' was indeed Alphonse, Oscar's warning that the fishermen did their prawning naked was perhaps a deliberate tactic to discourage Constance from getting involved in his routines – and indeed, bathing as they did from a sailing boat a long way off shore, the Worthing boys may themselves have swum naked; and possibly Wilde and Bosie too.

*

As her stay in Worthing proceeded, Constance's unhappiness was complemented by poor health. Cyril may have been looking 'marvellously well', but a seaside holiday in Worthing does not seem to have done much for his mother's physical well-being. On 11 September, the day before her holiday ended, Constance tells Georgina Mount Temple, 'I have not been well, and now I have got a bad sore throat, so I suppose that I have, in some mysterious way, taken cold!'

By 15 September, three days after her return to London, Constance's health is even worse:

> I have been so unwell for the past week that I can do nothing but the necessary things and these come to a good deal, since I have to put all the boys' things in order before they go to school. I have got most dreadful catarrh both bronchial and nasal, but tho' I am quite miserable, I fortunately have no fever, so I can get about, tho' I am stupid and headachy. I am going now to be dosed with tonics and my week at dear Babb. will set me up and make me strong again.

The reference to 'Babb.' is to Babbacombe Cliff, Lady Mount Temple's house in Devon, where Constance had been invited to spend a week in late September. The prospect of staying in the comfortable and well-ordered household of her affectionate surrogate mother must have seemed very appealing after the responsibilities Constance had been shouldering in Worthing – to say nothing of the emotional strain of being in close proximity for five weeks to a husband who so obviously loved Lord Alfred Douglas more than he loved her.

We know from Constance's 22 September letter to Georgina that on Friday 21 September the boys returned to their respective schools – 'It is so lonely without the boys who both went off yesterday to school' – and the same letter and one of 2 October tell us that between Monday 24 September and Monday 1 October Constance stayed at Babbacombe. Then Constance's loneliness returned as soon as she was back in London:

> I am very lonely up here in London without you, and I am too tired and headachey to do anything! How gloomy this sounds. But I am not really gloomy, and I carry about with me vivid memories of dear Bab, and the wonderful colouring of everything there – a contrast to dingy grey London.

At this time Oscar's mother needed much attention. Although Constance was 'terribly tired' on the evening of her return, she dutifully paid a visit to Lady Wilde, 'who seemed to me much weaker than she was a week ago'. She visited Lady Wilde again the following evening, writing on 3 October, 'I found Lady Wilde better last evening, but she is quite unable to walk.' On 6 October she has to write to Lady Mount Temple 'in great haste' because she has to 'fly up into town to get Lady Wilde's pension'. Afterwards she is going to lunch with Mrs Cowper,[47] then to a photographic exhibition, followed by evensong and dinner at seven o'clock with Emily Ford[48] – and then: 'Before I go to bed, I must see Lady Wilde, for she likes me to come sometime every day, and she is _so_ weak.' On 7 October Constance writes, 'This evening I shall be with Lady Wilde.' It was a demanding commitment.

During the same week Oscar Wilde, still in Sussex, had neither his mother nor his wife on his mind. In not one of Constance's six letters to Georgina Mount Temple over the period of twenty-five days since she had left Worthing is there a single word about her husband – perhaps because Oscar had had no desire or reason to write to her, and therefore Constance had no news of him to pass on.

Bosie had been with Oscar since the start of the month, and on 4 October they left Worthing for Brighton. Indeed, ironically, at the very time that Constance was paying dutiful attention to Oscar's mother, Oscar was nursing Bosie through a bout of influenza, and lavishing every attention on him, including the best fruit that money could buy. 'I got special grapes from London for you,' Wilde wrote later, 'as you did not care for those the hotel supplied.'[49] This solicitousness Bosie signally failed to reciprocate when Oscar himself fell ill a few days later. He behaved atrociously and then left for London, sending Oscar a letter that included the notorious statement: 'When you are not on your pedestal, you are not interesting. The next time you are ill I will go away at once.'[50]

It is an apt encapsulation of these various relationships that this chapter should end with a lonely Constance conscientiously attending to the needs of Oscar's mother, and with Bosie flouncing temporarily out of Wilde's life, leaving him solitary, ill, and sick at heart.

7

'My play is really very funny': *The Importance of Being Earnest*

'My play is really very funny: I am quite delighted with it.'
Oscar Wilde to Lord Alfred Douglas, 10 September 1894

The first mention of the play that was to become *The Importance of Being Earnest* is in a letter Wilde wrote to the actor-manager George Alexander, probably a week or two before he went down to Worthing.[1] 'The plot,' Wilde told Alexander, 'is slight, but, I think, adequate.' The outline he gives is very much as in the finished play, although there is no mention of plot devices such as the baby in the handbag; nor does the Ernest / earnest motif yet appear.

Only one character, Miss Prism, has her final name. Algernon at this point is Lord Alfred Rufford, the same name as Wilde gave one of the characters in *A Woman of No Importance* and confirmation, if any were needed, that the charming and feckless Algy was partly based on Bosie. Jack Worthing is Bertram Ashton, and his fictitious younger brother is not Ernest, but George. Lady Bracknell is the Duchess of Selby. Gwendolen Fairfax is Lady Maud Rifford. Cecily Cardew is Mabel Harford.

Like many of the world's greatest literary works, including the plays of Shakespeare and the novels of Dickens, *The Importance of Being Earnest* was a potboiler, composed for money by someone who wrote for a living. Wilde's need for money was at this point urgent. In a letter from Worthing to Charles Spurrier Mason, he wrote, 'I am in a very much worse state for money than I told you. But [I] am just finishing a new play which, as it is quite nonsensical and has no serious interest, will I hope bring me in a lot of red gold.'[2] Wilde hoped that the play might be produced not only by George Alexander but also by the American producer Albert Palmer. Palmer had put on a successful production of *Lady Windermere's Fan* in Boston and New York in early 1893, and Wilde told Alexander that Palmer was 'anxious to have a play from me for the States "with no real series interest" – just a comedy'. Wilde thought that the new play he had in mind would suit Palmer's purposes, and by the end of October he is telling Alexander that he has had 'very good offers from America for it'.[3]

Once he arrived in Worthing on 10 August, Wilde must have set to work at once, since by 25 August Constance was able to write to Georgina Mount Temple: 'Oscar has written a play here, so I <u>love</u> this place now!'

What Wilde had written in the first fortnight, however, can have been no more than an initial draft, since just over two weeks later, on 10 September,[4] Wilde is writing to Bosie to indicate that the play is not yet in its final form:

> I have been doing nothing here but bathing and playwriting. My play is really very funny: I am quite delighted with it. But it is not shaped yet. It lies in Sibylline leaves about the room, and Arthur has twice made a chaos of it by 'tidying up'. The result, however, was rather dramatic. I am inclined to think that Chaos is a stronger evidence for an Intelligent Creator than Kosmos is: the view might be expanded.[5]

The play was nonetheless sufficiently 'shaped' for the first draft to go to Mrs Marshall's Type Writing Office in the Strand a few days later. Although the original scheme Wilde had outlined to Alexander in July had been for a play in three acts, the play, which had the working title *Lady Lancing*, by now had four. The completed typescript of the first draft was stamped 19 September,[6] so it is possible that Constance took the manuscript to London with her when she and the children returned to the capital on 12 September.

The typing of the second draft took much of October, with

stamps at the end of each act as follows: Act I – 8 October; Act II – 18 October; Acts III and IV – both 25 October.[7]

The reason for these intervals may have been that Wilde was revising the play one act at a time, and sending each act to Mrs Marshall as he finished working on it. If so, the first act was probably dispatched just before Wilde and Bosie left Worthing.

At the end of October, Wilde sent Alexander the typescript, explaining that, although *Lady Lancing* was the title on the cover, the play's real title would be *The Importance of Being Earnest*. *Lady Lancing* was camouflage, there being no character of that name in the play.[8] By now most of the characters had their final names, apart from Algernon Moncrieff, who at that point was Algernon Montford, and Lady Bracknell, who was Lady Brancaster.

The wordplay on Ernest / earnest was probably suggested by the publication two years earlier of a volume of poems entitled *Love in Earnest* by the pederast schoolmaster John Gambril Nicholson.[9] Wilde took much interest in writings of this nature, and since the volume received a certain amount of attention – it was, for example, well reviewed in the *Artist*, a journal familiar to Wilde and his circle (a poem by Bosie appeared in the April 1894 issue) – it is unlikely that he was unaware of it. In a typical poem in the collection, 'Of Boys' Names', Nicholson runs through the associations that various names have for him, before ending each verse with 'Ernest sets my heart a-flame'. It is characteristic of Wilde that he thought nothing of the risk of being associated with so compromising a book.

George Alexander was initially uncertain whether the play was right for him, but the failure of a play by Henry James called *Guy Domville* – a section of the audience jeered James when he took a bow at the end of the play – meant there was a vacancy at the St James's Theatre; and Alexander decided to fill it with *Earnest*. In January 1895, he and Wilde met to discuss the play. Alexander said that he thought the third act of the four-act version superfluous and less good than the rest. Wilde fought for almost an hour to preserve the play as he had written it, but in the end gave way, with a typically Wildean flourish:

> The scene that you feel is superfluous cost me terrible exhausting labour and heart-rending nerve-racking strain. You may not

believe me, but I assure you on my honour that it must have taken fully five minutes to write.[10]

Wilde duly reduced the play to the three acts originally envisaged. The second and third acts of the four-act version were compressed to form the present second act, and a section featuring a lawyer called Gribsby was cut entirely.

Gribsby turns up at Jack Worthing's house in Hertfordshire to arrest Algy for debt. In a clear echo of Wilde's and Bosie's extravagant dining practices in real life – and Wilde's own parlous financial situation at the time he was writing the play – Algy has run up a debt of £176 14s 2d (about £17,600 today) dining at the Savoy. If he does not pay up, he will be taken to Holloway prison. The idea of going to a suburban prison appals Algy: 'I really am not going to be imprisoned in the suburbs for having dined in the West End.'

Gribsy tries to be reassuring:

The surroundings I admit are middle class; but the gaol itself is fashionable and well-aired; and there are ample opportunities of taking exercise at certain stated hours of the day. In the case of a medical certificate, which is always easy to obtain, the hours can be extended.

Within nine months or so of writing these lines, Wilde was himself in Holloway prison, which he did not find as fashionable as his fictional lawyer had promised. He was there for a month, from his arrest on 5 April 1895 until the first criminal trial ended on 7 May, when he was given bail after the jury failed to agree. Although Holloway proved unfashionable, conditions there were a great deal more pleasant than in the prisons where Oscar was incarcerated after his conviction. Since he was a remand prisoner, he was able to have his own clothes and furniture; and his meals were brought in from a nearby restaurant.

The four-act version of *Earnest* exists, and is occasionally performed. It was first published in 1903 in a German translation from a typescript which Robert Ross had sent to a German publisher. In 1956, the New York Public Library published the original typescripts and manuscripts, and in 1957 Wilde's younger son Vyvyan Holland used the German version as a 'template' for putting together an English four-act version from the various alternatives in the typescripts and manuscripts.[11]

The long Gribsby section, although amusing in parts, includes some weak exchanges; and much of the dialogue Wilde removed from elsewhere in the four-act version is also not up to the standard of what remains. Alexander was right, and he did both the author and the stage a favour by insisting that Wilde shorten the play.

*

Wilde was in the habit of using names for the characters in his plays derived from the area of England in which he was writing. Much of *Lady Windermere's Fan* was written while he was staying in the north of England, so, in addition to the title character, we have Lord Lorton, the Duchess of Berwick and Lord Darlington. Some of *A Woman of No Importance* was written in Norfolk, hence Lady Hunstanton. In *An Ideal Husband*, partly written, as we saw in Chapter 1, at Goring-on-Thames, we have Lord Goring, Lord Caversham, Mrs Cheveley and the Chilterns.

Similarly, when Wilde abandoned the names he gave Alexander in his original outline for *The Importance of Being Earnest*, several of the replacements had Sussex connections – most obviously, of course, Jack Worthing. But there were other names that appear to have been inspired by names in the *Worthing Gazette*.

The *Gazette*, published weekly on Wednesdays, was an eight-page broadsheet, much of it taken up with advertising. As well as local stories such as those featured in Chapter 3, there was national and international news, the latter often appearing in the form of rather pointless page fillers. Readers of the 22 August issue, for example, learnt in the 'At Home and Abroad' column that the German Social Democratic annual conference had been 'convened for Sunday, October 21st, at Frankfork[sic]-on-Main' and that 'after a desperate twenty-five round fight, Oberhardt, champion lightweight of Louisana, knocked out Stanton Abbott, the American champion'.

Wilde is likely to have read the *Gazette* each week during his holiday, not only in order to identify events that might give pleasure to his children, but also because he would have wanted to know what was being said about him. In addition, there is always much amusement to be had from the incongruities and parochialism of the local press.

A name almost certainly inspired by Wilde's perusal of the local press was that given to Algernon's imaginary invalid friend, Bunbury, who died abruptly when his existence became an embarrassment at the start of Act 3:

> ALGERNON: Poor Bunbury died this afternoon.
> LADY BRACKNELL: What did he die of?
> ALGERNON: Bunbury? Oh, he was quite exploded.
> LADY BRACKNELL: Exploded! Was he the victim of a revolutionary outrage? I was not aware that Mr. Bunbury was interested in social legislation. If so, he is well punished for his morbidity.
> ALGERNON: My dear Aunt Augusta, I mean he was found out! The doctors found out that Bunbury could not live, that is what I mean – so Bunbury died.
> LADY BRACKNELL: He seems to have had great confidence in the opinion of his physicians. I am glad, however, that he made up his mind at the last to some definite course of action, and acted under proper medical advice.

In the July 1995 issue of *The Wildean*, John Wagstaff devoted an entire article to the question of Bunbury.[12] He quotes an obituary notice in the *Worthing Gazette* for a certain Captain Bunbury, which a local historian had found forty years earlier. Captain Bunbury had served in the Army until he was twenty-nine, but the obituary says nothing of his subsequent career, so it cannot have been very remarkable. Wagstaff says that, ever since this discovery was made, it had been a Worthing tradition that this was Wilde's source for the name. We now know, however, that Wilde arrived in Worthing only on 10 August, so it is unlikely that he saw that particular issue of the *Gazette*.

However, there was no shortage of Bunburys in Sussex at that time, and Wagstaff found another report in which the name appears. The 12 September issue of the *Gazette* carried an amusing story about a recent hearing at Brighton magistrates' court. The usual stipendiary magistrate, Mr Heathcote, was on holiday, and his place was taken by the less competent Mr Bunbury, who made an elementary mistake when it came to passing sentence on one offender. A workhouse inmate was convicted of stealing some parish clothing, and Bunbury sentenced him to six months in prison. As is often the case among habitual offenders, the thief, as the *Gazette* put it, 'knew a thing or two' about the law. Resisting the gaoler's attempts to remove him from the dock, he 'maintained a running fire of commentaries of a more or less pointed and insolent nature, interlarded with exclamations so amusingly indignant as to send the court into roars of laughter'. He said that a month would have been enough. 'Six months for ten bobs' worth,' he said. 'That's a bit thick.' More importantly, he made the correct assertion that three months was the maximum sentence available for such an offence. Bunbury was forced to reconsider, and duly reduced the sentence to three months.

There was another, more direct connection between Wilde and the name Bunbury. At Trinity College Dublin, where Wilde had taken his first degree, Wilde had a friend called Henry S. Bunbury, to whom he wrote a letter in 1878, when Bunbury was living in Gloucestershire and Wilde was coming to the end of his time at Magdalen College, Oxford. If it was the newspaper report about the stipendiary magistrate that provided the initial inspiration for Bunbury's name, Wilde's memory of his student friend perhaps added piquancy to the choice.

In the case of Lady Bracknell, it is generally and plausibly held that Wilde's choice of name was due to the fact that Bosie's mother lived near the Berkshire town.[13] However, it is just possible that here too there may have been a stimulus provided by material in the *Worthing Gazette*.

In 1894, there were regular advisements in the paper for a patent preparation with the resonant name of Homocea. These were several versions of the advertisement, and it is the version that appeared on 15 August and again on 3 October that is of interest to us. It comes between two news items, and is designed to look like a news story itself, presented under the heading 'Servants' Characters'. The text says that, just as 'a good housekeeper would never think of engaging a servant without a character, and she would want that reference from a genuine source ... we (The Homocea Co.) do not ask the British public to take us on our own statement, but we publish testimonials such as no proprietor of Patent Medicines has ever received'. Four testimonials from satisfied users follow. The second of these reads as follows:

> Hillside, Bracknell, Berks
> LADY KEANE has much pleasure in recommending 'Homocea' as an invaluable remedy for Rheumatism, Cuts, Bruises, Piles, Sprains &c; she thinks so highly of it that she would not be without it in the house, as it has entirely cured her of Rheumatism and other ailments.

Lady Keane was clearly a martyr to her health, and it is fortunate that she had Homocea in her medicine cupboard. But the list she gives of ailments cured by Homocea is not exhaustive, since other grateful users quoted in the same advertisement testified to its efficacy as a cure for neuralgia, eczema and ringworm. Homocea's advertisements in other issues of the *Gazette* were variations on the same theme. In the 1 August issue, for example, the 'great African Explorer, Henry M. Stanley'[14] is quoted as saying, 'Your ointment, called Homocea, was found to be the most soothing and efficacious unguent that I could possibly have for my fractured limb.' Celebrities prostituting themselves to commerce is not a new phenomenon.

Caution should obviously be exercised when making connections on the basis of small pieces of evidence. Still, it is an odd coincidence that the words 'Bracknell' and 'Lady' should have appeared in such close proximity to each other in an advertisement published twice in a newspaper Wilde almost certainly read during the time he was writing *The Importance of Being Earnest*. Although we have conjectured that the second draft of the play went to Mrs Marshall's typing agency in stages, it is possible that the entirety of it was dispatched just before Wilde left Worthing on 4 October. At that point the Lady Bracknell character was called Lady Brancaster, so perhaps, a day or two after posting the manuscript, Wilde picked up the *Worthing Gazette*, saw the advertisement, and was inspired to make the name-change – the happy coincidence of a personal connection with the name cementing the idea, as in the case of Bunbury.

Lady Bracknell's first name – she was of course Algernon's Aunt Augusta – also has a link with Worthing. The town had a number of royal visitors in its early days, the longest visit being that of George IV's sister, Princess Augusta,[15] who stayed from November 1829 till March 1830. Afterwards the house where she stayed – on the seafront, about 350 yards to the west of the pier – was renamed Augusta House in her honour, and the street beside it Augusta Place. The princess's visit was usually mentioned in guidebooks to the town,[16] so Wilde may have read of it there; and he must sometimes have walked past Augusta Place and the four houses of Augusta Terrace during his stay in Worthing. What remained of Augusta House – the western half – had recently been converted into a hotel called Stanhoe Hall, which opened in May 1893 under the proprietorship of Mrs Thimm.[17]

Finally, in the context of connections between *Earnest* and Wilde's stay in Worthing, it is difficult to avoid the conclusion that Lady Bracknell's description of Miss Prism as 'a female of repellent aspect, remotely connected with education' was a conscious and unkind tribute to the 'horrid, ugly Swiss governess' whose presence at the Haven when Wilde arrived at the house on 10 August was so unwelcome to him. It is just possible too that, as hinted in Chapter 3, Wilde may have had in mind the extensive fictional output of Captain A. B. S. Fraser's mother, writing as 'Mrs Alexander', when he had Lady Bracknell refer to Miss Prism's magnum opus as 'a three-volume novel of more than usually revolting sentimentality'.

Some of the names in the play had inspirations outside Sussex. The solicitor Grigsby who appears in the four-act version works for the firm Parker and Grigsby, and Richard Ellmann suggests that the name Parker was chosen in reference to the Parker brothers with whom Wilde had been involved the previous year, and that Grigsby 'harked back to a character in du Maurier's aesthetic caricatures in *Punch*'. The two butlers were originally to be named after Wilde's publishers, John Lane and Elkin Mathews, with whom he had a fractious relationship, but, although the name Lane was retained, Mathews became Merriman.[18]

*

Although Wilde was adept at continuing to work through most

distractions, there was one distraction that was more of a problem than others. As we saw in Chapter 4, Bosie paid three visits to Worthing. The third visit, as Wilde makes clear in 'De Profundis', was one that he could have done without:

> I was trying to finish my last play at Worthing by myself ... Bored with Worthing, and still more, I have no doubt, with my fruitless efforts to concentrate my attention on my play, the only thing that really interested me at the moment, you insist on being taken to the Grand Hotel in Brighton.[19]

It is ironic that the love of Wilde's life should have been a barrier to his working on his greatest play. But Wilde claimed that it was always thus when Bosie was around:

> I am not speaking in phrases of rhetorical exaggeration but in terms of absolute truth to actual fact when I remind you that during the whole time we were together I never wrote one single line. Whether at Torquay, Goring, London, Florence or elsewhere. ... I had not sufficient influence with you to get you to leave me undisturbed as an artist should be left. Wherever my writing room was, it was to you an ordinary lounge, a place to smoke and drink hock-and-seltzer in, and chatter about absurdities.[20]

The assertion that Wilde makes in the first sentence quoted above is clearly preposterous. Much later Bosie countered the claim with 'rhetorical exaggeration' of his own. In his 1940 book *Oscar Wilde: A Summing-Up*, he furiously rejects Wilde's assertions that he never wrote anything when he was with him:

> But as in the (then) unpublished part of his letter to me from prison, 'De Profundis', he makes the amazingly and fantastically untrue statement that I interfered with his writing and that he *never wrote anything* while I was with him, I must again put on record the fact, which is susceptible of absolute proof, that from the time our close association began till the day he died he never wrote anything at all except when I was with him; generally I was actually staying in the same house and often sitting in the

same room with him while he wrote. He wrote the whole of *The Importance of Being Earnest* at a house in Worthing where I stayed with him, and most of it while I was sitting in the same room with him.[21]

It should be pointed out that much of the rewriting and revising of *Earnest* took place not in Worthing, but in Brighton and London during the late autumn. In addition, the claim that during their entire friendship Wilde never wrote anything except when Bosie was with him is just as absurd as Wilde's assertions to the contrary. Nor does the picture that Bosie paints of Wilde's concentrating on composing *Earnest* while he himself sat quietly and undemandingly in the same room carry much conviction.

At about the same time as Bosie was writing *Oscar Wilde: A Summing-Up*, he gave Marie Stopes – the birth-control pioneer, who became a friend of Bosie's towards the end of his life – a similarly Bosie-centric account of the composition of *Earnest*, telling her that he was 'personally with Wilde, staying with him and in and out of his study all the time he was writing [it]', and that a number of the jokes were based on his own 'repartee'.[22]

Probably neither Wilde's nor Bosie's versions of how things were during the writing of *Earnest* should be regarded as the entire truth. Wilde wrote 'De Profundis' when he was consumed by bitterness against Bosie. Much of his anger against Bosie at that time was therefore unfair, and indeed not entirely rational. We simply cannot know whether or not Bosie was, as Wilde says, a hindrance during the composition of *Earnest*; and perhaps, as Bosie suggests, some of the play's lines did indeed originate in badinage between the two of them.

This is not a preposterous assertion, for Bosie was undoubtedly an amusing conversationalist. Describing his first encounter with Bosie, in Cairo in February 1894, Robert Hichens[23] wrote in his autobiography, '[E. F. Benson] and Lord Alfred got on marvellously together, the wit of one seeming to call out and polish the wit of the other. Our dinners together in Louxour were without one moment of dullness.' A little later he refers to 'E. F. Benson and Lord Alfred Douglas, both so brilliant in their different ways, and so full of fun'.[24]

Even more persuasively Max Beerbohm, himself one of the wittiest men of the age, wrote on 12 March 1894 to Reginald Turner:

> Dear Bosie is with us. Is it you who have made him so amusing? Never in the summer did he make me laugh so much, but now he is nearly brilliant.[25]

Finally Wilde himself, admittedly at that time besotted by Bosie, referred in a letter of a few weeks before the Worthing holiday to 'the bright sword-play of your wit, the delicate fancy of your genius'.[26]

As time passed, however, Bosie tried to position himself closer and closer to the writing of the play; and eventually he perhaps convinced himself that he had been in constant proximity to its composition. It is amusing to note that, although in his vicious memoir of 1914 he was already keen to be associated with its composition – he says he was 'constantly with' Wilde when he wrote it – he is dismissive of all Wilde's plays:

> Wilde will not last as a dramatist ... His plays have been revived occasionally, and the glitter has been found in a great measure to have died out of them ... There are passages in all the plays which might have been written by a sentimental schoolgirl rather than by an artist, or by a giggling actor rather than a wit ... A man who boasted of the intellectual superiorities of which Wilde boasted, demeaned himself when he wrote them ... There are no plays of Wilde's and no books of Wilde's which can last on their literary merits.[27]

It is remarkable, in view of all that was going on in Worthing that summer, that Wilde found the time or mental space to write his bright, happy play full of manipulative and self-centred characters. The conditions under which he was working were far from ideal, with no room he could set aside for writing until Constance and the children left in mid-September and Arthur twice making chaos of the manuscript by 'tidying up'.[28] There were literary, theatrical and business matters to attend to – of the surviving twenty-six letters Wilde wrote from Worthing, over half (and almost all the longest) come into that category. There were the constant money worries. In the background there was the problem of the Marquess of Queensberry's campaign of harassment, which Oscar knew would become active again when he returned to London. There were the daily boat trips, and Oscar's relationship with Alphonse Conway. There was the long-suffering Constance, who got little attention, and the children, who received some. And of course – not the least of Oscar's problems – there was the egotistical Bosie. The fact that most of *The Importance of Being Earnest* came into being during so eventful and distraction-filled a summer is a tribute to Wilde's self-discipline, and to his ability to shut out the world in order to focus on his writing.

*

The first performance of *Earnest* took place on 14 February 1895. Allan Aynesworth, who played Algy, said later, 'In my fifty-three years of acting, I never remember a greater triumph than the first night of *The Importance of Being Earnest*. The audience rose in their seats and cheered and cheered again.'

Afterwards George Alexander, who played Jack Worthing, asked Wilde what he had thought of the performance.

'My dear Alec, it was charming, quite charming,' said Wilde. 'And, do you know,' he added, in reference to the many changes on which Alexander had insisted, 'from time to time I was reminded of a play I once wrote myself called *The Importance of Being Earnest*.'[29]

The reviews were mostly glowing.[30] In the *Speaker*, A. B. Walkley wrote:

Believe me, it is with no ironic intention that I declare Mr Oscar Wilde to have 'found himself' at last, as an artist in sheer nonsense ... there is no discordant note of seriousness. It is of nonsense all compact, and better nonsense, I think, our stage has not seen ... The laughter it excites is absolutely free from bitter afterthought.

In the *World*, William Archer wrote:

It is delightful to see, it sends wave after wave of laughter curling and foaming round the theatre ... an absolutely wilful expression of an irrepressibly witty personality ... 'farce' is too gross and commonplace a word to apply to such an iridescent filament of fantasy.

And in the *Pall Mall Gazette*, H. G. Wells wrote:

To the dramatic critic especially, who leads a dismal life, it came with a flavour of rare holiday ... It is all very funny, and Mr Oscar Wilde has decorated a humour that is Gilbertian[31] with innumerable spangles of wit that is all his own. We must congratulate him unreservedly on a delightful revival of theatrical satire.

Many years later, Hesketh Pearson eloquently summarised the unique charm of the play as follows:

It follows no rules and makes its own laws as it goes along. One cannot even call it perfect of its kind, because there is no kind. It is *sui generis*, perfect of itself, and the quintessence of Oscar ... Wilde said: 'The first act is ingenious, the second beautiful, the third abominably clever.' All of it is ingenious, all of it is abominably clever, and the whole is beautiful because perfection is beauty.

On 5 April 1895, the Queensberry libel trial collapsed and Wilde was arrested. The next day, the *Star* noted the effect the trial had had on the two plays of his being performed in London, *An Ideal Husband* at the Haymarket and *Earnest* at the St James's Theatre. The audiences were apparently much smaller than usual, but 'at neither place was there any hostile demonstration'. At the St James's, however, 'at one or two places slightly discordant remarks were made, especially when reference was made to the town of Worthing, but these chiefly came from the gallery and were of a trifling character'.[32]

On 6 April, George Alexander had Wilde's name covered up on the placards for *Earnest* with pieces of paper and blocked out on the programmes, and this principle remained in place for the rest of the run. He later claimed that this did this in order to help Wilde, this being the only way that he could prolong the run and thereby bolster Wilde's finances. Although Alexander's policy was imitated by Lewis Waller at the Haymarket for *An Ideal Husband*, this play was already scheduled to move to the Criterion, run by Charles Wyndham. Wyndham, admirably, said that he would not take the production unless Wilde's name appeared on the literature and advertising, and it was on this basis that *An Ideal Husband* ran at the Criterion from 13 to 27 April, the day after Wilde's first criminal trial began. *Earnest* was taken off on 8 May, twelve days before the start of the second trial.

8

'Absurd and silly perjuries': The Dramatist in the Dock

'You forced me to stay to brazen it out, if possible, in the box by absurd and silly perjuries.'
Oscar Wilde to Lord Alfred Douglas, 'De Profundis'

To some extent, everything had been put on hold during the two months that Oscar Wilde was in Worthing. It was an interlude. Indeed – if we exclude the affair with Alphonse Conway (quite a large exclusion, admittedly) – Wilde had by his standards been behaving respectably, too busy to get up to as much mischief as usual.

However, the problems in the offing had not gone away. The ridiculous but worrying correspondence between Bosie and his father had been continuing. Also, there had been an ominous event two days after Wilde arrived in Worthing. At midnight on 12 August, the police raided a house in Fitzroy Street in the East End of London that was being used as a meeting place for homosexuals. Among the eighteen men arrested were Alfred Taylor, who was to be Wilde's co-defendant in the criminal trials eight months later, and Charles Parker, who was to be one of the main prosecution witnesses. Although the magistrate had received letters indicating that most of the men brought before him were 'of the vilest possible character', there was insufficient evidence for them to be prosecuted, and Taylor, Parker and the others were given unconditional discharges.

Oscar was not overly concerned when he heard the news, writing a few days afterwards to Charles Spurrier Mason, with whom Taylor had gone through a mock marriage ceremony in 1893:[1]

I was very sorry to read in the paper about poor Alfred Taylor. It is a dreadful piece of bad luck, and I wish to goodness I could do something for him, but, as I have had occasion to write to him many times lately, as I have no play going on this season I have no money at all, and indeed am at my wits' end trying to raise some for household expenses and such tedious things.[2]

No direct ill consequence arose from the Fitzroy Street arrests, but it was a foretaste of things to come; and less than nine months later Alfred Taylor was back in court, this time with Oscar Wilde at his side.

*

After Bosie's appalling behaviour towards him while he lay ill in Brighton at the start of October 1894, Wilde resolved to end their relationship. According to his later account in 'De Profundis', he decided he would ask his solicitor to write to Bosie's father to tell him that he had 'determined never under any circumstances to allow you to enter my house, to sit at my board, to talk to me, walk with me, or anywhere and at any time to be my companion at all'; and write to Bosie to tell him what he had done.[3]

It is just possible that this time Wilde's resolve might have remained firm, but, as often in the Oscar Wilde story, fate made an unhelpful intervention. On 18 October – the day before Wilde himself left Brighton – Bosie's eldest brother, Viscount Drumlanrig, died from shotgun wounds at a shooting party. Although the inquest returned a verdict of accidental death, Drumlanrig's death was in some quarters held to be suicide.[4] He had been the private secretary to the Earl of Rosebery, who had succeeded Gladstone as Prime Minister in March 1894, and there were rumours that Drumlanig had been having a sexual relationship with Rosebery, and that this lay behind his death. Certainly Drumlanrig's father, the Marquess of Queensberry, was convinced of this, and referred in a letter to 'snob queers like Rosebery'. Rosebery's most recent biographer, however, believes that it is very unlikely that there was a homosexual relationship between the two men.[5]

Certainly there is no evidence that Drumlanrig was about to be exposed as Rosebery's lover, something that would have been impossible to prove and libellous to allege. Besides, Rosebery had more to lose from exposure than a relatively obscure young nobleman, and it does not seem likely that Drumlanrig should suddenly have been so overwhelmed with shame as to kill himself. And even if the curse of the blackmailer had struck, the money to pay him off would not have been difficult for a Prime Minister to find.

Whether accident or suicide, Drumlanrig's death had two implications as far as Wilde was concerned. The first was that he again took Bosie back into his life. The second was that Queensberry's determination not to – as he saw it – lose another son to homosexuality became an even greater obsession.

However, a few months passed before Queensberry took further action. In the meantime, Wilde's final two plays were being prepared for the stage. *An Ideal Husband* opened on 3 January 1895, to an enthusiastic first night audience and excellent reviews; and rehearsals for *The Importance of Being Earnest* began at about the same time.

On 17 January, Wilde and Bosie went to Algiers, where boys and hashish were freely available, and they partook freely of both. The French writer André Gide was also there. At that time he was still ambivalent about his sexual nature, but became less ambivalent after Wilde arranged for him to go to bed with an attractive young flute player. Meanwhile there was another dreadful quarrel between Wilde and Douglas, and Bosie went to Biskra with an Arab boy he had befriended.

Wilde returned to London and took rooms at the Avondale hotel in Piccadilly – he and Constance now rarely saw each other – and when Bosie returned from North Africa he joined Wilde there. Bosie's stay at the Avondale ended in acrimonious circumstances when he brought to the hotel 'a companion ... whose age, appearance, public and private profession, rendered him the most unsuitable companion possible for me in the terribly serious position in which I was placed'. Bosie took his young friend – whose 'private profession' was clearly that of male prostitute – to another hotel where, needless to say, Wilde paid for both.[6] This was an almost exact repetition of what had happened in Worthing at the end of the previous September.

Queensberry was now intent on forcing a confrontation more

decisive than his visit to Tite Street on 30 June the previous year, after which each man claimed a moral victory but nothing was resolved. Wilde had consulted his solicitor Charles Humphreys about a prosecution in May and again in July, but there were insufficient grounds to proceed. Queensberry too had consulted lawyers in the summer of 1893, after some letters from Wilde to Bosie had come into his hands. However, although their tone was unmistakeably homoerotic, for him also there was not enough on which to hang a case.

Queensberry's original plan was to disrupt the first night of *The Importance of Being Earnest* on 14 February by throwing vegetables at Wilde when he took his bow at the end of the performance. But Wilde and the actor-manager George Alexander learned of Queensberry's intentions, and Alexander cancelled his ticket and arranged for policemen to be on hand to prevent his admission to the theatre. Queensberry left his bouquet of carrots, cauliflowers and turnips at the box office.

Thwarted on 14 February, Queensberry went to Wilde's club four days later and left with the hall porter an open card on which were written five barely legible words. What Queensberry actually wrote was 'For Oscar Wilde, posing somdomite [*sic*]',[7] but by the time the case came to court he and his lawyers had decided that the words were 'posing as a so[m]domite', since this phrase would be easier to defend against the charge of libel.

The hall porter placed the card in an envelope, which he handed to Wilde on his next visit to his club on 28 February. His immediate reaction – and this was before he had spoken to Bosie – was given in a letter he wrote Robert Ross the same day: 'I don't see anything now but a criminal prosecution.'[8]

Bosie did all he could to bolster Wilde's resolve:

So to gratify [your hatred for your father], you gambled with my life, as you gambled with my money, carelessly, recklessly, indifferent to the consequence. If you lost, the loss would not, you fancied be yours. ... The prospect of a battle in which you would be safe delighted you. ... You thought simply of how to get your father into prison. To see him 'in the dock', as you used to say: that was your one idea.[9]

Like much of what Wilde wrote in 'De Profundis', this is to some extent unfair. Wilde was a party in the quarrel between father and son whether he liked it or not. It was disingenuous of him to suggest that it had nothing to do with him, as he asserted:

> Your quarrel with your father, again, whatever one may think about its character, should obviously have remained a quarrel between the two of you. It should have been carried on in a backyard. Such quarrels, I believe, usually are.[10]

Where Wilde was justified, however, was in pointing out that it was he, not Bosie, who was placing himself in jeopardy. It was also he that would have to be prepared to lie consistently and repeatedly – in due course on oath in court, but initially during meetings with his solicitor:

> What is loathsome to me is the memory of interminable visits paid to the solicitor Humphreys in your company, where in the ghastly glare of a bleak room you and I would sit with serious faces telling serious lies to a bald man, till I really groaned and yawned with *ennui*.[11]

The conventional view is that Wilde's decision to have Queensberry arrested for criminal libel was the fatal moment that brought about a disaster that would otherwise not have occurred. However if Wilde's association with Bosie had continued – as, in spite of their numerous hideous quarrels, it almost certainly would have done – Queensberry would have pursued other routes to ending a relationship that filled him with horror. Indeed, Queensberry had apparently been employing private detectives to look into Wilde's private life for some time before the calling-card was left, albeit without much success.[12]

It was, however, Queensberry, whether then or later, who was probably always going to be the key to Wilde's downfall. Wilde was not doomed simply because he conducted relationships with boys and young men with, often, a remarkable lack of discretion. Then, as today, men can get away with repeated sexual misdemeanours for surprising periods of time, sometimes indeed for a lifetime; and celebrity status, paradoxically, can make exposure less rather than more likely.

In addition, although after the Wilde trials the climate changed for ever, the law as it operated between 1885 and 1895 worked to the advantage of those whose sexual taste was for boys and young men. If a boy had sex with a man, he and the man were accomplices, and Wilde, Douglas and others like them could rely on this. If the case came to court, the elder participant would be deemed the more culpable, but both were offenders in the eyes of the law. Therefore no boy, particularly no boy of the lower classes, would have dreamt of going to the authorities. For a boy who felt aggrieved or underpaid, blackmail was the best available option, and indeed some made a profession of it. Bosie had been a victim in Oxford in the spring of 1892, and Wilde himself was the subject of a sustained blackmail attempt a year later. The blackmailers were Alfred Wood, then seventeen – a boy with whom Wilde had had a relationship and who was to feature prominently in the trials – and his accomplices, two professional blackmailers called Robert Cliburn and William Allen. Although Wilde brazened it out, the episode left him badly shaken.

The Act under which Wilde was prosecuted after the collapse of the libel trial was the Criminal Law Amendment Act of 1885. Prior to 1885, the law had taken no interest in sexual relations between males unless they involved buggery, for which the penalties had long been draconian. The Buggery Act of 1533 had made buggery, 'that abominable and detestable crime against nature', punishable by death; and it had ceased to be a capital offence only in 1861.

The 1885 Act came into being following public disquiet about the exploitation and prostitution of young girls, and its main purpose was to raise the age of heterosexual consent from thirteen to sixteen. A late amendment proposed by the Liberal MP Henry Labouchere made homosexual sex a crime – without any distinction of age – and introduced the catch-all offence of 'gross indecency' between males. The wording of the act did not specify what this meant, but in practice it covered any sexual activity between males other than buggery.

A notable trial soon after the act was passed was a case of September 1889 involving a homosexual brothel run by a man called Charles Hammond at 19 Cleveland Street in London. Its employees were telegraph boys aged between fifteen and seventeen, and its customers mainly men of the upper classes. Hammond fled abroad before the trial, as did some of his customers, notably Lord Arthur Somerset, the third son of the 8th Duke of Beaufort. The sentences passed on those that were brought to court were light. George Veck, aged forty, who was involved in the organisation of the brothel, received nine months with hard labour. Henry Newlove, an eighteen-year-old post office clerk who had procured telegraph boys to work at Cleveland Street, was given a four-month sentence. None of the brothel's customers were ever charged with any offence.

The case initially received little attention, but soon there were allegations that there had been a cover-up because of the importance of the brothel's clients – there were rumours that they included Prince Albert Victor, the eldest son of the Prince of Wales. Two further criminal trials followed. One, in January 1890, led to the jailing for twelve months of an investigative journalist called Ernest Parke, who had alleged that one of the brothel's customers was Henry Fitzroy, Earl of Euston. At the other trial, held in May, Arthur Newton, the solicitor who had acted for Veck and Newlove – and who was to be the solicitor for Wilde's co-defendant Alfred Taylor five years later[13] – was sentenced to six weeks for irregular contact with witnesses before the original trial. The brothel's customers continued to escape the law's attention.[14]

During the Wilde trials, as during the Cleveland Street trial, homosexual activity itself was the main issue, not the relative ages of the participants. When, in passing sentence on Wilde, Mr Justice Wills referred to his having been 'the centre of a circle of extensive corruption of the most hideous kind among young men',[15] it was the corruption that mattered more than the ages of those corrupted. The prosecuting barristers and the judges at the three trials gave the question of age a certain amount of attention, but mainly as an exacerbating circumstance.

*

On 2 March, Queensberry was arrested, charged with criminal libel, and bailed – whereupon the private detectives he had hired assiduously followed up every possible lead. Their most productive visit was to 13 Little College Street, where Alfred Taylor had rented four rooms for a year and eight months. In these 'sumptuously furnished' rooms – whose windows were never opened or cleaned, and whose curtains were always drawn – Taylor had 'burnt scent' and entertained numerous males aged between sixteen and thirty.[16]

Taylor came from a respectable and prosperous background. The son of a cocoa manufacturer, he had been educated at Marlborough College, one of England's leading public schools. In court during the first criminal trial he said that he had originally intended to go into the Army, but on coming of age came into a fortune of £45,000 (about £4,500,000 today) and thereafter 'had no occupation' but 'lived a life of pleasure'. By the time that he was living in Little College Street, however, he was bankrupt.[17] A louche individual, he had created around himself a homosexual milieu into which Wilde had drifted. Although the flat in Little College Street was not a brothel in the sense that the house in Cleveland Street had been, Taylor enjoyed introducing youths to men who would pay for the pleasure of their company.

At Little College Street, Queensberry's detectives found a cache of incriminating letters and a number of addresses that led directly or indirectly to most of the boys and young men who were to make statements, and who would have appeared as witnesses at the libel trial had it not collapsed. Most were subsequently to be named in the charges against Wilde and to give evidence in the two criminal trials, although not Walter Grainger and Alphonse Conway, since Wilde's involvement with them had been in Oxfordshire and Sussex, and therefore outside the jurisdiction of the Central Criminal Court.

Wilde knew nothing of Queensberry's investigations, and indeed it had never occurred to him that Queensberry would be able to track down the youths he had had sexual relations with over the past three years. When, on 1 or 2 April, Wilde was presented with Queensberry's Plea of Justification, which named no fewer than ten boys and young men, it was a devastating blow. Since it had been decided that 'posing as a sodomite' was the phrase Queensberry had to defend, Wilde had thought his main role would be to demonstrate that his writings were not sodomitical in character

– what became known as 'the literary part of the case'. Of course he had known that he would also be questioned about Bosie, but this had not greatly concerned him, not least because there was no question of Bosie's giving evidence. However, it would be almost impossible to contradict the evidence of so many witnesses – and yet Wilde did not change course.

A common view – and the one that Wilde developed at great length in 'De Profundis' – is that pressure from Bosie was largely to blame for Wilde's decision to continue, and that he lost the will to think independently. However, there were other factors that contributed to his decision. Although it was a huge risk to proceed, attempting to bluff it out was an option that was in many ways less unpalatable than the alternative. Indeed, Wilde had been considering what to do about Queensberry for at least a year, so he was not facing a dilemma into which much thought had not already gone.

And then there was Wilde's supreme self-confidence. Charm, intellectual dexterity and forcefulness of character had got him out of awkward situations in the past. Why should it be any different this time? He doubtless saw himself a match for any barrister in the land. In the libel trial he would present himself as an aesthete and a democrat – a befriender of youths, certainly, but a man whose instincts recoiled from the squalid activities that would be alleged by Queensberry's witnesses. The Old Bailey would be Wilde's biggest stage yet, but there was no reason why it could not be the scene of another triumph.

Pride was at stake too; and there were the practical consequences of not proceeding. Withdrawal would have been tantamount to an acceptance that he was not only a 'posing somdomite' but a sodomite *tout court*. Humiliation and a long period of exile would have been inevitable. 'I could not bear life if I were to flee,' he told his friend Robert Sherard between the two criminal trials. 'I cannot see myself slinking about the Continent, a fugitive from justice.'[18] Indeed, Wilde could never have returned to England while Queensberry remained alive, since the moment that he did so the Queensberry legal machine would have started up again. In the event Queensberry was to die at the relatively young age of fifty-five – in January 1900, ten months before Wilde – but he was only ten years older than Wilde. The actuarial probability, therefore, was that Wilde would have had to remain an exile for much of the rest of his life. If the gamble paid off, however, and Wilde won the case, the threat from Queensberry would be neutralised for good. In addition, once Wilde had been exonerated by a successful conclusion to the libel case, it would have been difficult for any subsequent case to be brought against him for sexual relations with boys. So, while the risks of continuing with the libel action were great, so were the potential rewards.

After the libel trial collapsed, Bosie and Wilde's other friends urged him to flee to the Continent during the few hours available before his arrest; but Wilde prevaricated until it was too late. His resistance to a lifetime of exile had not changed, and there was always the possibility that he might be acquitted, not least because most of the witnesses were tainted in one way or another. According to Bosie, Wilde's optimism, such as it was, was bolstered by the result of the first criminal trial: 'He looked upon the disagreement of the jury as a sort of verdict in his favour, and was under the impression that he stood a very good sporting chance of being found not guilty at the second trial.'[19]

*

The Queensberry libel trial began at the Central Criminal Court on 3 April 1895. To begin with, Wilde and Edward Carson, Queensberry's counsel, were evenly matched. Indeed, during the literary part of the case Wilde often had the upper hand: it was difficult to better him on his own territory. But Carson did not much mind if he did not win the literary debate, since these were merely the preliminaries. In the end it was not going to be crucial to the case whether or not a sodomitical interpretation could be placed on Wilde's published writings or his more florid letters to Bosie. Carson had his witnesses waiting. And once Carson moved on to the boys' evidence, the tone of the proceedings changed. Wilde's answers became shorter; there was less intellectual sparring, and there were fewer witty sallies.

Because much that Wilde said during the libel trial was clever, amusing and defiant, the view is sometimes taken that it was one of his finest hours. But that is to ignore the crucial fact that he was trying to get an innocent man sent to prison. The twelve-month sentence passed on Ernest Parke for suggesting that the Earl of Euston had been one of the customers of the Cleveland Street brothel demonstrates that the law took a stern approach to those that accused others of homosexual conduct without proof. Wilde's prosecution of Queensberry was at best ignoble, at worst wicked. 'Absurd and silly perjuries'[20] do not become admirable just because they are elegantly expressed and wittily phrased.

Another, lesser area that is awkward for Wilde's reputation was his attitude to social class as revealed during the trials – an attitude that provided Edward Carson with much ammunition during the libel trial. Wilde may, four years earlier, have written a long essay called 'The Soul of Man under Socialism', but it is difficult not to conclude that he was what would today be called a champagne socialist. Indeed, in his venomous account in *Oscar Wilde and Myself*, Bosie accuses Wilde of being a vulgar social climber, who was 'too much the tuft-hunter and the snob ever to be liked by the people for whose acquaintance he sighed ... He dearly loved a lord and would put up with a great deal of pain and inconvenience on the mere chance of a casual word or two with a duchess.' 'Wilde's socialism,' adds Bosie mystifyingly, 'was a species of socialism which looks very revolutionary but which is really designed to benefit the rich rather than the poor.'[21]

While these comments were malicious – and, to be fair to Bosie, it should be noted that he later repudiated the book[22] – there is some truth in them. Wilde had an air of effortless superiority about him that could be confused with snobbishness, but – although some of his answers in court might suggest the contrary – he was not by nature patronising. It is, however, hardly surprising that he was uncomfortable when Carson repeatedly referred to the social difference between him and the young men whose company he enjoyed.

Wilde had no alternative but to claim, improbably, that he was a man entirely indifferent to all distinctions of class. Thus, questioned about his association with Alfred Wood, Wilde said, 'If anybody interests me or is in trouble and I have been asked to help him in any way, what is the use of putting on airs about one's own social position? It is childish.'[23] When Carson asked if he knew that

Charles Parker had been a valet, Wilde replied, 'I never heard it, nor should I have minded. I don't care twopence about people's social positions.'[24] And when, a little later, Carson again asked if he knew that one of the Parker brothers was a valet and the other a groom, Wilde said that he did not know, repeating, 'Nor should I have cared ... I don't think twopence for social position; if I like them, I like them. It is a snobbish and vulgar thing to do.'[25] Finally, when Carson returned yet again to his theme, asking Wilde what he had in common with a young man of Charlie Parker's class, Wilde replied:

> Well, I will tell you, Mr Carson, I delight in the society of people much younger than myself. I like those who may be called idle and careless. I recognise no social distinctions at all of any kind and to me youth – the mere fact of youth – is so wonderful that I would sooner talk to a young man half an hour than even be, well, cross-examined in court. *(Laughter.)*[26]

Although Wilde largely maintained a consistent – if unconvincing – position as a man indifferent to class distinction, he dropped his guard when the opportunity for a witty riposte presented itself in the context of the clothes he had given Alphonse Conway. Carson suggested that he had bought Conway the clothes 'in order that he might look more like an equal'. 'Oh, no,' Wilde replied, 'he never would have looked that.' *(Laughter.)*[27]

In addition, Wilde demonstrated again and again how conscious he was of the intellectual gap between himself and his young friends; and indeed he made humorous capital out of this, something just as 'vulgar' as making social distinctions. However, he made an exception in the case of Alphonse Conway, for whom he clearly retained more affection than for any of the others. Although his guard had slipped when it came to Alphonse's new clothes, he was protective of him when it came to his lack of education:

> CARSON: He was an uneducated lad, wasn't he?
> WILDE: Oh, he was a pleasant, nice creature. He was not culti-
> vated. *(Laughter.)* Don't sneer at that. He was a pleasant, nice
> creature.[28]

Admirable though it was that Wilde would not countenance Alphonse's lack of cultivation being the cause of mirth, in the process he used a term that emphasised the social difference between them – he would not have called Robert Ross or Bosie a 'creature', nor, for that matter, a youth with intellectual interests such as Edward Shelley.

Although Alphonse's lack of education was off limits, Wilde rarely missed an opportunity for humorous comment at the expense of most of his other unintellectual companions. When Carson asked him whether Charles Parker – a youth with whom Oscar had become involved in November 1892 – was 'an educated man', Wilde replied, to laughter, 'Culture was not his strong point.'[29] And when, a little later, a letter from Parker was produced and read, and Carson asked if Wilde had any other of Parker's letters, Wilde replied, 'I never thought his correspondence sufficiently interesting to preserve.'[30]

Wilde responded in similar terms when Carson moved on to Fred Atkins and asked whether Atkins had discussed literature with him. There followed this exchange:

WILDE: Oh, I would not allow him. *(Laughter.)*
CARSON: That was not his line?
WILDE: No, the art of the music hall was as far as he had got. *(Laughter.)*[31]

Sometimes during the trials there were small, unguarded, foolish moments that revealed much. During the first criminal trial, for example, Charles Gill, the lead prosecutor, questioned Wilde about the cigarette cases that he gave as a matter of course to almost any youth that caught his eye; and Wilde remarked, more patronisingly than pertinently, 'Boys of that class smoke a good deal of cigarettes' – as though heavy smoking were vulgar behaviour confined to the lower classes, rather than a habit to which he himself was also addicted.[32]

A similarly patrician moment came during the second criminal trial, when Wilde was asked if he denied that there had been unusual stains on his bedsheets at the Savoy Hotel during his stay there in March 1893: 'I do not examine bed linen when I arise,' he replied. 'I am not a housemaid.'[33]

By the time of the second criminal trial Wilde was worn down and tired, and, although there were still flashes of brilliance, his tone was notably less assured than it had been during, in particular, much of the libel trial. Also, he was no longer thinking so nimbly or defensively. This sequence during his cross-examination by Sir Frank Lockwood is telling:

> WILDE: I admit that I am enormously fond of praise and admiration, and that I like to be made much of by my inferiors – inferiors socially. It pleases me very much.
> LOCKWOOD: What pleasure could you find in the society of boys much beneath you in social position?
> WILDE: I make no social distinction.
> [This mantra now seems very tired and unconvincing, not least in that it immediately follows Wilde's use of the word 'inferiors'.]
> LOCKWOOD: What did you do with them?
> WILDE: I read to them. I read one of my plays to them.
> [Improbable, surely?]
> LOCKWOOD: Did it not strike you that in your position you could exercise a considerable influence over these lads for good or ill?
> WILDE: No, I am bound to say I don't think it did. The only influence I could exercise on anybody would be a literary influence. Of course in the case of these young men that would be out of the question. [In that case, what was the point of reading them his play?] Otherwise I don't see what capacity I have for influencing people.[34]

In reality, Wilde was posing when he made himself out to be a man without social distinctions. He did not seek out members of the lower classes unless they were young, male and sexually amenable. What remains surprising, however, is the tone that he often took in court. It is as if he had forgotten where he was. His humorous comments were of the kind he might have made had he been among friends. At that time, and indeed through much of the twentieth century, liaisons between educated homosexuals and working-class boys or young men were common. When a man was among other members of his own tribe, light-hearted comments about the gaucheries and ignorance of the desirable youth were not unusual; and they caused no harm or hurt, since the young man was not present. It helped deflate the underlying embarrassment of the social and intellectual mismatch. But courtesy and common sense dictate that the ignorance and vulgarity of your bedmates should not be mocked in public. Whom did Wilde think he was addressing? Bosie or Robbie Ross?

In court, Wilde was not among like-minded literary homosexuals in tune with his arch asides. He was in the arena of the enemy. A playwright, above all men, should know his audience, but the script Wilde had brought to the Old Bailey was light comedy, while the tone of the drama was dark. It was a strategy of sorts, but it was flawed; and in the end – as we shall see in a moment – his playing to the gallery had disastrous consequences.

The question of who Wilde chose to sit down to dinner with provoked further inconsistency. Asked during the libel trial why he had invited the eighteen-year-old groom Ernest Scarfe to dinner, Wilde replied, 'Because I am very good-natured, because it is one of the best ways perhaps of pleasing anybody, particularly anyone not in one's social position, to ask him to dine.'[35]

Then, within minutes, Wilde took a different attitude to sitting at table with someone not in his social position – the reason being that the boy was Walter Grainger, one of his servants at Goring in 1893. Wilde was not prepared to extend the principle of democratic dining to an employee, even an employee with whom he shared his bed. When Carson asked whether Grainger had ever dined with him, Wilde was vehement: 'Never in my life ... It is really trying to ask me such a question ... He waited on me at table; he did not dine with me.' Carson commented, waspishly but pertinently, 'I thought he might have sat down. You drew no [social] distinction.' Wilde's response could almost have come from the lips of Lady Bracknell: 'If it is people's duty to serve, it is their duty to serve; if it is their pleasure to dine, it is their pleasure to dine and their privilege.'[36]

This comment was immediately followed by the most damaging moment in the trial, when Carson asked whether Wilde had ever kissed Walter Grainger. 'Oh, no, never in my life,' Wilde replied. 'He was a peculiarly plain boy ... very ugly ... I pitied him for it.' Wilde had fatally dropped his guard, and Carson homed in on him relentlessly. Cornered, Wilde stammered out unconvincing answers, and finally, lamely and humiliatingly, claimed that as the result of Carson's trying to 'unnerve' him he had given 'a flippant answer' when he should have spoken 'more seriously'. It was the turning point of the trial.[37]

But not only was this answer immensely damaging, since it demonstrated that Wilde would happily kiss good-looking boys, but not ugly ones; it was also an unforgivable thing to say of someone with whom he had had sexual relations. Once again, Wilde spoke as if he was among friends. Not only did Wilde, not for the first time, seem to think that servants did not have ears; he also did not seem to be concerned about their feelings – not a very socialist position. Although Grainger was not in court, he might have been called to give evidence at any moment, so Wilde knew that he could not be far away. With what relish did Queensberry perhaps return to the safe house where his witnesses were being kept to tell Grainger what Wilde had said.

The remark was not only unforgivable. It was not forgiven. It cannot be a coincidence that when, after Wilde's release from prison, Constance was preparing divorce proceedings – these never came to fruition – it was Walter Grainger that was to be the principal witness, as Wilde told Bosie in 'De Profundis':

> I, naturally, know nothing of the details. I merely know the name of the witness on whose evidence my wife's solicitors rely. It is your own Oxford servant, whom at your special request I took into my service for our summer at Goring.[38]

*

In the nineteenth century, 'Greek love' was commonly used to describe intimate relations between men, whether physical or not; the word homosexuality was not yet in common use. Greek love was an undercurrent to the trials, but Wilde avoided using the term. This was well advised, since Greek love had become a convenient cloak of semi-respectability which its adherents tried to drape over what was otherwise regarded as unnatural vice. The point at which Greek love almost rose to the surface was when part of Douglas's poem 'Two Loves' was quoted, including the resonant phrase 'the Love that dare not speak its name'. This was during the first of the two criminal trials, and Wilde's response was to deliver what was in effect a speech in defence of Greek love:

> The 'Love that dare not speak its name' in this century is such a great affection of an elder for a younger man as there was between David and Jonathan, such as Plato made the very basis of his philosophy, and such as you find in the sonnets of Michelangelo and Shakespeare. It is that deep, spiritual affection that is as pure as it is perfect. It dictates and pervades great works of art like those of Shakespeare and Michelangelo, and those two letters of mine, such as they are. It is in this century misunderstood, so much misunderstood that it may be described as the 'Love that dare not speak its name', and on account of it I am placed where I am now. It is beautiful, it is fine, it is the noblest form of affection. There is nothing unnatural about it. It is intellectual, and it repeatedly exists between an elder and a younger man, when the elder man has intellect, and the younger man has all the joy, hope and glamour of life before him. That it should be so, the world does not understand. The world mocks at it and sometimes puts one in the pillory for it.

This powerful speech was greeted with loud applause mingled with some hisses, causing Mr Justice Charles to say, 'If there is the slightest manifestation of feeling I shall have the Court cleared.'

As a sincere and emotional tribute to his love for Bosie – and that is what, in effect, it was – these sentiments cannot be faulted. But Wilde was not on trial for Bosie, and it was not on account of 'a deep, spiritual affection' that he was where he was. In the overall context of the trial, Wilde's words were hollow and hypocritical, as he well knew. Indeed, 'Greek love' as it was usually practised in the Victorian age was not something the Greeks would have recognised, the exchange in ancient Athens being, in simple terms, that the man gave the boy the benefit of his wisdom and experience, and the boy gave the man his body. Michael S. Foldy explains this:

> The Platonic relationship described by Socrates was precisely the opposite of the kind of (sexual) love that Wilde had sought with Parker, Wood, and the rest of the young men. Wilde's disingenuous but skilful appeal to the authority of Plato and the Bible proved successful because it was interpreted literally by those in the courtroom.[39]

It is true that, since Wilde was not allowed to defend his sexual adventures in the honest and hedonistic terms he would prefer to have used, his only option was high-flown hypocrisy. But there was nothing Greek about his relationships with the boys and young men with whom he was involved. As Foldy says, 'according to the ancient Athenian pederastic model, the youthful partner was supposed to benefit emotionally, intellectually, and spiritually from his relationship with the adult male'.[40] It is also true that in Wilde's relationships there was an element of companionship, and more so with Alphonse Conway than any of the others. He enjoyed giving boys dinner, although this was partly because he loved to be the centre of attention; and he occasionally provided help to his young friends – he at least 'made enquiries' about the Merchant Navy on behalf of Alphonse Conway. However, sexual desire was the driving force, not some philosophical principle dating back over 2,000 years.

Indeed, Carson's suggestion about how Wilde might alternatively have treated Conway – made during the libel trial just before the prosecution was withdrawn and the trial ended – was arguably closer to the spirit of Greek love than anything in Wilde's practice:

> I could understand the generous instincts of a man who would say, 'Here is a smart boy at Worthing whom I have met at the pier. I will try and get him employment; I will educate him; I will give him some money; I will try and assist him in any way I can.' But is it any assistance to a boy like Conway to do as Wilde did, to take him up and dress him and take him about giving him champagne lunches and all the rest of it?[41]

It might also be pointed out that that one of the principles that lay at the heart of Greek love was that the man took up with a single youth, not a whole seraglio of them, as Wilde and Douglas did. Ironically, it was as the result of the Oscar Wilde trials that Greek love could never again be a convenient excuse for the activities of educated pederasts. The trials exposed the late nineteenth-century variant of Greek love for what it was. Like Bunbury, it was 'quite exploded'.

*

On the whole, the English justice system dealt fairly with Wilde.

The principal blot – and it was one of which none of the judges or barristers were aware – is that it appears that some of the offences Wilde was charged with related to instances where Bosie was the culprit. In 'De Profundis' – written under prison censorship – Wilde was as explicit as he could be without incriminating Bosie:

> The sins of another were being placed to my account. Had I so chosen, I could on either trial have saved myself at his expense, not from shame indeed but from imprisonment. Had I cared to show that the Crown witnesses – the three most important – had been carefully coached by your father and his solicitors, not in reticences merely, but in assertions, in the absolute transference, deliberate, plotted, and rehearsed, of the actions and doings of someone else on to me, I could have had each one of them dismissed from the box by the Judge, more summarily than even the wretched perjured Atkins was.[42]

In *Oscar Wilde and Myself*, Bosie flatly denied that this was true. He cites a passage from Robert Sherard's 1906 biography where Wilde is quoted as saying after his release, 'Five of the counts referred to matters with which I had absolutely nothing to do. There was some foundation for one of the counts.' To have told his defence team this, Wilde added, 'would have meant betraying a friend'. But Bosie insists that Wilde was guilty on all six counts, adding, 'Wilde was not of the stuff that goes to hard labour with the name of a friend in his bosom when, by mentioning that name, he could have cleared himself.'[43] The general consensus, however, is that there was truth in Wilde's claims; and, if witnesses were indeed persuaded to attribute to Wilde activities they had indulged in with Bosie, that is indeed shocking. Doubtless Queensberry justified the tactic by telling himself that, since Wilde had perjured himself in order to try to get him imprisoned, it was reasonable that his witnesses should return the favour.

The jury in the first criminal trial found Wilde and Taylor not guilty on some of the charges, but could not agree on the rest, and it was duly discharged. In such circumstances it was by no means inevitable that a new trial would be ordered. Indeed, Carson asked the Solicitor-General, Sir Frank Lockwood, who was to be the lead prosecutor in the final trial, why the Crown would not 'let up' on Wilde. Lockwood replied that they dared not abandon the trial, because 'it would at once be said, both in England and abroad, that owing to the names mentioned in Q's letters we were forced to abandon it'.[44] These letters supposedly implicated Rosebery and others. In other words, Queensberry seems to have been blackmailing the English legal system. Only by sending Wilde to prison could the scandal be contained.

It was an exceptional step to bring in the Solicitor-General to lead the prosecution team at the second criminal trial. This not only gave the prosecution additional authority. There was also the curious principle that if the Solicitor-General was prosecuting a case he, rather than the defence, was allowed the advantage of the last word – an invidious privilege that Sir Edward Clarke pointed out he himself had never once exercised during his own six-year period as Solicitor-General.[45] It was clear that what we would today call the Establishment was determined that Wilde should be convicted.

Nonetheless, the third trial, like the others, was conducted fairly. Mr Justice Wills is best remembered for the ferocity of his remarks in passing sentence, but in other respects his conduct of the case was as impartial as that of the other two judges. Wills had had to sit through a lengthy recitation of 'absurd and silly perjuries' delivered in high-minded tones, and this undoubtedly influenced the character of his final comments. In any case, in being shocked and appalled by the offences of which Wilde was found guilty, he was merely reflecting what most people of the time felt – and indeed what the majority of those that study the evidence attentively today would doubtless feel. Nonetheless, if this was truly, as he claimed, the worst case he had ever tried,[46] Mr Justice Wills must have led a sheltered judicial life.

*

A common canard among those who know a little about Wilde is that he was a martyr to Victorian injustice and hypocrisy. However, as we have indicated, the trials were conducted fairly; and Wilde was fortunate that the maximum sentence available to the judge was two years, which Mr Justice Wills described as 'wholly inadequate for such a case'. Today men who have sexual relations with boys under sixteen can be sentenced to up to fourteen years in prison, and paying for sex with a boy of sixteen or seventeen carries a sentence of up to seven years. Wilde probably committed the first of these offences,[47] and he was certainly guilty of the second.

Hostility to Wilde was almost universal. When the sentence was announced, people danced with joy in the streets. A few prostitutes kicked up their skirts with glee, and one said, "'e'll 'ave 'is air cut reglar now', to much laughter.[48] Then, six months later, on 13 November 1895, when Wilde was being transferred from Wandsworth to Reading, he endured a hideous humiliation at Clapham Junction, where he had to change trains:

> From two o'clock till half-past two on that day I had to stand on the centre platform of Clapham Junction in convict dress and handcuffed, for the world to look at ... Of all possible objects I was the most grotesque. When people saw me they laughed. Each train as it came up swelled the audience. Nothing could exceed their amusement. That was of course before they knew who I was. As soon as they had been informed, they laughed still more. For half an hour I stood there in the grey November rain surrounded by a jeering mob.[49]

Today the whores might not have danced, and the rail travellers might not have been allowed to jeer unchecked, but Wilde would have been pilloried in different ways, not least in the vicious British press of which he had written so presciently in 'The Soul of Man under Socialism'. He would have been called a 'child abuser' and a 'predatory paedophile', terms which – freely if inaccurately used for offences right up to the age of consent – bring so much convenient baggage with them. His plays would have been taken off the stage, probably more quickly than they were in 1895. His name would have disappeared from the newspapers, except when some cameraman with a long lens captured him talking to a fisher boy on a Mediterranean beach, whereupon the front page of the paper would have printed a spiteful story about a pervert returning to his former ways.

No reasonable person condones adult males engaging in sexual acts with prepubescent boys. When it comes to teenagers, however, we are in more complex territory, and blanket condemnation is unhelpful. Some such relationships are supportive, even valuable; others are exploitative and damaging. The age, maturity and personality of the boy – and the difference in age between him and the man – all need to be considered, as do the context and the circumstances. The man's attitude, too, is relevant; and Wilde gets little credit in this respect. We quoted in the first chapter of this book his later comment: 'I grew careless of the lives of others. I took pleasure where it pleased me and passed on.' His obsession with Bosie left no space for emotional involvement with anyone else.

Even within one individual there may be variations, and this applied in Wilde's case. The relationship with Alphonse Conway seems to have been relatively benign and – at least until the scandal broke in the spring of 1895 – untraumatising. The relationship with Walter Grainger, however, had a darker side. As a servant, Grainger was in a position where he perhaps did not have much choice when it came to Wilde's advances. Also, uniquely among Queensberry's witnesses, Grainger alleged that Wilde had warned him of the importance of telling no one about the activities they engaged in, saying that if he did the boy would be in 'serious trouble' and would go to prison.[50] The kindest interpretation of this is that Grainger may have been rather slow witted, with little common sense or knowledge of the law, and that Wilde thought he was more likely than the others to blurt out something compromising; but it still does not make comfortable reading.

Wilde himself, however, was in no doubt that he was a better man than those that brought him down:

> I never came across anyone in whom the moral sense was dominant who was not heartless, cruel, vindictive, log-stupid, and entirely lacking in the smallest sense of humanity. Moral people, as they are termed, are simple beasts. I would sooner have fifty unnatural vices than one unnatural virtue.[51]

*

Wilde was ill equipped to cope with the rigours of the harsh prison regime of those days, or with the almost total lack of human contact – prisoners were not allowed to speak to each other, and few visits were allowed. At Reading, where Wilde spent the last eighteen months of his sentence, the governor for the first eight of these months was Colonel Isaacson, a martinet with a passion for petty rules and punishment, and Wilde's time under him was miserable. Under Isaacson's successor, Major Nelson, a more humane regime prevailed, and Wilde was allowed more books, and indeed the writing materials that allowed him to write the long letter to Bosie that became known as 'De Profundis'.

Wilde was released from prison on 19 May 1897, and later the same day he took the ferry to Dieppe. He never returned to England. The remaining three and a half years of his life were spent in France and Italy. His exile was not altogether unhappy. There were intermittent humiliations when he was recognised by hostile strangers, or cut by people he had seen as friends. He was almost always short of money, and he drank too much. Although he had long ago stopped loving Constance, it was a grief to him that he never saw his sons again. He had to depend for financial and practical support on unreliable people, not least Bosie.

But it was not all unhappiness. Wilde was rarely alone. There were inevitable reconciliations and estrangements with Bosie. There were loyal friends such as Frank Harris and Robbie Ross. There was no longer any need to hide his attraction for teenage boys, or to pretend that it had anything to do with Greek love, and he had sexual relations with numerous French and Italian boys.

But he had lost the urge to write. There was just one final work of substance – *The Ballad of Reading Gaol* – and after that Wilde's genius fell silent. There was no spark left, and, equally importantly, no audience.

He did, however, contemplate writing one more poem, as he told Frank Harris in December 1898, when he was staying at the Hôtel des Bains at La Napoule, near Cannes:

'I should like to write *The Ballad of a Fisher Boy*,' said Oscar, and he fell to dreaming. ... 'I shall do this joy-song much better than I did the song of sorrow and despair.' ... 'I have composed three or four verses of it. I have got them in my head.' And he recited two or three, one of which was quite good, but none of them startling.[52]

Wilde told Harris that *The Ballad of a Fisher Boy* was to be 'a sort of companion to *The Ballad of Reading Gaol*; in which I sing of liberty instead of prison, joy instead of sorrow, a kiss instead of an execution'. The never-written poem was inspired by scenes on the beach at La Napoule, where 'romance ... comes in boats, and takes the form of fisher-lads, who draw great nets, and are bare-limbed: they are strangely perfect'.[53] But perhaps Wilde also sometimes remembered the happy, good-humoured boy who had been his companion on so many swimming and fishing expeditions in Sussex four years earlier.

*

The penultimate section of this chapter is a catalogue of deaths.

Constance Wilde, who in October 1895 took for herself and her sons the name Holland – a remote name within her family[54] – in order to avoid the shame and embarrassment associated with her husband's name, died on 7 April 1898, following an unsuccessful operation on her back.

Oscar Wilde died on 30 November 1900 at the Hotel d'Alsace in Paris, with Robert Ross and Reginald Turner at his bedside. Bosie came as soon as he could, but arrived two days too late.

Wilde's elder son, Cyril Holland, became an Army officer, and three months after the start of the First World War was promoted to the rank of captain. He was killed by a German sniper on 9 May 1915 during the Battle of Festubert.

Wilde's younger son, Vyvyan, also served in the First World War, and afterwards became an author and translator. He died on 10 October 1967. The direct line of descent from Oscar Wilde continues, however. Lucian Holland, the only child of Vyvyan Holland's son Merlin, followed his great-grandfather to Magdalen College, Oxford in 1997 and, like him, achieved a double first in Greats.

The Marquess of Queensberry died on 31 January 1900, less than a year before Wilde. His eldest surviving son, Percy, who had taken Wilde's side in 1895, visited him on his deathbed, and Queensberry found the energy to spit at him. Bosie stayed away.

Robbie Ross and Bosie, once close friends, became acrimonious adversaries in the aftermath of Wilde's death, and remained so until

Ross – the most steadfast and loyal of Wilde's supporters and his literary executor – died on 5 October 1918.

Bosie repudiated both Oscar Wilde and homosexuality. On 4 March 1902 he married Olive Custance, a young poet who had written to him admiringly about his verse. For ten years the marriage was happy, but they did not live together as man and wife after 1913, although they mainly remained friends. Appalled and humiliated by 'De Profundis', the long letter that Wilde had written to him in Reading prison, Douglas was for many years vitriolic in his denunciations of his one-time lover and friend. As the years passed, however, he more or less came to terms with the relationship that had dominated his life and in whose shadow he lived till his death. He died on 20 March 1945.

Bosie and Olive had one child, Raymond, born on 17 November 1902, who began to show signs of mental illness in his early twenties and was diagnosed with schizophrenia. The condition gradually worsened, and he spent the last twenty years of his life in a mental institution. He did not marry or have children, and died on 10 October 1964.

Most of the boys and young men with whom Wilde had been involved in the first half of the 1890s were never heard of again, and nothing is known for certain about what happened afterwards to Alphonse Conway – although, there is evidence that he and his mother may have put 10,000 miles between themselves and the Wilde scandal, and forged a new life in Australia.[55]

*

Meanwhile, Worthing initially did its best to forget its uncomfortable brush with genius, and the Wilde trials were not reported in the local press.

Today the town's links with Wilde are almost universally celebrated. A few years ago, however, there was a minor controversy that made the pages of the national newspapers. In January 2009 – a few months after the publication of a book about Worthing's history that devoted a few pages to Oscar Wilde's time in the town[56] – it was reported that John 'Steve' Stevens DFC, a former Second World War fighter pilot and veteran moral crusader,[57] was concerned that the link with Wilde brought 'the wrong sort of people' to Worthing. Stevens was quoted in the *Observer* as follows:

> This town is going downhill tremendously fast and people feel so strongly that we have to stand up and fight against that. This was a beautiful area and we shall have no truck with remembering the likes of Oscar Wilde and all the worst things in life. I myself would fight tooth and nail for any campaign to erase a link between Worthing and a child abuser.[58]

As indicated earlier, it is incorrect to describe Wilde as a child abuser. Until half a century or so ago, men attracted to teenage boys were known, as in ancient Athens, as pederasts; today psychologists use the term ephebophile. However, regardless of what terminology is used, Wilde's sexual activities still pose difficult questions today.

The passage of the years has a curious relationship with awkward truths. Embracing the redeeming effect of time can result in inconsistencies. In the case of Wilde, the convenient solution is to pretend that his sexual taste was for young men, and in this respect the Wilde story is sometimes told with deliberate dishonesty. In the 1997 film *Wilde*, for example, the youths with whom Wilde was involved are presented as young adults. Charles Parker, who was seventeen when Wilde had a sexual relationship with him[59] – and a couple of years older at the time of the trials – was played by a twenty-six year old actor. That is distorting the past for the convenience of the present.[60]

Comments such as Stevens's at least have the merit of forcing us to address our illogicalities and hypocrisies. The journalist and broadcaster Tom Sutcliffe cogently addressed the issue in his column in the *Independent* on 6 January 2009 in response to the Stevens story:

> It did get me wondering about the statute of limitations on social transgression though. After all, there's little doubt that if Wilde was a contemporary playwright his predilection for teenage boys would effectively guarantee the end of his career … It isn't impossible either to imagine crimes that could still end Wilde's career, or make new productions a lot more awkward. What

if, say, a literary historian discovered irrefutable proof that he had violently raped pre-pubertal children? Would we still be as charmed by his epigrams about scandal, still be as inclined to argue the toss about different cultural norms? None of the jokes in the works would have changed a bit, none of the word-play or the paradoxes would be less sparkling – but I doubt that audiences would feel free to indulge the wit so readily. It's easy to mock those who set out to retrospectively police the social and sexual attitudes of our forebears – but it's worth remembering that there's usually a line none of us would cross.

Stevens's reference to 'erasing the link' between Wilde and Worthing related to a suggestion that the blue plaque commemorating Wilde's visit be removed from Esplanade Court, the hideous modern building that stands on the site of the terrace where Wilde and his family stayed.[61] But this campaign never amounted to much.

As it happens, all the main physical links between Wilde and Worthing have already been erased, since all four buildings in the town that we know Wilde spent time inside are gone.

The Haven, where the Wilde family stayed in the summer of 1894, was demolished with the rest of the Esplanade at the end of the 1960s. The Marine Hotel, where Wilde entertained Bosie, Alphonse and Stephen to lunch on or around 21 August 1894, was demolished in 1965, the present pub and restaurant being the second building that has stood there since then. The Assembly Rooms, later the New Theatre Royal – where Wilde was cheered when he and Cyril entered on 7 September – closed in 1929 and was demolished in 1934; today a toy shop occupies the site. And the pavilion at the sea end of the pier, where Wilde delivered his amusing speech on 13 September, was destroyed by fire in 1933 and replaced by an art deco structure, recently restored as tearooms and a venue for private parties and weddings.

However, Oscar Wilde's stay in Worthing has a permanent memorial that no one can destroy – for *The Importance of Being Earnest* will continue to give delight for as long as plays are performed in the English language.

Notes

For the convenience of the reader, a book's full title, publisher, and date of publication are given the first time a book is cited in any given chapter, rather than just on its first appearance anywhere in the notes. In subsequent citations within each chapter a short version is used.

Six books proved indispensable during the writing of the first and last chapters of this book, which deal with Oscar Wilde's life before and after the Worthing holiday. These are: Richard Ellmann, *Oscar Wilde* (Hamish Hamilton, 1987); Merlin Holland, *Irish Peacock & Scarlet Marquess: The Real Trial of Oscar Wilde* (Fourth Estate, 2003); Merlin Holland and Rupert Hart-Davis, eds, *The Complete Letters of Oscar Wilde* (Fourth Estate, 2000); H. Montgomery Hyde, *Lord Alfred Douglas* (Methuen, 1984); H. Montgomery Hyde, *Trials of Oscar Wilde* (William Hodge, 1948); and Neil McKenna, *The Secret Life of Oscar Wilde* (Century, 2003). Specific information derived from these books for these two chapters is referenced in the notes, but what might be described as general information may not be.

1 'Three is company and two is none': A Disruptive Friendship

1. The journalist and art critic Robert Ross (1869–1918) was ever-present in Wilde's life from 1886 till Wilde's death. Although his place in Wilde's affections was to some extent taken by Bosie, he never wavered in his devotion to Wilde, and he remained on good terms with Bosie. During Wilde's imprisonment and exile, however, the relationship between Ross and Bosie became acrimonious, and after Wilde's death they were bitter enemies.
2. Frank Harris, *Oscar Wilde, His Life and Confessions*, Vol. 2 (Constable, 1938), p. 486. This conversation took place in December 1898 when Wilde was staying at the Hôtel des Bains at La Napoule, near Cannes.
3. Richard Ellmann, *Oscar Wilde* (Hamish Hamilton, 1987), p. 262, using material from a letter of Otho Holland to Arthur Ransome of 28 February 1912.
4. Letter from Robert Sherard to A. J. A. Symons, 8 May 1935.

5. Vyvyan Holland, *Son of Oscar Wilde* (E. P. Dutton, 1954), p. 24.
6. Merlin Holland and Rupert Hart-Davis, eds, *The Complete Letters of Oscar Wilde* (Fourth Estate, 2000), p. 732.
7. Lord Alfred Douglas, *The Autobiography of Lord Alfred Douglas* (Martin Secker, 1929), p. 64.
8. This is the figure arrived at by the rigorous calculations of Josephine M. Guy and Ian Small in *Oscar Wilde's Profession: Writing and the Culture Industry in the Late Nineteenth Century* (Oxford University Press, 2000), p. 111. Guy and Small reject the 'mythical' figure of £7,000, 'which has passed into scholarly folklore'. I am grateful to Donald Mead for this reference.
9. Neil McKenna, *The Secret Life of Oscar Wilde* (Century, 2003), p. 174.
10. *Complete Letters*, p. 795.
11. A May date lies between two other dates given elsewhere. On p. 27 of *Lord Alfred Douglas* (Methuen, 1984), H. Montgomery Hyde writes, 'It was also probably at this time, during the Easter vacation, in 1892, that Bosie eventually gave in to Wilde.' Neil McKenna says that 'the love of Oscar and Bosie was consummated in the early hours of a June morning at Tite Street' (*The Secret Life of Oscar Wilde*, p. 185), but no source is given.
12. Letter from Lord Alfred Douglas to Frank Harris, 20 March 1925.
13. *Complete Letters*, p. 689.
14. *Complete Letters*, pp. 687–8, 767–8.
15. Alfred Bruce Douglas, *Oscar Wilde and Myself* (John Long, 1914), pp. 84–6.
16. Douglas, *Oscar Wilde and Myself*, pp. 96–7, 102, 112–13. Bosie later repudiated this book – see Chapter 8, note 22.
17. *Complete Letters*, p. 730.
18. *Complete Letters*, p. 692.
19. *Complete Letters*, p. 715.
20. *Complete Letters*, pp. 685–6.
21. For information about Lady Mount Temple, see pp. 88–9.
22. Franny Moyle, *Constance: The Tragic and Scandalous Life of Mrs Oscar Wilde* (John Murray, 2011), pp. 213–16.
23. See McKenna, *The Secret Life of Oscar Wilde*, pp. 238–40.
24. Constance Wilde to Georgina Mount Temple, undated, BR 57/14 /93.
25. Ellmann, *Oscar Wilde*, p. 262, using material from Otho Holland's letter to Arthur Ransome of 28 February 1912.
26. *Complete Letters*, p. 784.
27. *Complete Letters*, p. 694.

2 'Anything is better than London': The Haven in Worthing

1. The bibliographic information for Constance Wilde's letters to Georgina Mount Temple is given in notes 7 and 8 to Chapter 6.
2. Merlin Holland and Rupert Hart-Davis, eds, *The Complete Letters of Oscar Wilde* (Fourth Estate, 2000), p. 594.
3. *Complete Letters*, p. 597.
4. *Complete Letters*, p. 598. Ernesto was probably Ernest Scarfe, a youth with whom Wilde had become sexually involved early in 1894. Wilde had met

Scarfe through Alfred Taylor, who had picked him up at the roller-skating rink in Knightsbridge. See Neil McKenna, *The Secret Life of Oscar Wilde* (Century, 2003), p. 276

5. *Complete Letters*, p. 598.
6. James Gregory, 'Lady Mount Temple and Her Friendship with Constance Wilde', Section I (online article) suggests this only as a possibility. On p. 243 of Franny Moyle, *Constance: The Tragic and Scandalous Life of Mrs Oscar Wilde* (John Murray, 2011), it is presented as a fact. Moyle is presumably following Gregory, but she provides no additional evidence.
7. *Worthing Gazette*, 15 August 1894.
8. Merlin Holland, *Irish Peacock & Scarlet Marquess: The Real Trial of Oscar Wilde* (Fourth Estate, 2003), p. 237.
9. Wilde certainly cannot have travelled down to Worthing with Humphreys on the Saturday, because the family lunch he described to Bosie on the day of his arrival in Worthing – *Complete Letters*, p. 598 – is clearly not the lunch with Humphreys.
10. Merlin Holland points out that 'the margin for error [in the transcribed text of the Queensberry trial] is considerable', with much potential for 'mishearings of the proceedings and misreadings of their own notes' by the different shorthand writers (Holland, *Irish Peacock & Scarlet Marquess*, p. xl).
11. This sum clearly included food and servants' wages, and probably the rent as well.
12. The list of the household that Constance gave her brother Otho in the letter of 31 August seems to be the only place where Arthur Fenn's surname appears.
13. Hesketh Pearson writes that the two men 'were shown into the library by the seventeen-year-old footman, who was small in stature and tremblingly nervous at the sight of the ex-champion and his fellow-bruiser', Hesketh Pearson, *The Life of Oscar Wilde* (Penguin, 1960; first published by Methuen, 1946), p. 270. Pearson does not provide a reference – his book has no notes – but at the back he lists as 'Authorities' some 150 books he has consulted, so presumably the information is reliable.
14. *Complete Letters*, p. 602.
15. Richard Ellmann, *Oscar Wilde* (Hamish Hamilton, 1987), p. 429.
16. McKenna, *The Secret Life of Oscar Wilde*, p. 212; Holland, *Irish Peacock & Scarlet Marquess*, p. 117.
17. On p. 90 of Anon [Christopher Millard], *Oscar Wilde Three Times Tried* (Ferrestone Press, 1910), Wilde's denial that he had ever had a servant called 'Ginger' is followed by the editorial comment that 'Ginger was the nickname of a page-boy in Wilde's employment'. I am indebted to Donald Mead for this reference, and indeed for his deduction that Arthur Fenn and 'Ginger' were probably the same person.
18. These famous comments are part of the account of the episode that Wilde gave in court during the Queensberry libel trial (Holland, *Irish Peacock & Scarlet Marquess*, pp. 58–9). He cast himself as the clear victor in their exchanges, and said that at the end he 'went out into the hall followed by Lord Queensberry' and addressed these remarks to his servant. In his brief reference to the confrontation in 'De Profundis' (*Complete Letters*, pp.

699–700), however, Wilde – after focusing on Queensberry's behaviour and 'loathsome threats' – stated that Queensberry 'had to leave the room first'. Queensberry himself claimed in a letter that Wilde 'had shown him the white feather' (Ellmann, *Oscar Wilde*, p. 396).
19. See McKenna, *The Secret Life of Oscar Wilde*, pp. 238–40. The unfortunate Walter Grainger was the boy who, during the Queensberry libel case, was gracelessly described by Wilde as too ugly to kiss, a foolish comment that proved to be the turning point of the trial (see pp. 138–9). Grainger was born in 1876 (Holland, *Irish Peacock & Scarlet Marquess*, p. 321, note 209), so he would have been sixteen or seventeen in the summer of 1893.
20. Vyvyan Holland, *Son of Oscar Wilde* (E. P. Dutton, 1954), pp. 43, 176.
21. Franny Moyle writes that Cyril and Vyvyan 'had an aquarium with them' (*Constance*, p. 246), but in fact each boy had one of his own. Although the 'S' in Constance's letter of 11 August to Lady Mount Temple is small, it is definitely present; and indeed it makes sense – two small boys with a shared aquarium would have been a recipe for ructions, broken glass, and crabs on the carpet.
22. Vyvyan Holland, *Son of Oscar Wilde*, p. 25.
23. Franny Moyle incorrectly gives the 4 September date as the date of Constance's departure (*Constance*, p. 249).
24. The multiple daily postal collections and deliveries in late Victorian England made the post a much faster means of communication than it is today.
25. The 'concert letter', *Complete Letters*, pp. 607–8, and printed verbatim in Appendix B.

3 'The beauty and grace of everything': Oscar Wilde and the Worthing Festivals

1. Robert Elleray, *Sussex Theatres: An Illustrated Survey and Gazetteer, c. 1750–2000* (2000), p. 38. The New Theatre Royal closed on 9 February 1929 – Elleray, *Worthing Theatres, 1780–1984* (1985), p. 14 – and was demolished in 1934. The interior of the building underwent extensive restructuring in 1897 and 1906, but Elleray believes that the outside remained much as it had been when it was the Assembly Rooms, although the glass canopy to protect queuing patrons from the rain seen in illustration 27 was probably an addition dating from 1897 or 1906 (telephone conversation, 13 October 2011). Oddly, an advertisement for a play called *Theodora* in the *Worthing Gazette* of 5 September 1894 uses the name 'Theatre Royal, Worthing' for the venue, so that name was evidently already sometimes in use in Wilde's time.
2. Information from www.clanfraser.ca/admiral_fraser.htm and www.victorian-research.org/atcl/show_author.php?aid=459. The birth and death dates of the members of the Fraser family are as follows: General Alexander Fraser (1824–98), Caroline Fraser, *née* Small (1829–1908), Captain Alexander Fraser (1847–1933), Captain Campbell Fraser (1850–1926), Charlotte Smith (1861–1946), Lieutenant-Colonel Cecil Fraser (1885–1951), Admiral Bruce Fraser (1888–1981). Captain A. B. S. Fraser was a farmer, first at West Tarring

Farm, just north-west of Worthing – where he won prizes for his cows Betsy in 1897 (*Country Life*, 1897) and Perry Farm Pansy in 1902 (*Journal of the Royal Agricultural Society of England*, 1902) – and then at Withdean Farm near Brighton. When he died in 1933, *The Sussex County Magazine* reported, 'Sussex has lost one of its most prominent public men.'

3. Merlin Holland and Rupert Hart-Davis, eds, *The Complete Letters of Oscar Wilde* (Fourth Estate, 2000), pp. 607–8.
4. See pp. 65, 178.
5. By an odd coincidence, there was a group of singers called the Olympian Quartet active in America at the same time. The *New York Sun* reported on 2 May 1894, 'There are few brand-new things in the variety theatres this week. La Belle Tina made her American debut at the Union Square on Monday, and displayed a deal of grace in posing and balancing in midair. Here, too, are Wood and Sheppard and the Olympian Quartet, which was for a long time associated with Evans and Hoey [a well-known vaudeville act of the period]. The list of performers is long.' Performances by this Olympian Quartet are also noted in the *New York Times* of 16 July 1901 (they had performed 'a long list of new and old favourites' at Keith's Union Square Theatre) and the *Monroe County Mail* of 27 February 1902, which reports that the Olympian Quartet of Rochester 'gave an entertainment in Grange Hall Saturday evening'. Worthing would have been an unlikely destination for vaudevillians from New York, so it is improbable – though not impossible – that the American quartet were the singers that performed in the town in the summer of 1894.
6. Arthur Law (1844–1913) was a prolific playwright of the time. *The New Boy* was a great success, and was also performed on Broadway.
7. Weedon Grossmith (1854–1919) was an English writer, painter, actor, playwright and impresario, best known as co-author of *The Diary of a Nobody* (1892) with his brother George (1847–1912), an actor and music hall comedian. George Grossmith was the first to play the part of the Wilde-inspired aesthetic poet Bunthorne in Gilbert and Sullivan's *Patience*, and Oscar wrote to him in April 1881 to ask him to 'reserve a three-guinea box' for the first night 'if there is one to be had ... I am looking forward to being greatly amused'. See *Complete Letters*, p. 109.
8. Questioned by Edward Carson during the Queensberry libel trial about the evening he seduced Alphonse Conway, Wilde claimed never to have seen Alphonse in the evening 'with the exception of twice when I gave him tickets for the theatre'. Alphonse seems to have been a keen theatregoer, since not only did he apparently twice patronise the Assembly Rooms in Worthing at Wilde's expense but also – after Wilde decided that Portsmouth, Alphonse's first choice, was too far – selected Brighton for their overnight trip in late September 'because he wished to go to a theatre'. Wilde paid for the ticket, but did not go himself (perhaps Alphonse's choice of play was not to his taste). Merlin Holland, *Irish Peacock & Scarlet Marquess: The Real Trial of Oscar Wilde* (Fourth Estate, 2003), pp. 146, 150.
9. In the Victorian age billposting was a profitable business, and in Worthing at that time the service was provided by the Worthing and District Bill Posting

and Advertising Company Limited at 16 Ann Street (Proprietor: Frederick J. Bast), which promised 'Bills Posted in Every Part of Sussex at Reasonable Prices – Boards or Men Supplied by the Day or Week' (*Long's Worthing Directory 1892*).
10. The Aerated Bread Company Ltd, which operated from 1862 to 1955, was a national firm of bakers, confectioners and light refreshment contractors. In Worthing it had premises at 33 Warwick Street.
11. The Sangers, members of a circus dynasty dating back to early in the nineteenth century, were of course not real lords. John Sanger (born 1816) died in 1889, but his son continued to run the circus under the same name. George Sanger (born *c*. 1825) was murdered with a hatchet in 1911 by one of his employees, who then committed suicide.
12. At the time of the 1891 census, the entire population of Worthing was 19,177. Even though the crowd would have been swollen by visitors from the other Sussex coastal towns that had sent their lifeboats to the event, it is improbable that 25,000 people were lining the seafront on 22 August 1894.
13. Brock's Fireworks was a famous British firework company that dated back to the early eighteenth century. The open-air displays they organised came to be known as 'Brock's Benefits'. The company survived until 1988, when it was bought by Standard Fireworks, although the Brock's name was still used on some products into the present century.
14. *Complete Letters*, p. 607.
15. *A Descriptive Account of Worthing* (W. T. Pike & Co, 1895), p. 7.
16. In view of the previous year's typhoid epidemic, praise of the town's water supply was tactful and welcome.

4 'You will come, won't you?': Bosie

1. *The Complete Letters of Oscar Wilde*, eds, Merlin Holland and Rupert Hart-Davis (2000), p. 697.
2. The following biographies of Bosie were consulted during the search for information about his stays in Worthing: Patrick Braybrooke, *Lord Alfred Douglas: His Life and Work* (1931); Rupert Croft-Cooke, *Bosie: The Story of Lord Alfred Douglas, His Friends and Enemies* (1963); H. Montgomery Hyde, *Lord Alfred Douglas* (1984); Douglas Murray, *Bosie: A Biography of Lord Alfred Douglas* (2000); and Caspar Wintermanns, *Alfred Douglas: A Poet's Life and His Finest Work* (2006). Most barely mention Bosie's time in Worthing, and none give dates. The information Hyde gives in his brief passage about Worthing (p. 63) all seems to come from Wilde's letters or the transcript of the Queensberry trial, and his saying that 'Bosie stayed for about a week in a hotel' on the first visit is almost certainly conjecture based on his own reading of the letters, since the period of 'about a week' is not verified anywhere else. It is unlikely that Hyde was here making use of information that came directly from Bosie – whom he had known, albeit forty years before he wrote his biography – as in that case there would be other fresh material in the passage about Worthing, and there is none. Bosie's own autobiographical writings include no date evidence.

3. In *Complete Letters*, p. 598, this letter is given only the general date 'July–August 1894'.
4. *Complete Letters*, pp. 598–9.
5. Wilfrid Scawen Blunt, *My Diaries: Being a Personal Narrative of Events 1888–1914* (single-volume edition 1932; originally published in two volumes 1919), pp. 147–8.
6. Lord Alfred Douglas, *Without Apology* (Martin Secker, 1938), pp. 37–8.
7. Letter from Wilfrid Scawen Blunt to Judith, Lady Wentworth, 11 August 1894 (BL 54115). I am indebted to Colin Peters for going to the British Library to read this letter and the letter referred to in the next footnote and copying down relevant extracts.
8. Letter from Blunt to his wife, Lady Anne Isabella Noel Blunt, 15 August 1894 (BL 54103). Lady Blunt was a granddaughter of the poet Byron.
9. Both sides of the postcard are reproduced on p. 244 of Merlin Holland, *Irish Peacock & Scarlet Marquess: The Real Trial of Oscar Wilde* (Fourth Estate, 2003).
10. Queensberry's letters of 21 and 28 August 1894 were read out in court by Sir Edward Clarke on 4 April 1895 during the libel trial. The quotations are taken from Holland, *Irish Peacock & Scarlett Marquess*, pp. 217–8.
11. The footnote on p. 401 of Richard Ellmann, *Oscar Wilde* (1987), which mentions the date of the signing of the contract and names Bosie as the witness, provides further support to the already very strong case for Bosie's having arrived in Worthing on 14 August. Although there is no direct evidence for Wilde's and Bosie's having travelled down to Worthing together, the fact that they had been at the signing of the *Oscariana* contract earlier that day makes it all but certain that they did.
12. Alfred Douglas, *Oscar Wilde: A Summing Up* (Duckworth, 1940), pp. 114–15.
13. Rupert Croft-Cooke, *The Unrecorded Life of Oscar Wilde* (W. H. Allen, 1972), p. 9.
14. Vyvyan Holland, *Son of Oscar Wilde* (E. P. Dutton, 1954), p. 43.
15. *Complete Letters*, pp. 601–2, and printed in full in Appendix B.
16. The Henry referred to was perhaps Lord Henry Somerset, a homosexual expatriate whose brother Lord Arthur Somerset, also homosexual, had been involved in the Cleveland Street Scandal (see pp. 129–30). Bosie had been in correspondence with him in 1893 and had published a poem of his in *The Spirit Lamp*, the journal he edited in his last year at Oxford. In a letter to Charles Kains-Jackson in April 1894, in which Bosie said he was about to go to Florence, Bosie asked Kains-Jackson if Somerset was currently there. See H. Montgomery Hyde, *Lord Alfred Douglas* (Methuen, 1984), pp. 55–6.
17. Richard Ellmann, *Oscar Wilde* (Hamish Hamilton, 1987), p. 397, citing a letter from Douglas to Robert Ross quoted in the *Daily Telegraph* on 19 April 1913.
18. *Complete Letters*, p. 695.
19. Ellmann mixes up his Percys on p. 397 of *Oscar Wilde*. The Percy referred to in the 'storm letter' of 10 September was not Bosie's brother, Lord Percy Douglas, but the boy who often joined Alphonse and Stephen on the sailing boat outings with Wilde and Bosie.

20. The 'concert letter', *Complete Letters*, pp. 601–2, and printed in full in Appendix B.
21. Under cross-examination by Sir Edward Clarke, 4 April 1895, Holland, *Irish Peacock & Scarlet Marquess*, p. 237.
22. *Complete Letters*, p. 697.
23. At the start of the passage in 'De Profundis' (*Complete Letters*, pp. 696–9) in which Wilde briefly describes Bosie's final trip to Worthing, he refers to Bosie's conduct towards him 'on three successive days, three years ago'. A casual reading of this confusingly sequenced section might suggest that this phrase relates to – and therefore establishes the length of – Bosie's final stay in Worthing. However it in fact refers to three days (10–13 October) in Brighton when Wilde was prostrated by influenza and Bosie behaved appallingly.
24. In his account in 'De Profundis' Wilde wrote that he and Bosie had stayed at the Grand Hotel, but his memory was at fault, since it was at the adjacent Metropole that they stayed from 4–7 October. The hotel bill was still unpaid at the time of Wilde's arrest. See Holland, *Irish Peacock & Scarlett Marquess*, p. 310, note 118.
25. *Complete Letters*, p. 697.
26. George Bernard Shaw wrote in a letter to Bosie, 'That flowerlike sort of beauty must have been a horrible handicap to you.' Mary Hyde, ed., *Bernard Shaw and Alfred Douglas: A Correspondence* (Ticknor & Fields, 1982), p. 4.
27. The Elementary Education (School Attendance) Act of 1893 had just increased the minimum school-leaving age, but only from ten to eleven. In 1894, many boys in their early teens were in some kind of employment.
28. Edward Colman was Bosie's literary executor. The eighteenth-century house where he lived, today known as Monk's Farm Presbytery, is in North Road, Lancing.

5 'A happy, good-humoured companion': Alphonse

1. H. Montgomery Hyde, *Trials of Oscar Wilde* (William Hodge, 1948), p. 13.
2. Richard Ellmann, *Oscar Wilde* (Hamish Hamilton, 1987), p. 410.
3. www.barriesgenealogy.co.uk/html/st_andrews_baptisms_1888-1900
4. England & Wales, Free BMD Death Index: 1837–1915.
5. I am grateful to Geoffrey Godden for alerting me to Mrs J. Conway's appearance in an 1887 Worthing directory, which prompted me to return to the directories and follow her back to 1883–84.
6. Merlin Holland and Rupert Hart-Davis, eds, *The Complete Letters of Oscar Wilde* (Fourth Estate, 2000), p. 145.
7. Wagstaff, 'The Wildes in Worthing: Part 2, Alphonse Conway', *The Wildean*, No. 6 (January 1995), p. 34.
8. The complete Queensberry trial transcript is printed in Merlin Holland, *Irish Peacock & Scarlet Marquess: The Real Trial of Oscar Wilde* (Fourth Estate, 2003). A painstakingly compiled but incomplete and unreliable version of the libel trial (and the two criminal trials) appeared ninety years earlier in Anon [Christopher Millard], *Oscar Wilde: Three Times Tried* (Ferrestone Press, 1912). This was the basis for the version in Hyde, *Trials of Oscar Wilde*.

9. Alphonse Conway's witness statement is quoted from in Neil McKenna, *The Secret Life of Oscar Wilde* (Century, 2003), pp. 298–9.
10. McKenna, *The Secret Life of Oscar Wilde*, p. 297. McKenna and Holland have had access to the witness statements, but they are not available for general inspection. In the statement, the word 'about' is used to qualify the date (private information from Neil McKenna).
11. Under cross-questioning by Edward Carson during the Queensberry trial, Wilde referred to the second boy who helped with the boats on the first day only as 'a younger boy in flannels'. McKenna refers to Stephen as the boy who was with Alphonse on the first day and at the Marine Hotel on the second (*The Secret Life of Oscar Wilde*, pp. 297–8), so presumably Alphonse's witness statement makes clear that Stephen and not Percy was the boy in flannels.
12. Information from Conway's witness statement, McKenna, *The Secret Life of Oscar Wilde*, p. 298.
13. The West Pier was just over half a mile from the Royal Albion, but was probably where the paddle steamer from Worthing would have stopped in 1894, since the nearer Chain Pier was semi-derelict by then. The Palace Pier, just opposite the hotel, was still under construction.
14. McKenna, *The Secret Life of Oscar Wilde*, p. 299, citing Conway's witness statement.
15. Wagstaff, 'The Wildes in Worthing: Part 2, Alphonse Conway', p. 37.
16. It closed in 1900, and did not reopen until 1913.
17. John Wagstaff does not take a firm view as to which hotel Wilde and Alphonse stayed at, but inclines towards the hotel in Queen's Road (Wagstaff, 'The Wildes in Worthing: Part 2, Alphonse Conway', p. 37). Merlin Holland does not offer the Royal Albion option, but mentions only the Queen's Road establishment (*Irish Peacock & Scarlet Marquess*, p. 317).
18. *Complete Letters*, pp. 583–4.
19. McKenna, *The Secret Life of Oscar Wilde*, p. 306.
20. Ellmann, *Oscar Wilde*, p. 415.
21. McKenna, *The Secret Life of Oscar Wilde*, p. 348.
22. McKenna, presumably drawing on information from the boy's witness statement, refers to Alphonse's having had dinner at the Haven on 'two or three occasions' (*The Secret Life of Oscar Wilde*, p. 298). In court, Wilde did not specify the number of dinners he and Alphonse shared, saying only, 'He has dined with me' (Holland, *Irish Peacock & Scarlet Marquess*, p. 145).
23. Alphonse Conway gave his address to Queensberry's solicitor Charles Russell as 1 Bath Place (Holland, *Irish Peacock & Scarlet Marquess*, note 163, p. 316).
24. Holland, *Irish Peacock & Scarlet Marquess*, p. 317. Holland says that it was Brockwell who arrested Wilde at the Cadogan Hotel on 5 April 1895, but McKenna (*The Secret Life of Oscar Wilde*, pp. 377–8) indicates that, while Brockwell was in charge of the case, the detectives who arrested Wilde were Detective-Inspector Richards and Detective-Sergeant Allen.
25. The terrace from No. 7 upwards is different in style from Nos 3 and 5, and slightly lower, and probably dates from early in the twentieth century.

26. McKenna, *The Secret Life of Oscar Wilde*, p. 348.
27. Holland, *Irish Peacock & Scarlet Marquess*, p. xxxvii.
28. Hyde, *Trials of Oscar Wilde*, p. 319.
29. Hyde, *Trials of Oscar Wilde*, p. 315.
30. Wilde, under cross-examination by Charles Gill, lead prosecutor in the first criminal trial, Hyde, *Trials of Oscar Wilde*, p. 241.

6 'No-one to talk to': Constance

1. When she wrote the 3 September letter, Constance probably did not remember having briefly mentioned her trip to the photographer to Lady Mount Temple five weeks earlier, so the word 'just' probably simply implies 'recently', and is unlikely to indicate a further or alternative visit to Mendelssohn's studio in late August during a trip up to London from Worthing.
2. Merlin Holland and Rupert Hart-Davis, eds, *The Complete Letters of Oscar Wilde* (Fourth Estate, 2000) contains twenty-six letters from Wilde in Worthing; and there were undoubtedly many others that have not survived. One of the more important (*Complete Letters*, p. 617) was a letter published in the *Pall Mall Gazette* on 2 October 1894 in which Wilde asked to be allowed 'to contradict, in the most emphatic matter, the suggestion, made in your issue of Thursday last, and since then copied into many other newspapers, that I am the author of *The Green Carnation*. I invented that magnificent flower ... The flower is a work of art. The book is not.' The book in question was a thinly disguised fictional account of the relationship between Wilde and Bosie by their friend Robert Hichens. In his response in the following day's edition of the *Pall Mall Gazette*, the anonymous reviewer attributed the fact that other newspapers had taken his suggestion about its authorship seriously to 'stupidity', and the fact that Wilde had done the same to 'the disastrous effect of the bracing air of Worthing'. I am grateful to Donald Mead for alerting me to the reviewer's response and sending me a scan of it.
3. The letters written by Constance Wilde to Lady Mount Temple are in the Broadlands Archive at the University of Southampton. This part of the archive was deposited in the University Library in 1987 and has been open for research since then, although the formal purchase and acquisition was not concluded until early 2012 (information from Professor Woolgar of Southampton University, 23 April 2012). The letters from Constance Wilde seem not to have attracted significant attention until Philip Hoare used a few of them in *England's Lost Eden* (2005). The first full account of the correspondence between Constance and Lady Mount Temple was James Gregory's long article 'Lady Mount Temple and Her Friendship with Constance Wilde', published in the November/December 2006 issue of the online publication *The Oscholars* (Vol. III, No. 12, Issue No. 31), and some of the material from the article was included in Gregory's book, *Reformers, Patrons and Philanthropists: The Cowper-Temples and High Politics in Victorian England* (2010). I learnt of the existence of the letters – and the important fact that there were a number from the Worthing period – when I read Franny Moyle, *Constance: The Tragic and Scandalous Life of Mrs Oscar Wilde* (John Murray, 2011).

4. 31 August 1894. I am grateful to Merlin Holland for sending me a scan of this letter, which is in his private collection, and for giving me permission to quote from it.
5. 11 August 1894, British Library, Eccles Collection, 81732.
6. The contract for *Oscariana* was signed on 14 August by Wilde and Humphreys, and witnessed by Bosie. The book was privately printed in January 1895, but not published until 1910: see Richard Ellmann, *Oscar Wilde* (Hamish Hamilton, 1987), p. 401. Fifty copies were produced in January 1895, and in May a further 200 (*Complete Letters*, p. 604, footnote).
7. I am grateful to the Broadlands Archive for providing me with photocopies of the letters from Constance Wilde to Lady Mount Temple in 1894, and to Merlin Holland for allowing me to quote from them. Since all quotations from or references to these letters in this book give the date of the letter in question, the bibliographical information needs to be given only once. The archival reference numbers for the letters from Worthing are as follows: 7 August, BR 57/20/10; 11 August, BR 57/20/11; 17 August, BR 57/20/12; 20 August, BR 57/20/13; 25 August, BR 57/20/14; 2 September, BR 57/20/15; 3 September, BR 57/20/16; 4 September, BR 57/20/17; and 11 September (incomplete), BR 57/21/1. All the letters use the Wildes' 16 Tite Street writing paper, but Constance methodically crosses out the printed address and replaces it with the Worthing address. An exception is the 17 August letter, which retains its Tite Street heading, and since Constance indicates in it that she had gone up to London the previous day, she may still have been at 16 Tite Street when she wrote it.
8. The letters to Lady Mount Temple from 16 Tite Street that were consulted for the purposes of this chapter are: 4 August, BR 57/20/9; 15 September, BR 57/21/2; 22 September, BR 57/21/3; 2 October, BR 57/21/4; 3 October, BR 57/21/5; 6 October, BR 57/21/6; and 7 October, BR 57/21/7.
9. Although the 'Mount-Temple' variant often appears (including in the nineteenth century, as in the passage quoted in note 13), the Mount Temple name should correctly be written without a hyphen. Lord Mount Temple's full title was 'Baron Mount Temple of Mount Temple in the County of Sligo', and Mount Temple is therefore not a 'double-barrelled' name like the family name, Cowper-Temple. The Broadlands Archive catalogue uses 'Mount Temple' (though does not hyphenate 'Cowper Temple') and the Rossetti Archive uses 'Mount Temple' and 'Cowper-Temple', as does James Gregory in *Reformers, Patrons and Philanthropists*. Lord Mount Temple's title was a revival of the junior title held by the Viscounts Palmerston, which had become extinct along with the viscountcy on Palmerston's death in 1865.
10. An e-mail query of James Gregory, author of *Reformers, Patrons and Philanthropists*, produced this response (24 April 2012): 'It's usually said in the secondary literature that he was the natural son of Lord Palmerston, and the striking similarity between the two was detected by contemporaries. Though it was not something I found any allusion to in William Cowper-Temple's papers, my view was that he probably was.'
11. There are descriptions of Babbacombe Cliff on pp. 44–5 of Vyvyan Holland, *Son of Oscar Wilde* (E. P. Dutton, 1954) and p. 186 of Moyle, *Constance*.

12. The book of Ruskin's letters to the Mount Temples runs to over 400 pages: *The Letters of John Ruskin to Lord and Lady Mount-Temple*, ed. John Lewis Bradley (1964).
13. The report in *The British Medical Journal* (19 May 1888) of a vegetarian supper held at the Walmer Castle Coffee Tavern, Seymour Place 'for 100 *employés* of the Vestry of St Marylebone' includes this: 'Apologies [for absence] were read from Lords Waldegrave, Claud Hamilton, and Mount-Temple (who stated that Lady Mount-Temple had been a vegetarian for many years).'
14. The sources for the information in this paragraph are too numerous to list, but all facts have been cross-checked.
15. *The Nineteenth Century and After*, vol. 139, 1 January 1946, p. 228.
16. Franny Moyle states that Arthur Humphreys stayed the night (*Constance*, p. 244), but it is clear that he did not. Although on 7 August Constance had written to Lady Mount Temple that 'on Saturday Mr Humphreys comes until Sunday evening', on 11 August, the evening of the visit, she wrote that they had 'had Mr Humphreys down for the day'.
17. Moyle, *Constance*, pp. 242, 243: 'Constance is feeling towards an affair' and 'These signals were clearly responded to and acted on'. Moyle relies for her first statement on this passage from the letter that Constance wrote to Humphreys on 1 June 1894: 'But if we are to be friends, as I hope we may be, you must trust me. Indeed I can be trusted, as I believe that you can be. I am the most truthful person in the world, also I am intuitive.' Moyle's second statement derives from her interpretation of the 11 August letter – but, although she quotes this letter almost in its entirety, she omits the crucial sentence about Arthur's love making Constance 'good'. Ellmann (*Oscar Wilde*, p. 401) writes that Constance 'may have had a brief affair with Humphreys', while pointing out that 'she was away for much of the time in late summer and autumn'.
18. British Library, Eccles Collection, 81732. I am grateful to Colin Peters for going to the British Library to examine and copy out this letter for me.
19. I am grateful to Joanna Nortcliff for adding her female instincts to my own deliberations.
20. The footnote on p. 401 of Ellmann, *Oscar Wilde* gives this date for the signing of the contract and says that Bosie witnessed it.
21. Only four letters from Constance to Arthur Humphreys appear to survive – dated 1 June, 11 August and 22 October 1894, and 27 February 1898 (see note 31) – but there were almost certainly others.
22. British Library, Eccles Collection, 81732.
23. Neil McKenna, *The Secret Life of Oscar Wilde* (Century, 2003), p. 295.
24. Constance Wilde's letter of 22 October 1894 to Arthur Humphreys is in the collection of the William Andrews Clark Memorial Library, UCLA, which kindly provided a scan.
25. The Society for Psychical Research, which had been founded in 1882, was often referred to as 'the Psychical Research Society', hence Constance's acronym. Frederic Myers (1843–1901), a poet, critic and academic, was one of the founders and became its president in 1901. Other famous members

included Arthur Balfour, Charles Lutwidge Dodgson (Lewis Carroll), W. B. Yeats and Carl Jung.
26. *Complete Letters*, pp. 604, 611 and 623–4.
27. *Complete Letters*, pp. 599–600.
28. McKenna writes that this play was 'reputedly to be called *Constance*' (*The Secret Life of Oscar Wilde*, p. 295) and Moyle, probably drawing on McKenna's statement, says that it was 'provisionally entitled *Constance*' (*Constance*, p. 245). However McKenna does not give a source for his information, and there is no reference to the proposed play's title in the letter to George Alexander in which Wilde set out the plot. While it is possible that Oscar may have had the temporary title *Constance* in his head – and shared the thought with, say, Bosie – it is surely inconceivable that he would have used his wife's name as the final title of a play about adultery.
29. *Complete Letters*, p. 673. Wilde accidentally wrote 'Charles' instead of 'Arthur'. Charles Humphreys was his solicitor during his trials.
30. *Complete Letters*, pp. 879–80.
31. Constance Wilde to Arthur Humphreys, 27 February 1898, quoted on p. 119 of Jonathan Fryer, *Wilde* (Haus Publishing, 2005). The present location of the letter is not given.
32. Gregory, 'Lady Mount Temple and Her Friendship with Constance Wilde', Section I, online article (see note 3 for details). Moyle, *Constance*, p. 244 includes further information about Eyton's and Lilley's radical political sympathies.
33. Certainly Lilley's first name does not appear in any of the letters studied for the present article. He is always 'Mr Lilley'.
34. Sir Joshua Fitch (1824–1903) was a distinguished educationalist and an advocate of higher education for women.
35. Conrad Roden Noel (1869–1942), known as 'the Red Vicar of Thaxted', was a prominent British Christian Socialist and a founding member of the British Socialist Party. He hung inside his church the red flag and the flag of Sinn Féin alongside the flag of St George, leading to the long-running 'Battle of the Flags' between 1919 and 1922, during which there were several large demonstrations in the small Essex town. The chancellor of the Diocese of Chelmsford eventually insisted on Noel's removing the offending flags.
36. G. K. Chesterton, *The Autobiography of G. K. Chesterton* (Hutchinson, 1936), p. 165.
37. When he was charged, Evans replied, 'Do you call it sacred wine? If you do, it has made me drunk.' He had a number of previous convictions and was sentenced to four years' penal servitude. www.oldbaileyonline.org/print.jsp?div=t19100405
38. The 'Luini crucifixion at Lugano' was the *Passion and Crucifixion* fresco at Santa Maria degli Angeli in Lugano, painted by Bernardino Luini (*c*. 1480/82–1532). Franny Moyle states that Lilley visited Constance in Worthing on 7 August (*Constance*, pp. 243–4), but it is clear from the 7 August letter that Constance is describing a visit that took place on the Sunday before she left London – that is, 5 August.
39. The fact that Constance was not just a Sunday churchgoer is confirmed in her

3 October letter from 16 Tite Street, in which she tells Lady Mount Temple, 'I go to evensong at Holy Trinity at 6 every evening, & I shall try & do this thro' the winter, tho' I may of course be prevented; one seldom manages what one wants to do.'

40. This was Henry Drummond's theological work *Lowell Lectures on the Ascent of Man*, published that year, which concerned itself with the appropriate Christian response to Darwin's theory of evolution. Drummond was an evangelist who urged Christians to embrace all nature as the work of 'an immanent God, which is the God of Evolution', a God 'infinitely grander than the occasional wonder-worker, who is the God of an old theology'.
41. Walter Pater (1839–94), the art critic and proponent of the cult of aestheticism, was an important influence on Wilde.
42. This humorous Anglo-Jewish novel portrays a fictitious character who lorded it over the London Ghetto at the close of the eighteenth century.
43. Marcus Aurelius's *Meditations* expresses a philosophy of service and duty, describing how to find equanimity in difficult times by following nature as a source of guidance.
44. This novel, the first by the author of *The Secret Garden* and *Little Lord Fauntleroy*, is heavy both on religion and on use of Yorkshire dialect.
45. See, for example, pp. 127–8 of Merlin Holland, *The Wilde Album* (Fourth Estate, 1997).
46. Merlin Holland, *Irish Peacock & Scarlet Marquess: The Real Trial of Oscar Wilde* (Fourth Estate, 2003), p. 238.
47. This was Lord Mount Temple's American sister-in-law, Jessie Cowper (Gregory, 'Lady Mount Temple and Her Friendship with Constance Wilde', Section I, online article).
48. Emily Ford (1850–1930) was an artist who became the vice-chairman of the Artists' Suffrage League. There are five of her paintings in the Leeds University Art Collection and Gallery. Her sister was the writer, social reformer and fellow-suffragist Isabella Ford.
49. *Complete Letters*, p. 697.
50. Wilde's account in 'De Profundis' indicates that Bosie's illness was for 'four or five days' from the night of their arrival in Brighton, therefore from 4 October until about 8 October; Bosie's appalling letter arrived on 16 October, Wilde's fortieth birthday (*Complete Letters*, pp. 697–700). Oscar and Bosie stayed at the Metropole – not the Grand, as Oscar incorrectly remembered – for four nights, 4 to 7 October; and moved into lodgings on 8 October (see Holland, *Irish Peacock & Scarlet Marquess*, p. 310, note 118).

7 'My play is really very funny': *The Importance of Being Earnest*

1. Merlin Holland and Rupert Hart-Davis, eds, *The Complete Letters of Oscar Wilde* (Fourth Estate, 2000), p. 595. The letter is given the conjectural date '? July 1894', but, since we now know that Wilde went to Worthing on 10 August, an early August date is possible.
2. *Complete Letters*, p. 603. Charles Spurrier Mason had been – and possibly still was – the lover of Wilde's co-defendant, Alfred Taylor. See Chapter 8, note 1.

3. *Complete Letters*, pp. 597, 620.
4. See Appendix B for the dating of this letter.
5. *Complete Letters*, p. 602.
6. Melissa Knox, *Oscar Wilde in the 1990s: The Critic as Creator* (Camden House, 2001), p. 43.
7. Auction catalogue for the sale at Christie's East, 219 East 67th Street, New York on 6 February 1981. The catalogue says of the date for the completion of Act I 'not 3 October as noted by Dickson'.
8. *Complete Letters*, p. 620 and footnote.
9. *Love in Earnest* by Timothy d'Arch Smith (Routledge & Kegan Paul, 1970) gives a detailed account of Nicholson and other pederastic writers of the 1890s.
10. Hesketh Pearson, *The Life of Oscar Wilde* (Penguin, 1960; first published by Methuen, 1946), p. 252.
11. I am grateful to Donald Mead for providing me with this summary of the history of the four-act version of *The Importance of Being Earnest*.
12. John Wagstaff, 'The Wildes in Worthing, Part 3: Why Bunbury?', *The Wildean*, No. 7 (July 1995), pp. 35–9.
13. 'We hardly ever saw him [Queensberry] either in London or at my mother's country house, the Hut, three miles from Bracknell, in Berkshire, which we inhabited during the summer months' and 'He [Wilde] also stayed at my mother's house near Bracknell.' *The Autobiography of Lord Alfred Douglas* (Martin Secker, 1931), pp. 8, 86. I am indebted to Donald Mead for these references.
14. Sir Henry Morton Stanley (1841–1904) is most famous for his search for David Livingstone and for supposedly – and not necessarily apocryphally – having uttered the words 'Dr Livingstone, I presume?' when he found him in November 1871 near Lake Tanganyika.
15. Princess Augusta (1768–1840) was the second daughter of George III and the sister of George IV and William IV. George IV was on the throne at the time of her visit to Worthing.
16. Princess Augusta's visit is, for example, mentioned on p. 7 of *Guide to the Borough of Worthing* (published by G. D. S. Kirshaw, 1891) and on p. 3 of *A Descriptive Account of Worthing* (published by W. T. Pike & Co., 1895).
17. *A Descriptive Account of Worthing*, p. 33. Stanhoe Hall, later renamed the Stanhoe Hotel, was demolished in 1948, and an undistinguished modern block called Augusta House now stands in its place. In Wilde's time Augusta Place was a short cul-de-sac running north from the seafront a few yards to the east of the Stanhoe Hotel.
18. Richard Ellmann, *Oscar Wilde* (Hamish Hamilton, 1987), p. 399.
19. In fact it was the Metropole Hotel. See Merlin Holland, *Irish Peacock & Scarlet Marquess: The Real Trial of Oscar Wilde* (Fourth Estate, 2003), p. 310, note 118.
20. *Complete Letters*, pp. 685, 767.
21. Douglas, *Oscar Wilde: A Summing Up* (Duckworth, 1940), pp. 114–15.
22. Diary of Marie Stopes, 18 March 1939, quoted in H. Montgomery Hyde, *Lord Alfred Douglas* (Methuen, 1984), p. 310.

23. Robert Hichens (1864–1950) was a prolific author, but is remembered today mainly for his authorship of *The Green Carnation* in 1894 (see Chapter 6, note 2).
24. Robert Hichens, *Yesterday: The Autobiography of Robert Hichens* (Cassell, 1947), pp. 64–5.
25. Rupert Hart-Davis, ed., *Max Beerbohm's Letters to Reggie Turner* (Lippincott, 1964), p. 91. Reginald Turner (1869–1938) was one of Wilde's most loyal friends and was at his bedside when he died.
26. *Complete Letters*, p. 594.
27. Alfred Bruce Douglas, *Oscar Wilde and Myself* (John Long, 1914), pp. 237, 301–2.
28. *Complete Letters*, p. 602.
29. Pearson, *The Life of Oscar Wilde*, p. 255.
30. These review extracts are taken from Pearson, *The Life of Oscar Wilde*, p. 256.
31. The influence on *The Importance of Being Earnest* of W. S. Gilbert, the librettist for Sir Arthur Sullivan's Savoy operas, has been widely noted.
32. *Star*, 6 April 1895, quoted on p. 55 of Michael S. Foldy, *The Trials of Oscar Wilde: Deviance, Morality, and Late-Victorian Society* (Yale University Press, 1997).

8   'Absurd and silly perjuries': The Dramatist in the Dock

1. During the second criminal trial Alfred Taylor was questioned about this 'burlesque' marriage ceremony, information about which had come from Charles Parker. See H. Montgomery Hyde, *Trials of Oscar Wilde* (William Hodge, 1948), p. 281. Charles Spurrier Mason (1868–1940) was twenty-five or twenty-six in 1894. Opinions differ as to whether the references Wilde made in the two letters he wrote Mason from Worthing to Mason's being married – Merlin Holland and Rupert Hart-Davis, eds, *The Complete Letters of Oscar Wilde* (Fourth Estate, 2000), p. 603 – refer to Mason's genuinely being married to a woman or are light-hearted references to his being 'married' to Taylor.
2. *Complete Letters*, p. 603.
3. *Complete Letters*, p. 700.
4. George Murray, who had spoken a few days after the incident to his cousin H. J. Mordaunt, a member of the shooting party, wrote to Rosebery on 22 October: 'To add to the mystery, he was shot through the mouth upwards, a circumstance almost impossible to produce by accident.' Mordaunt, the two other members of the shooting party and the doctor all thought it was suicide. Leo McKinstry, *Rosebery: Statesman in Turmoil* (John Murray, 2005), p. 364.
5. McKinstry, *Rosebery*, pp. 355–64.
6. *Complete Letters*, pp. 703, 795–6.
7. R. E. Alton studied Queensberry's handwriting and established that the semi-legible words were 'posing somdomite' – see Richard Ellmann, *Oscar Wilde* (Hamish Hamilton, 1987), note 3 to Chapter XVII, p. 577. Curiously,

Ellmann then gives the definitive version as 'To Oscar Wilde, posing somdomite' (p. 412), when no handwriting expert is needed to see that the first word is 'For'.
8. *Complete Letters*, p. 634.
9. *Complete Letters*, pp. 707, 708, 709.
10. *Complete Letters*, p. 771.
11. *Complete Letters*, p. 759.
12. H. Montgomery Hyde, *Lord Alfred Douglas* (Methuen, 1984), pp. 71, 74. On p. 71 Hyde has 'detective' and on p. 74 'detectives'.
13. Arthur Newton was not the only link between the Cleveland Street trials and the Oscar Wilde trials. The barrister who defended Veck in the first trial and Newton in the third was Charles Gill, who was to appear against Oscar Wilde in the three trials in 1895. Charles Willie Mathews, who was junior counsel against Parke, was on Sir Edward Clarke's team in the three Wilde trials. Parke was defended by Frank Lockwood QC, who was to be lead prosecutor in the final Wilde trial. Junior counsel for Parke, incidentally, was H. H. Asquith, later Prime Minister.
14. The information about the Cleveland Street trials is taken from H. Montgomery Hyde, *The Cleveland Street Scandal* (W. H. Allen, 1976).
15. Hyde, *Trials of Oscar Wilde*, p. 339.
16. Hyde, *Trials of Oscar Wilde*, p. 199.
17. Hyde, *Trials of Oscar Wilde*, pp. 242–3.
18. Robert Sherard, *Oscar Wilde: The Story of an Unhappy Friendship* (Greening & Co., 1905), p. 161.
19. Alfred Bruce Douglas, *Oscar Wilde and Myself* (John Long, 1914), p. 115.
20. *Complete Letters*, p. 691.
21. Douglas, *Oscar Wilde and Myself*, pp. 69–70, 75.
22. On pp. 231–2 of *Son of Oscar Wilde*, Vyvyan Holland prints a letter to him from Bosie that includes this: 'It is true that I attacked him in my book, *Oscar Wilde and Myself*, but I did it under frightful provocation [namely what Wilde had written about Bosie in 'De Profundis'], and I have now repudiated the book.' On p. 171 of his book Holland says that this letter was written 'in about 1929'. In September 1944, Bosie wrote on a blank page at the front of Donald Sinden's copy of the book, 'This book (nearly all of which was written by T. D. H. Crosland) has long since been repudiated by me. It does not represent my real views about Wilde as I have explained in numerous places. I much regret that it was ever published.' I am grateful to Donald Mead for sending me a scan of this page.
23. Merlin Holland, *Irish Peacock & Scarlet Marquess: The Real Trial of Oscar Wilde* (Fourth Estate, 2003), p. 119.
24. Holland, *Irish Peacock & Scarlett Marquess*, p. 164.
25. Holland, *Irish Peacock & Scarlett Marquess*, p. 166.
26. Holland, *Irish Peacock & Scarlett Marquess*, pp. 174–5.
27. Holland, *Irish Peacock & Scarlett Marquess*, p. 149.
28. Holland, *Irish Peacock & Scarlett Marquess*, p. 145.
29. Holland, *Irish Peacock & Scarlett Marquess*, p. 165.
30. Holland, *Irish Peacock & Scarlett Marquess*, p. 178.

31. Holland, *Irish Peacock & Scarlett Marquess*, p. 185.
32. Hyde, *Trials of Oscar Wilde*, p. 241.
33. Hyde, *Trials of Oscar Wilde*, p. 321.
34. Hyde, *Trials of Oscar Wilde*, p. 316.
35. Holland, *Irish Peacock & Scarlett Marquess*, p. 199.
36. Holland, *Irish Peacock & Scarlett Marquess*, p. 207.
37. Holland, *Irish Peacock & Scarlett Marquess*, pp. 208–9.
38. *Complete Letters*, p. 704.
39. Michael S. Foldy, *The Trials of Oscar Wilde: Deviance, Morality, and Late-Victorian Society* (Yale University Press, 1997), p. 118.
40. Foldy, *The Trials of Oscar Wilde*, p. 121.
41. Holland, *Irish Peacock & Scarlett Marquess*, pp. 279–80.
42. *Complete Letters*, p. 714.
43. Alfred Bruce Douglas, *Oscar Wilde and Myself*, pp. 118-9.
44. H. Montgomery Hyde, *The Life of Sir Edward Carson, Lord Carson of Duncairn* (William Heinemann, 1953), p. 143.
45. Hyde, *Trials of Oscar Wilde*, pp. 88–9.
46. Hyde, *Trials of Oscar Wilde*, p. 339.
47. In her statement to Queensberry's solicitors Jane Cotta or Cotter, a chambermaid at the Savoy, where Wilde and Bosie stayed in March 1893, said that she saw 'a common boy, rough-looking' aged about fourteen in Wilde's bed. In court later she raised the age to eighteen or nineteen. See Neil McKenna, *The Secret Life of Oscar Wilde* (Century, 2003), p. 219 and Hyde, *Trials of Oscar Wilde*, p. 220. Wilde was in the habit of kissing the young pageboys at the Savoy and then tipping them the generous sum of half a crown. These included Herbert Tankard, who was thirteen or fourteen at the time (McKenna, *The Secret Life of Oscar Wilde*, p. 221–2). Queensberry's Plea of Justification included the allegation that Wilde 'did take indecent liberties with one Herbert Tankard'.
48. Hyde, *Trials of Oscar Wilde*, p. 92.
49. *Complete Letters*, p. 757.
50. McKenna, *The Secret Life of Oscar Wilde*, pp. 239–40.
51. Letter to Leonard Smithers, probably 28 November 1897, *Complete Letters*, p. 996.
52. Frank Harris, *Oscar Wilde: His Life and Confessions*, Vol. 2 (1916), pp. 131, 138.
53. Letter to Leonard Smithers, 13 January 1899, *Complete Letters*, p 1119.
54. An enquiry of Merlin Holland about the source of the Holland name produced the following response (27 January 2014): 'Constance's paternal grandfather, John Horatio, married a Caroline Holland Watson and the name was used by their son Horace as a sort of middle name when he christened his son, Otho. Otho then used it as a surname when he left England and was being pursued by his creditors in the late 1880s. Constance then did the same in 1895. It was close enough to be significant but not so close that people were immediately going to make the link between Constance Holland and Oscar Wilde.'
55. See Appendix H.

56. Chris Hare, *Worthing: A History* (Phillimore, 2008), pp. 127–30.
57. 'Steve' Stevens, who died in 2011 at the age of ninety, was one of the founders of the 1970s moral crusade the Festival of Light, and was for many years active in trying to purge Worthing of anything that smacked of licentiousness. In 1973, he succeeded in preventing the film *Last Tango in Paris* being shown. He repeatedly campaigned against a Worthing sex shop, carrying a placard reading, 'Our men did not die for today's moral depravity' (*Worthing Herald*, 5 December 2007). In 2008, he was instrumental in preventing a lap-dancing club being opened in the town.
58. *Observer*, 4 January 2009.
59. Holland, *Irish Peacock & Scarlett Marquess*, p. 165.
60. In *The Trials of Oscar Wilde*, Michael S. Foldy gives the ages of those in connection with whom Wilde was charged (note 91, p. 183): '*Star* (May 1, 1895) reports Frederick Atkins was twenty years old when he testified, which makes him seventeen or eighteen years old when the alleged events took place in November of 1892. Charles Parker was twenty-one when he testified, placing him in the eighteen–nineteen year range (*Star*, April 26, 1895). Edward Shelley testified that he was "a lad of eighteen or nineteen" when he met Wilde (*Star*, May 22, 1895). Alfred Wood was referred to as "the lad" (*Star*, April 27, 1895), as indeed were Atkins, Parker, Shelley, and all the rest of the young men who gave evidence against Wilde.'
61. At the time of writing, the blue plaque is located on the wrong part of the replacement building, as the result of incorrect deductions made when the location of the Haven was investigated prior to the plaque being placed there in 1994. See Appendix E.

APPENDIX A

Chronology of the Worthing Holiday of 1894

Tuesday 7 August
Constance Wilde, Cyril and Vyvyan arrive at the Haven,[1] presumably with the boys' Swiss governess[2] – who seems, however, no longer to have been part of the household by the end of the month.[3] Arthur Fenn, the servant Constance described as her 'page-boy', comes to Worthing either at the same time as Constance and the children or a few days later with Oscar.[4] The other servants at the Haven during the Wildes' holiday – a cook and a housemaid – are employees of Miss Lord, the owner of the house; and the 'cook's little boy' completes the household.[5]

Thursday 9 August
Oscar Wilde writes to Lord Alfred Douglas (Bosie) to say that he is going down to Worthing the next day and to suggest that Bosie join him there in due course.[6]

Friday 10 August
Oscar Wilde arrives in Worthing.[7] After lunch on the day of his arrival he writes a brief, hasty letter telling Bosie not, after all, to come.[8]

Saturday 11 August
Arthur Humphreys, who is shortly to publish *Oscariana*,[9] spends the day in Worthing with the Wildes. While he is still at the Haven, Constance writes him a letter telling him how much she loves him.[10]

Monday 13 August
Lord Alfred Douglas, who is in Stratford-upon-Avon at the end of a 'pilgrimage' to Shakespeare's tomb with his distant cousin Wilfrid Scawen Blunt, returns to London 'in a hurry' because he has 'an engagement to stay with Oscar Wilde at Worthing'.[11]

Tuesday 14 August
Bosie, now in London, sends the Marquess of Queensberry the notorious postcard in which he threatens to shoot him.[12] Wilde is also in London, to sign the contract for *Oscariana* with Arthur Humphreys. Bosie witnesses the document. Wilde returns to Worthing, bringing Bosie with him.[13]

Chronology of the Worthing Holiday of 1894

Thursday 16 August
Constance goes to London to see Lady Wilde and to discuss the publishing of *Oscariana* with Arthur Humphreys – and to receive his response to the intimate letter she wrote five days earlier.[14]

Monday 20 August
Wilde and Bosie meet Alphonse Conway and Stephen for the first time.[15]

Tuesday 21 August
Wilde entertains Bosie, Alphonse and Stephen to lunch at the Marine Hotel.[16]

Wednesday 22 August
Wilde attends the Lifeboat Demonstration.[17]

Saturday 25 August
The initial draft of *The Importance of Being Earnest* is perhaps already all but finished, for Constance writes to Lady Mount Temple, 'Oscar has written a play here, so I *love* this place now!'

Monday 3 September
Constance writes to Lady Mount Temple, 'I have had no-one to talk to, and I have been rather depressed.' Constance's complaining of loneliness – added to other evidence[18] – suggests that Bosie's first visit to Worthing has not yet ended. However, Constance adds that 'tomorrow Mr Lilley [a clergyman friend of hers] comes to stay with us', so on – or by – 4 September the coast was probably clear of Bosie.

Tuesday 4 September
Around this date Bosie leaves Worthing, with Percy – the third boy on the boat trips – leaving a day later.[19] Constance's friend Leslie Lilley comes to stay overnight with the Wildes.[20]

Wednesday 5 September
Wilde attends the Worthing Annual Regatta.[21]

Friday 7 September
Wilde goes to London for lunch with the actor-manager George Alexander, and returns to Worthing by the 4.30 train in time for dinner. In the evening, Wilde and Cyril attend the concert given by the Olympian Quartet ('the vagabond singers of the sands') in the Assembly Rooms.[22]

Saturday 8 September
Wilde writes Bosie the 'concert letter' in which the visit to London and the musical event of the previous day are mentioned.[23]

Sunday 9 September
Wilde, Alphonse and Stephen get caught in a severe storm while returning from Littlehampton in their sailing boat.[24]

Monday 10 September
Wilde writes Bosie the 'storm letter', describing the 'dangerous adventure' of the previous day.[25] Wilde says that his new play is 'really very funny' and that he is 'quite delighted with it', but he adds (*pace* Constance's comment to Lady Mount

Wednesday 12 September
Constance and the children return to the Wildes' house at 16 Tite Street,[26] but Arthur Fenn remains in Worthing with Wilde.[27]

Thursday 13 September
Bosie returns to Worthing.[28] Wilde attends the Venetian Fete, gives away the prizes and makes an amusing speech.[29]

Saturday 15 September
Wilde and Bosie take the ferry from Newhaven to Dieppe.[30]

Wednesday 19 September
Wilde and Bosie return from Dieppe, and Bosie then probably stays in Worthing for a few more days.[31] The first typed draft of *The Importance of Being Earnest* – Wilde is at this point using the working title *Lady Lancing* – is stamped 19 September, this almost certainly being the date the typing was completed.[32]

Friday 21 September
Cyril and Vyvyan leave 16 Tite Street and go back to their respective schools.[33] Wilde gives Alphonse Conway a copy of a book called *The Wreck of the Grosvenor*.[34]

Monday 24 September
Constance leaves 16 Tite Street and goes to stay with Lady Mount Temple at Babbacombe.[35]

Thursday 27 September
Wilde and Alphonse Conway go to Brighton and spend the night at the Royal Albion Hotel.[36]

Sunday 30 September
Bosie arrives in Worthing for the third time, bringing with him a 'companion' so unsuitable that Wilde is not prepared to entertain him at the Haven; so Bosie and his friend stay elsewhere.[37]

Monday 1 October
Bosie's companion 'returns to the duties of his profession' and Bosie re-locates to the Haven. Constance's stay at Babbacombe ends and she returns to 16 Tite Street.[38]

Thursday 4 October
Oscar Wilde and Lord Alfred Douglas leave Worthing and check in at the Metropole Hotel in Brighton.[39]

Notes

1. On Saturday 4 August Constance wrote to Lady Mount Temple: 'On Tuesday [7 April] we go off to Worthing for 4 or 5 weeks.' On 7 August she wrote again: 'Here am I settled with my two dear boys and Oscar comes, I believe, on Friday [10 August].'
2. In the letter Wilde wrote as soon as he arrived in Worthing (*Complete Letters*, pp. 598–9), he told Bosie that there was 'a horrid ugly Swiss governess' at the Haven, who had been looking after Cyril and Vyvyan for a year. The governess almost certainly travelled down to Worthing with Constance and the children.
3. On 31 August, Constance gave a full list of the household at the Haven in a letter to her brother Otho, but the governess referred to in Oscar's letter to Bosie does not appear on it.
4. On 11 August, Constance wrote to Lady Mount Temple, 'I have my page-boy Arthur down here to take them [Cyril and Vyvyan] out on the sands and in boats on the sea, so I am not much troubled about them.' This suggests that Arthur had been *in situ* since 7 August rather than that he had arrived the previous day with Oscar, but it is not conclusive.
5. See note 3.
6. This date is exact only if the 10 August date for Wilde's arrival is correct (see note 7). In *Complete Letters*, p. 598, this letter is given the date-range '[July–August 1894]'.
7. Since Wilde was nothing if not impulsive in his arrangements, we cannot be certain that he did actually arrive on the 10 August date projected in Constance's letter of 7 August. However, he cannot have arrived any later, since Arthur Humphreys came to Worthing on 11 August and Oscar was certainly present, because Constance wrote to Lady Mount Temple that evening to say, '*We* [my italics] have had Mr Humphreys down here for the day.' Wilde's reply in court on 4 April 1895 when Sir Edward Clarke asked, 'When was it you went down to Worthing?' was 'I think the 1st of August I went there.' Therefore, either Wilde's memory was badly adrift or '1st August' was mis-transcribed as '10th August' when the court reporter wrote up his shorthand notes.
8. *Complete Letters*, pp. 598–9. Wilde wrote 'Letter – No. II' at the top of this letter. Letter No. I was probably the letter written the previous day from London in which Wilde had encouraged Bosie to come to Worthing, a suggestion contradicted in Letter No. II.
9. *Oscariana* was a collection of epigrams from Wilde's works, which was published privately the following year.
10. See pp. 90–1.
11. See pp. 60–1. The words in inverted commas are Blunt's.
12. See pp. 61–2.
13. Richard Ellmann, *Oscar Wilde* (1987), p. 401, footnote. Although there is no direct evidence for Wilde's and Bosie's having travelled down to Worthing together, the fact that they had been at the signing of the *Oscariana* contract earlier that day makes it all but certain that they did.
14. See p. 95.

15. In his witness statement to Queensberry's solicitors, Alphonse said only that he met Wilde 'about 20 August' (private information from Neil McKenna), so the 20 August date we give for their first meeting may not be exact.
16. The accuracy of this date depends on the accuracy of the previous date. At the Queensberry libel trial Wilde said that the four of them lunched at the Marine Hotel on 'the second day', a statement evidently supported by Alphonse's witness statement.
17. See pp. 37, 47–51.
18. See next note.
19. In the 'storm letter', written on 10 September, Wilde says, 'Percy left the day after you did.' This phrase suggests that Percy's and Bosie's departures were recent events, so the dates five and six days earlier that have been deduced from the circumstantial evidence in Constance's letters must be, if not exact, at least very close.
20. See p. 101.
21. See pp. 37, 51–2.
22. These events are described in the 'concert letter' (*Complete Letters*, pp. 607–8).
23. *Complete Letters*, pp. 607–8.
24. This is the only possible date for the dangerous storm in which Wilde and the boys got caught – see Appendix B. *Complete Letters* (pp. 601–2) follows John Wagstaff (*The Wildean*, No. 8, January 1996), in giving the incorrect date of 13 August.
25. *Complete Letters*, pp. 601–2.
26. Constance had originally planned to return on 4 September, but in the event returned on 12 September. See pp. 35–6.
27. In a letter to Lady Mount Temple from 16 Tite Street on 15 September, Constance mentions that one of her servants is still in Worthing. Since – if we exclude the Swiss governess, who, even if still in Worthing until 12 September, would have returned to London with Constance and the children on that day – Arthur was the only servant from the London household who went down to Sussex, it must have been he.
28. This date relies on Bosie's having opted for Wilde's suggestion in the 'concert letter' that he come back to Worthing 'say on Thursday' rather than the alternative suggestion that they meet 'at Newhaven on the 15th'.
29. See pp. 52–6.
30. This date relies on the day Wilde suggested for the departure to France having been adhered to. The suggestion was made on 8 September in the 'concert letter'.
31. In the 'concert letter', Wilde said he could 'only manage three days' in Dieppe, while in court on 4 April 1895 he said he went to Dieppe 'for four days'. We opt for four nights / three full days. The suggestion that Bosie stayed on in Worthing afterwards is supported by the fact that, in reference to Bosie's third and final visit, Oscar wrote in 'De Profundis' (*Complete Letters*, p. 697) 'the two [other] visits you had paid me had ended'. The context – and the fact that Bosie's first visit had been for about three weeks – suggests that the second visit consisted of more than just two nights in Worthing and three in Dieppe.

Indeed it is plausible that Oscar's trip to Brighton with Alphonse nine days later was by way of compensation for Wilde's trip to Dieppe with Bosie, in which case it is possible that Bosie stayed on in Worthing for the best part of a week, with Oscar unable to organise Alphonse's trip to Brighton until Bosie had gone.

32. The manuscript was therefore probably sent to the typing agency just before the trip to Dieppe; or perhaps Constance took it back with her to London on 12 September.
33. Letter from Constance to Lady Mount Temple, 22 September.
34. In court on 3 April 1895, Edward Carson read out the inscription Wilde wrote in the book: 'Alphonso Conway from his friend Oscar Wilde. Worthing, September 21st 1894' (Merlin Holland, *Irish Peacock & Scarlet Marquess*, p. 147).
35. Letter from Constance to Lady Mount Temple, 22 September. See pp. 106–7.
36. The 27 September date for the trip to Brighton may not be exact. Queensberry's Plea of Justification, using information from Alphonse's witness statement, says the acts alleged to have occurred at the hotel in Brighton took place 'on or about the twenty-seventh day of September'.
37. See *Complete Letters*, p. 697.
38. Letter from Constance to Lady Mount Temple, 2 October. See p. 107.
39. Wilde wrongly remembered the hotel where he and Bosie stayed as the Grand. See Holland, *Irish Peacock & Scarlet Marquess*, p. 310, note 118.

APPENDIX B

Four Letters from Oscar Wilde to Lord Alfred Douglas

The Letters

Wilde to Douglas, probably 9 August 1894

16 Tite Street [London]

Dearest Boy,

    I hope to send you the cigarettes, if Simmonds will let me have them. He has applied for his bill. I am overdrawn £41 at the bank: it really is intolerable the want of money. I have not a penny. I can't stand it any longer, but don't know what to do. I go down to Worthing tomorrow. I hope to do work there. The house, I hear, is very small, and I have no writing room. However, anything is better than London.

    Your father is on the rampage again – been to Café Royal to enquire for us, with threats etc. I think now it would have been better for me to have had him bound over to keep the peace, but what a scandal! Still, it is intolerable to be dogged by a maniac.

    When you come to Worthing, of course all things will be done for your honour and joy, but I fear you may find the meals, etc., tedious. But you will come, won't you? at any rate for a short time – till you are bored.

    Ernesto has written to me begging for money – a very nice letter – but I really have nothing just now.

    What purple valleys of despair one goes through! Fortunately there is one person in the world to love. Ever yours

    Oscar

Wilde to Douglas, probably 10 August 1894

[The Haven, Worthing]

Letter – No. II.

Dearest Bosie,

    I have just come in from luncheon. A horrid ugly Swiss governess has, I find, been looking after Cyril and Vyvyan for a year. She is quite impossible.

Also, children at meals are tedious.

Also, you, the gilt and graceful boy, would be bored.

Don't come here. I will come to you. Ever yours

Oscar

Wilde to Douglas, 8 September 1894 (The 'Concert Letter')

[The Haven, Worthing]

My own dear Boy,

Your sweet letter arrived this morning, and this moment I have received your delightful telegram – delightful because I love you to think of me. What do you think of three days at Dieppe? I have a sort of longing for France, and with you, if you can manage to come (I could only manage three days, as I am so busy).

I went yesterday up to town for the afternoon, lunched with George Alexander at the Garrick, got a little money from him, and returned by the 4.30 for dinner, so I can pay my rent, and Cyril's (little wretch and darling) school-fees. I dare not lodge the money in the bank, as I have overdrawn £40, but I think of hiding gold in the garden.

Could you meet me at Newhaven on the 15th? Dieppe is very amusing and bright. Or would you come down here first? Say on Thursday: and we could go on?

I saw Gatty, by chance, as I was driving through Pall Mall. He stopped my cab and we had a long chat about you, of course. He is one of your many admirers. Last night (see other letter) you, and I, and the Mayor figured as patrons of the entertainment given by the vagabond singers of the sands. They told me that our names, which have been placarded all over the town, excited great enthusiasm, and certainly the hall was crammed. I was greeted with loud applause, as I entered with Cyril. Cyril was considered to be you.

Dear boy, this is a scrawl, is it not? I find farcical comedies admirable for style, but fatal to handwriting.

Do write to me, and do come to France. Is Basil here? If so, of course come here. With fondest love, ever devotedly yours

Oscar

Wilde to Douglas, 10 September 1894 (The 'Storm Letter')

[The Haven, Worthing]

My own dearest Boy,

How sweet of you to send me that charming poem. I can't tell you how it touches me, and it is full of that light lyrical grace that you always have – a quality that seems so easy, to those who don't understand how difficult it is to make the white feet of poetry dance lightly among flowers without crushing them, and to those 'who know' is so rare and so distinguished. I have been doing nothing here but bathing and playwriting. My play is really very funny: I am quite delighted with it. But it is not shaped yet. It lies in Sibylline leaves about the room, and Arthur has twice made a chaos of it by 'tidying up'. The result, however, was rather dramatic. I am inclined to think that Chaos is a stronger evidence for an Intelligent Creator than Kosmos is: the view might be expanded.

Percy left the day after you did. He spoke much of you. Alphonso is still in favour. He is my only companion, along with Stephen. Alphonso always alludes to you as 'the Lord', which however gives you, I think, a Biblical Hebraic dignity that gracious Greek boys should <u>not</u> have. He also says, from time to time, 'Percy was the Lord's favourite,' which makes me think of Percy as the infant Samuel – an inaccurate reminiscence, as Percy was Hellenic.

Yesterday (Sunday) Alphonso, Stephen, and I sailed to Littlehampton in the morning, bathing on the way. We took five hours in an awful gale to come back! did not reach the pier till eleven o'clock at night, pitch dark all the way, and a fearful sea. I was drenched, but was Viking-like and daring. It was, however, quite a dangerous adventure. All the fishermen were waiting for us. I flew to the hotel for hot brandy and water, on landing with my companions, and found a letter for you from dear Henry, which I send you: they had forgotten to forward it. As it was past <u>ten</u> o'clock on a Sunday night the proprietor could not <u>sell</u> us any brandy or spirits of any kind! So he had to <u>give</u> it to us. The result was not displeasing, but what laws! A hotel proprietor is not allowed to sell 'necessary harmless' alcohol to three shipwrecked mariners, wet to the skin, because it is Sunday! Both Alphonso and Stephen are now anarchists, I need hardly say.

Your new Sibyl is really wonderful. It is most extraordinary. I must meet her.

Dear, dear boy, you are more to me than any one of them has any idea; you are the atmosphere of beauty through which I see life; you are the incarnation of all lovely things. When we are out of tune, all colour goes from things for me, but we are never really out of tune. I think of you day and night.

Write to me soon, you honey-haired boy! I am always devotedly yours
Oscar

The Dates

These are the only four letters written to Bosie during the Worthing period that survive, but there were certainly others. One lost letter is referred to in the 'concert letter'; and there must have been letters relating to the arrangements for Bosie's first and second visits to Worthing.

Unfortunately Oscar Wilde rarely dated his letters, and it is often possible to calculate only approximately when they were written.

Sometimes, however, internal or other evidence allows letters to be dated more or less exactly, and happily this applies to the letter that Wilde wrote to Bosie the day before he set off for Sussex and to the three surviving letters to Bosie from Worthing.

Oscar almost certainly arrived in Worthing on Friday 10 August. As we saw in Chapter 2, Constance wrote to Lady Mount Temple on Tuesday 7 August to tell her that she had arrived in Worthing, adding 'Oscar comes, I believe, on Friday'. Since the date lay in the future, we cannot be certain that he did arrive on the Friday, but he was certainly at the Haven by Saturday 11 August, when Arthur Humphreys came down for the day. If the 10 August date for Oscar's arrival is correct, then the 'probable' dates given for the first two letters printed in this appendix are exact; if that date is not correct, the dates are at most a day or two out.

In my article about Bosie's stay in Worthing in *The Wildean*, No. 39 (July 2010), I christened the third and fourth of the letters printed here the 'concert letter' and the 'storm letter', for ease of reference; and the same terms are used in this book.

In his article 'The Wildes in Worthing: Part 4, Two Letters Newly Dated' (*The Wildean*, No. 8, January 1996), John Wagstaff dated the concert letter to Saturday 8 September. This dating is unassailable, since Wagstaff matched the event to a report in the *Worthing Gazette* of a concert given by the Olympian Quartet and 'various [other] performers' on Friday 7 September. This was certainly the same occasion, since the brief report refers to the concert's having been under the 'patronage of the Mayor, Lord William [*sic*] Douglas and Mr Oscar Wilde' and describes the Olympian Quartet as 'four vocalists who have given performances on the sea-front during the season'. In his letter, Wilde refers to the Olympian Quartet as 'the vagabond singers of the sands'.

Further proof that the concert letter was written on Saturday 8 September is that Wilde, in proposing that he and Bosie take a trip to Dieppe on 15 September, suggests that Bosie first come to Worthing – 'say on Thursday'. He is clearly referring to the week immediately following.

Wagstaff was, however, incorrect in his dating of the storm letter. He turned to the weather records of the summer of 1894 in search of a Sunday that fitted. However, he was following Rupert Hart-Davis's conjectural dating of the letter to '? August 1894' in *The Letters of Oscar Wilde* (1962) and thus did not examine the weather records for September. Instead, he settled on the only Sunday in August that provided appropriate weather – 12 August – and dated the letter to 13 August.

This mid-August date is contradicted by several pieces of irrefutable evidence that were not available to Wagstaff, who was writing in the belief that Wilde came to Worthing on 1 August and not, as we now know, on or around 10 August. In addition, Wagstaff was not aware of the evidence that Bosie arrived on 14 August. Finally, Alphonse Conway's witness statement in which he says that he met Wilde 'about 20 August' had not yet come to light.

The storm letter makes it clear that Wilde's friendship with Alphonse was well established by the time the letter was written, and that Bosie's first stay had ended several days earlier. So clearly a much later date than 13 August needed to be found.

Wagstaff's enquiries of the Met Office had eliminated the possibility of any other Sunday in August. Therefore the 'dangerous adventure' must have taken place on a Sunday in September. My own enquiry of the Met Office, about Worthing's weather in September 1894, produced this response, in an e-mail from Steve Jebson on 23 February 2011:

The only Sunday in September 1894 that really fits was Sunday 9 September. On this day high pressure was situated to the north-west of the British Isles, with low pressure centred over northern Germany. This situation produced a strong north or north-easterly flow of wind across the British Isles. Looking at observations from a number of resorts along the south coast of England, the weather on this day was fairly blustery with sunshine and blustery showers, some of which were heavy with thunder. The wind along the English Channel was strong, blowing at Force 5 (fresh breeze) to Force 7 (moderate gale) at times during the evening. The sea state was classed as either rough or very rough during the evening, especially to the east of the Isle of Wight.

This cohered exactly with the events of the day as Wilde described them. We know from *Son of Oscar Wilde* (1954), the autobiography of Wilde's younger son, Vyvyan, that their father took him and Cyril out sailing only 'when it was not too breezy' and – even though Alphonse and Stephen were older and were doubtless experienced sailors – Wilde would not have been so irresponsible as to go out to sea had the weather outlook been dangerously stormy. Indeed, we know from the storm letter that they set off in the morning and bathed on the way to Littlehampton – at a time that day when, according to the Met Office summary, there was a mixture of sunshine and blustery showers in that area. Wilde's account and the Met Office report are then again in accord in indicating that the storm blew up in the evening. There could be little doubt that it was on 9 September that they were caught in a storm.

We know that Wilde and Bosie were in Dieppe on Sunday 16 September; and Sunday 23 September could also be ruled out, since a letter written as late as Monday 24 September would not have included references to Percy's departure and to *Earnest*'s being 'not shaped yet'.

However I wanted to be absolutely certain that 2 September could not be a candidate for the day of the storm, and made a further enquiry of Steve Jebson, who responded on 28 February 2011 as follows: 'There were no reports of any particularly stormy weather on Sunday 2 September 1894. The wind direction was from the east or north-east and blowing at Force 4 (moderate wind) or Force 5 (fresh wind). The sea states during the evening in the eastern Channel were moderate to heavy swell.' A fresh wind and a moderate to heavy swell do not match the severe and dangerous conditions Wilde describes on the night of the storm, so 2 September could also be ruled out.

The concert letter and the storm letter were thus written two days apart, indicating a concentrated burst of epistolary activity between Wilde and Bosie at this point. This made perfectly good sense. Constance and the children were returning to London on 12 September, so the Haven would soon be free of family encumbrances; and Wilde was keen to have Bosie back in Worthing.

To summarise the activities of that weekend. Wilde and Cyril went to the concert on the Friday evening. On Saturday, Bosie's 'sweet letter' and 'delightful telegram' arrived, and Wilde wrote the concert letter. Sunday was the day Wilde, Alphonse and Stephen got caught in the storm. Then, on the Monday, a 'charming poem' arrived from Bosie, and Wilde wrote the storm letter, in which he praises the poem and recounts his and the boys' adventure of the previous night.

There was a third letter, which has not survived. We know this from the interpolation '(see other letter)' in the concert letter. This could refer only to a letter which was written at the same time and probably enclosed in the same envelope.

Could this third letter be the storm letter? The storm took place the day after the concert letter was written, so this could be the case only if the concert letter was not posted till the Monday and the words '(see other letter)' were a last-minute postscript written above the line of the rest of the text. However the William Andrews Clark Memorial Library provided me with a scan of the concert letter, and the bracketed words turned out to form part of an unbroken and continuous passage in Wilde's handwriting – and therefore could not have referred to a letter written two days afterwards.

Since the concert letter and the missing letter were almost certainly Oscar's first letters to Bosie after Bosie left Worthing in early September, it might seem odd that Oscar's news about progress with *Earnest* and about Percy's departure appeared only in the subsequent storm letter. These omissions, however, can be explained by the fact that the concert letter was 'a scrawl', written on a day when Wilde did not have time for a leisurely narrative – he rattles through his various points at high speed – and that its main purpose was to propose the trip to Dieppe. It is curious, however, that the storm letter includes no further reference to the Dieppe plan, set out two days earlier, with Wilde ending the letter merely by expressing the hope that Bosie will write soon.

APPENDIX C

Speech Given by Oscar Wilde on 13 September 1894

On 13 September 1894, a so-called Venetian Fete was held in Worthing. Afterwards a concert was held in the pavilion at the sea end of the pier, following which Oscar Wilde gave away the prizes for the best decorated boats and delivered a short speech.

The report in the *Worthing Gazette* of 19 September, quoted in full in Chapter 3, uses indirect speech. This reconstruction into direct speech was prepared for the visit to Worthing of members of the Oscar Wilde Society on 12 August 2012, when the present writer spoke Wilde's words for the first time for nearly 120 years, within a few yards of where they were first delivered.

Although we cannot be certain if this was the entire speech, it looks as though it is. The report in the *Gazette* says that Wilde began by proposing a vote of thanks to the committee. The first sentence that follows seems to be the opening of the main part of the speech; and the fact that the last sentence given in the report was followed by applause suggests that it was Wilde's conclusion.

*

I congratulate Worthing on the extremely beautiful scene of this evening.

Worthing has already arranged some extremely pretty shows. I have been much struck at the Regatta, at the Lifeboat Demonstration, and other festivals with the beauty and grace of everything I have seen.

There was, however, one thing that marred the Regatta. There was a sailing boat, not belonging to Worthing, but coming from some wicked, tasteless spot [probably the rival resort of Brighton], bearing a huge advertisement of a patent pill. I hope that boat will never be allowed to enter Worthing again. *(Much laughter.)*

I cannot help feeling the change that has taken place this year in the town, and expressing the great pleasure it gives visitors to return. I consider that such a charming town will become one of the first watering places on the South Coast. It has beautiful surroundings and lovely long walks – which I recommend to other people, but do not take myself. *(Laughter.)*

As for the excellent water supply, I am told that the total abstainers who

Speech Given by Oscar Wilde on 13 September 1894

visit Worthing are so struck with the purity and excellence of the water that they wish everybody to drink nothing else. *(Laughter.)*

Above all things I am delighted to observe in Worthing one of the most important things, having regard to the fashion of the age – the faculty of offering pleasure. To my mind few things are as important as a capacity for being amused, feeling pleasure, and giving it to others. I hold that whenever a person is happy he is good – although, perhaps, when he is good he is not always happy. *(Laughter.)* There is no excuse for anyone not being happy in such surroundings.

This is my first visit, but it will certainly not be my last. *(Applause.)*

APPENDIX D

Three Extracts from the Transcript of the Queensberry Libel Trial

The Queensberry libel trial – *Regina (on the prosecution of Oscar Wilde)* v. *John Douglas, Marquess of Queensberry* – was held from Wednesday 3 April to Friday 5 April 1895 at the Central Criminal Court before Mr Justice Collins and a jury. The trial ended abruptly on the Friday morning, as explained at the end of the third of these extracts.

The complete transcript of the trial, which came to light only in 2000, was published in 2003 in Merlin Holland's *Irish Peacock & Scarlet Marquess*. The extracts given here – the passages that relate to Alphonse Conway and Worthing – are printed by kind permission of Merlin Holland. Because Queensberry's Plea of Justification uses the spelling 'Alfonso', Holland standardised to this spelling throughout his book; but 'Alphonso' is the version of the name that appears in the original transcript, and is used here.

*

Edward Carson QC, Lead Counsel for the Marquess of Queensberry, Questions Oscar Wilde (Afternoon of 3 April 1895)

CARSON: Did you become intimate with a young lad named Conway?
WILDE: I beg your pardon.
CARSON: Did you become intimate with a young man named Conway?
WILDE: Oh, yes, at Worthing.
CARSON: What was his Christian name?
WILDE: Alphonso.
CARSON: He sold newspapers on the pier at Worthing?
WILDE: No, never to my knowledge.
CARSON: What?
WILDE: Never.
CARSON: Or at the kiosk?

WILDE: No, never.
CARSON: What was he doing?
WILDE: Oh, enjoying himself in being idle.
CARSON: He was a loafer at Worthing?
WILDE: I call him a very happy, idle nature. You can call him what you like.
CARSON: He had no money?
WILDE: Oh, none. When I say none, his mother had a house at Worthing.
CARSON: No occupation?
WILDE: No, he had no occupation.
CARSON: Did you know or have you ever heard that his previous occupation had been selling newspapers?
WILDE: Never in my life.
CARSON: Would it astonish you to hear that he had so much industry?
WILDE: I think it would.
CARSON: Was he a literary character?
WILDE: Oh, not at all. (*Laughter.*)
CARSON: Was he an artist?
WILDE: No.
CARSON: What age was he?
WILDE: I suppose about eighteen – about eighteen, I should think.
CARSON: About the same age as Shelley?
WILDE: Yes, if Edward Shelley was that age. I don't know Edward Shelley's age.
CARSON: How did you come to know him?
WILDE: To know Alphonso Conway? When I was at Worthing last August, Lord Alfred Douglas and I were in the habit of going out in a sailing boat and one afternoon while this boat, which was high-beached, was being dragged down by the boatmen, Conway, and a younger boy who was in flannels, were helping to draw down the boat. I said to Lord Alfred Douglas when we reached the sea: 'Shall we bring them out for a sail?' or, 'Shall we ask them whether they would like a sail?' and he said: 'Yes.'
CARSON: Then, he was assisting you in putting out the boat?
WILDE: No, I wasn't taking that trouble. He and the boy – younger who was in flannels – amused themselves by helping the two boatmen to drag down our boat which was high-beached. I amused myself with contemplation and as they had been taking the trouble to do this and so on, I said to Lord Alfred Douglas: 'Shall we ask them whether they would like to have a sail?' and they seemed very delighted and they came out for a sail. They came out every day.
CARSON: They came out every day?
WILDE: Yes, every day.
CARSON: Did you become intimate with Alphonso?
WILDE: Oh, yes. We were great friends.
CARSON: Great friends?
WILDE: Great friends.
CARSON: Did you ask this boy that you met upon the beach to lunch with you?
WILDE: To lunch with me?
CARSON: Yes.
WILDE: He has dined with me.

CARSON: Where?
WILDE: At my house in Worthing.
CARSON: At the Haven?
WILDE: At the Haven.
CARSON: Did he also have a meal with you at an hotel there?
WILDE: Oh, yes, – I remember – yes, the second day.
CARSON: At the Marine Hotel?
WILDE: Yes he lunched with me and Lord Alfred and the other friend.
CARSON: Was his conversation literary?
WILDE: No, it was, on the contrary, quite simple and easy to be understood. (*Laughter.*)
CARSON: He was an uneducated lad wasn't he?
WILDE: Oh, he was a pleasant, nice creature. He was not cultivated. (*Laughter.*) Don't sneer at that. He was a pleasant, nice creature. His ambition was to be a sailor.
CARSON: What was his class in life?
WILDE: If you ask me what his class in life was, his father had been an electrical engineer who had died young. His mother had very little money and kept a lodging house – at any rate she had one lodger. That he himself was the only child, that he had been sent to school where naturally he had not learned much. His desire was to go to sea as an apprentice in a merchant ship. One thing he cared about was the sea. His mother was to a certain extent reluctant for him to leave her. That was the story he told me.
CARSON: And you conceived a great fondness for Alphonso?
WILDE: A most pleasant creature.
CARSON: Now, did you ask him to meet you by appointment on the parade in the evening at about nine o'clock?
WILDE: On the parade? I didn't know there was such a place at Worthing.
CARSON: Isn't the Haven near the end of the parade?
WILDE: I have never – I don't think I have ever seen Alphonso with the exception of twice when I gave him tickets for the theatre – no, I have never seen him in the evening.
CARSON: Did you take him one evening after nine o'clock to walk towards Lancing?
WILDE: No.
CARSON: Are you quite sure of that?
WILDE: Yes, quite certain. Yes.
CARSON: Is Lancing near there?
WILDE: It is about two miles off.
CARSON: Is it a lonely road?
WILDE: I have never been there in the daytime. It is a road by the sea.
CARSON: Did you kiss him on the road?
WILDE: Certainly not.
CARSON: Did you put your hands inside his trousers?
WILDE: No, certainly not.
CARSON: And had you any familiarities with him of any kind?
WILDE: None of any kind.
CARSON: Did you give him anything?

WILDE: Oh, yes.
CARSON: Money?
WILDE: I don't think I ever gave Alphonso any money – no, I don't think so.
CARSON: No money?
WILDE: No money.
CARSON: Did you give him sums from time to time amounting to fifteen pounds?
WILDE: Good heavens! No, certainly not.
CARSON: Why should that be astonishing?
WILDE: Because it didn't happen.
CARSON: He was a poor boy?
WILDE: I don't know about that. I say his mother had a house of her own.
CARSON: Did you know his mother?
WILDE: No, I did not.
CARSON: Did you ever go into his house?
WILDE: Never.
CARSON: Did you give him a cigarette case?
WILDE: I think I might have – yes, that I might have done. I forgot about that. I remember certain things I gave him.
CARSON: What did you call him?
WILDE: Alphonso.
CARSON: Did he call you Oscar?
WILDE: No.
CARSON: Are you quite sure of that ?
WILDE: Yes.
CARSON: This is the cigarette case you gave him?
WILDE: I dare say, yes.
CARSON: Did you put this inscription in it 'Alphonso from his friend Oscar Wilde'?
WILDE: Whether I wrote it or he, I don't know until I see it.
CARSON: Will you look at it?
WILDE: It is more than probable I wrote it. Yes, that is my writing.
CARSON: You gave him your photograph?
WILDE: Yes.
CARSON: Just take that please and tell me if that is your writing?
WILDE: It is sure to be on my photograph, yes, that is my writing, certainly.
CARSON: 'Oscar Wilde to Alphonso'?
WILDE: Yes.
CARSON: And you gave him a book?
WILDE: Yes.
CARSON: *The Wreck of the Grosvenor*. 'Alphonso Conway from his friend Oscar Wilde. Worthing, September 21st 1894.'
WILDE: Yes.
CARSON: You gave him that?
WILDE: I gave him – well, I don't know.
CARSON: You were fond of this boy?
WILDE: I liked him. He had been my companion for six weeks.
CARSON: He had been your companion for six weeks?
WILDE: A month, I suppose.

CARSON: Would you be surprised to hear that the only occupation that he ever had was this selling of newspapers?
WILDE: I never thought Alphonso had any past. I don't know why I should be asked if I would be surprised – yes, I would be rather – from what he said to me, that would surprise me – he told me that he had no profession of any kind. Certainly that would surprise me.
CARSON: Did you give him a walking stick?
WILDE: Yes, I gave him a walking stick.
CARSON: For a newspaper boy. Just look at that! He was a newspaper boy out of employment.
CLARKE: I beg your pardon.
WILDE: It is like the way you talked of Edward Shelley.
CARSON: You bought that for Conway?
WILDE: Yes.
CARSON: What did that cost?
WILDE: Five or six shillings.
CARSON: This is silver.
WILDE: Ten shillings or something.
CARSON: Fifteen shillings?
WILDE: It is not beautiful.
CARSON: It was a handsome stick for a boy of that class.
WILDE: I don't think it a beautiful stick myself. I don't think it a beautiful stick, but the choice was his. (*Laughter.*)
CARSON: It is not real art, I suppose?
WILDE: I don't think so.
CARSON: Did you bring this boy away with you to Brighton?
WILDE: Yes.
CARSON: How was he dressed?
WILDE: A suit of clothes I had given him – a suit of blue serge clothes that I had given him.
CARSON: That you had given him?
WILDE: Yes.
CARSON: What kind of a hat had he?
WILDE: That I forget; I fancy, a straw hat.
CARSON: A straw hat with a red-and-blue ribbon?
WILDE: Yes, with a red-and-blue ribbon.
CARSON: Did you select the red-and-blue ribbon?
WILDE: No, that belongs to the Corps – it was an unfortunate selection of his own – I mean, because I believe the colour pleased him. (*Laughter.*)
CARSON: You paid for the hat?
WILDE: Yes, I did, certainly. I gave him a suit of clothes, straw hat, flannels, a book to read – I gave him a lot of things.
CARSON: You dressed him up to bring him to Brighton?
WILDE: Not to bring him to Brighton.
CARSON: You dressed him up for Worthing?
WILDE: Yes, oh, certainly. Yes, for a regatta to which he was very anxious to go.
CARSON: In order that he might look more like an equal?

WILDE: Oh, no, he never would have looked that. (*Laughter.*) No, in order that he shouldn't be ashamed, as he told me he was, of his shabby and ordinary clothes – because he desired to have flannels and blue serge and a straw hat.
CARSON: He was ashamed of his shabby clothes?
WILDE: Yes, he was in a certain degree.
CARSON: Did he look better when he was dressed up?
WILDE: Yes, he looked much nicer, much nicer.
CARSON: You took him to Brighton?
WILDE: Yes.
CARSON: Did you take a bedroom for him?
WILDE: We stayed at the hotel.
CARSON: Did you take a bedroom for him?
WILDE: Yes.
CARSON: He had no money?
WILDE: Yes, of course. I took him as a trip to Brighton.
CARSON: Was the bedroom communicating with your own?
WILDE: That I forget; it might have been so.
CARSON: Green baize folding doors?
WILDE: Green baize folding doors?
CARSON: On the first floor?
WILDE: It was on the first floor, yes – it was on the first floor – sitting room and two bedrooms, yes.
CARSON: The Albion?
WILDE: At the Albion Hotel.
CARSON: Did he come into your bed that night?
WILDE: No.
CARSON: Are you certain of that?
WILDE: Quite certain of that.
CARSON: What did you take him to Brighton for?
WILDE: I took him to Brighton because I had promised that before I left Worthing I would take him some trip, to any place where he wished to go, because he had been a very pleasant, happy, good-humoured companion to myself and my children. He wished to be at Portsmouth, because he wanted to be a sailor. I, having been abroad – to France – I came back then to Worthing. I said I couldn't take him to Portsmouth – it was too far for me to go – I was just finishing a play. I said I couldn't afford the time. He then asked me whether I would take him to Brighton, as he wished to go to a theatre and that he would regard it as a trip. I expressed my surprise, he living so close to Brighton, that he should consider it as a trip. It was his own choice. If I had had time I should have brought him to Portsmouth.
CARSON: Did you go to the theatre?
WILDE: I didn't, no – I sent him.
CARSON: Did you take him to dine there at a restaurant?
WILDE: Yes.
CARSON: How was it that he was such a pleasant companion for you?
WILDE: Because he was a pleasant, bright, simple, nice nature. That is what I call him.

CARSON: A nice personality?
WILDE: I would not say for him personality, no.
CARSON: When did he go back to Worthing?
WILDE: We went back the next day.
CARSON: Did you go back with him?
WILDE: Yes.
CARSON: Did you ever take another boy to the Albion?
WILDE: I have stayed at the Albion. I don't know what you mean. Just kindly tell me exactly what you mean. I have stayed with my friends at the Albion often.
CARSON: I am not talking of friends. Did you on any other occasion bring a youth about the same age – eighteen or twenty – to the Albion?
WILDE: Lord Alfred Douglas – I stayed with him at the Albion.
CARSON: Not Lord Alfred Douglas.
WILDE: No.
CARSON: Are you sure?
WILDE: Quite sure, yes.
CARSON: No one else?
WILDE: No one else.

Sir Edward Clarke QC, Lead Counsel for the Prosecution, Questions Oscar Wilde (Afternoon of 4 April 1895)

CLARKE: With regard to Alphonso Conway at Worthing, when was it you went down to Worthing?
WILDE: I think the 1st of August I went there.
CLARKE: And about how long did you stay there?
WILDE: I stayed, I think, two months at Worthing.
CLARKE: Did you stay there continuously or did you leave Worthing to go to London for a time and go back there?
WILDE: No, I went once to Dieppe; that was for four days. I came up to London once for a day to see a theatrical manager. But I was there continuously with the exception of four or five days.
CLARKE: What house was it that you had at Worthing or rooms? Did you have a home?
WILDE: Yes, it was a house: my wife and my children and myself lived in a furnished house that we had taken from a friend of my wife's.
CLARKE: It was a furnished house that was taken for a time?
WILDE: Yes.
CLARKE: Did your wife and your boys go to Worthing at the same time you did?
WILDE: Yes.
CLARKE: And remained there during your stay?
WILDE: At the beginning. Sometime in September – I can hardly say exactly when – both my boys had returned to school; my wife returned to town with them to prepare them for going back to school and I stayed on for, I fancy, a fortnight after that.
CLARKE: And did Mrs Wilde re-join you?
WILDE: No, she went visiting in the country.

CLARKE: You have told us, with regard to this boy, the circumstances under which you met him. He was not at that time in any employment so far as you know?
WILDE: None at all.
CLARKE: Did you ever hear of his having been employed as a newspaper boy?
WILDE: No, I had no idea; no, certainly not. I never heard of it, nor had any idea that he had any connection with literature in any form. (*Laughter.*)
CLARKE: So far as your information went as to his desires or wishes as to employment, what was that desire and wish?
WILDE: Oh, an intense desire to go to sea in the Merchant Service as an apprentice.
CLARKE: And did he go out from time to time sailing with you?
WILDE: He used to go out every day after I met him with myself, with my son, with my son's friend and with other friends who were there. We went out every morning and bathed from this boat and fished in the afternoon.
CLARKE: Was Mrs Wilde acquainted with Conway?
WILDE: Oh, yes.
CLARKE: Did she see Conway?
WILDE: Oh, yes, constantly.
CLARKE: Where?
WILDE: After bathing we would return to the beach. My wife would meet us, that is my son and myself and my son's friends, and, of course, I introduced Conway to her – she knew him quite well. He had also been to a children's tea at our house while my wife was there. He was a great friend of my son's as well as myself.
CLARKE: When did you leave Worthing?
WILDE: I fancy about the 2nd or 3rd of October I went round to Brighton.
CLARKE: Have you ever seen Conway since then?
WILDE: No, I have never seen him since then – no. I have written to him one letter.
CLARKE: Do you remember when that was?
WILDE: Writing the letter?
CLARKE: Yes.
WILDE: I think it was in the month of November last. It was with reference to his becoming an apprentice in the Merchant Service. I had consulted a gentleman who was a great friend of mine who has many ships and so on, and asked him the circumstances under which it could be done, and I wrote to Conway and told him the circumstances of the case.

The Last Part of Edward Carson's Opening Speech for the Defence (Morning of 5 April 1895)

I take now in contrast to the case of Parker, the case of Conway – Alphonso Conway. Why I am now taking Conway in contrast to the other case is for this reason: Conway was not procured by Taylor, but was procured by Wilde himself. Wilde at the time was living in Worthing and he had not Taylor at hand when these horrible lusts came upon him to procure a boy and so let us see how he gets at poor Conway. Now, was there ever a more audacious story confessed in a court of justice than that confessed by Wilde in relation to Conway? What is it? He sees a boy upon the beach at Worthing; he knows nothing whatsoever about him except that he is a boy there assisting about the different boats. His real history, as Wilde proved to you, is this: he had previously sold newspapers at Worthing at the pier at one of these kiosks, and I must say that I do not think a more flippant answer ever was given by a witness than what Mr Wilde said yesterday. When he was asked if he knew anything about Conway being previously connected with selling newspapers, he told us he did not know that he had had any previous connection with literature. No doubt he thought in many of his answers he was making very smart repartee and probably that he was scoring off counsel who was cross-examining, or something of that kind, but Conway is upon the beach and he helps Mr Wilde to take out his boat and through that an intimacy springs up. Now, if you had not heard it proved by Mr Wilde himself, could you have believed that within a day or two that boy was lunching with Wilde, was brought to his house and if Wilde's evidence is true, which I hope sincerely it is not, was introduced to his children and to his family. At the time when he first met Conway, it appears his wife was not at Worthing, but I rather gathered from him that his children were; at all events, he said that at some time or other Conway had been in association with his children, an extraordinary fact – this young man Conway of twenty being told to you to be in association with two little boys of eight and nine – well, you find Conway lunching. Now, what happens? Of course Wilde could not bring about this boy, there or anywhere else, looking in his extraordinary condition, and what does he do? And – now, it is really here that the disgraceful audacity of the man comes in – he procures him a suit of clothes and he dresses him up like a gentlemen and he puts some of these public school colours, something of that kind, upon his hat and he makes him look as if he were a proper person to be associating with him. Really, really, gentlemen of the jury, the thing is past belief. It is almost past belief; if we had proved that, as against Mr Wilde [stating it], you would have almost not believed it. But Mr Wilde knew that we had the witnesses to prove it all, we had all the things here to produce as you saw and Wilde dare not deny it. What did he dress Conway up for? I venture to say that if he was really anxious to assist Conway, the very worst thing he could have done was to take Conway out of his proper sphere and to begin, as he did with Parker, giving him champagne lunches, taking him to his hotel, treating him in a manner which, of course, Conway in the future could never expect to live up to. I could understand the generous instincts of a man who would say: 'Here is a smart boy at Worthing whom I have met at the pier. I will try and get him employment; I will educate him; I will give him some money; I will try and assist him in any way I can,' but is it any assistance to a boy like Conway to do as Wilde did, to take him up and dress him and take him about giving him champagne lunches and all the rest of it? (Here Carson pauses.) Would your lordship excuse me for a moment?

*

Sir Edward Clarke and his junior, Willie Mathews, returned to the court at this point, having been absent for about ten minutes. Clarke plucked Carson by the gown, and they conferred inaudibly. Clarke was informing Carson that Wilde had decided to withdraw his prosecution. Clarke and Carson then each addressed the judge, and the judge directed the jury to find the Marquess of Queensberry not guilty; which they duly did.

APPENDIX E

The Location of the Haven

The confidence – indeed the certainty – with which pictures of the Haven, the house in Worthing where Oscar Wilde stayed in 1894, are presented among the illustrations in the centre of this book (illustrations 22–24 and 32–34) might suggest that the location of the house is a long-established fact.

In reality, it was only after a prolonged and detailed investigation early in 2011 that a correct and conclusive identification of which house was the Haven was arrived at.

This appendix consists of a slightly revised version of an article published in *The Wildean* No. 39 in July 2011. Although this piece is likely to prove too detailed for all but the most determined, it is important that the full evidence be set down, in view of the fact that the blue plaque commemorating Wilde's stay is at present on the wrong part of the modern building that replaced the Esplanade. The hope must be that one day it will be moved.

*

Although the Esplanade was demolished less than half a century ago, it is extraordinarily difficult to establish which house the Haven was. There seems to be no historical memory in Worthing of the configuration of the Esplanade, and Worthing Borough Council has no relevant documents available. Therefore, the only evidence is indirect, and comes principally from old directories and town plans.

Setting down the evidence in conclusive detail is made particularly important by the fact that no fewer than three different locations for the Haven have previously been suggested – and none has been correct.

The Haven was not, as Kim Leslie and John Wagstaff (in 1994) and I (in my first *Wildean* article in January 2011) had all decided, a house in the centre of the terrace. Nor was it the house marked with a printed X on an Oscar Wilde commemorative postcard of 1994 produced by Crossroad Postcards, which identifies the house as the most westerly of the four semi-detached houses that, as we shall see, also had Esplanade addresses. And it was not the house at the sea end with the curved balcony, identified as the Wilde house by Worthing historians

Ron Kerridge and Mike Standing in their 2001 photographic history of the town, an identification followed in at least one other book about Worthing.

In Wilde's time 'The Esplanade' was the official name for three separate and distinct geographical features: the eight houses that included the Haven; a promenade running along part of the seafront; and a short north-to-south street leading from Brighton Road to the seashore. Today, only the last of these names remains in use.

A modern visitor entering the street from the Brighton Road end passes, on the west side, first No. 10 and then Nos 9 and 9a, The Esplanade, followed by the eastern end of New Terrace. These buildings did not exist in 1894, when the area was open ground.

On the eastern side of the Esplanade there now stands an ugly modern block of flats, with a car dealership on the Brighton Road side. In the centre of the west-facing side of this block is a blue plaque to alert passers-by to the fact that it was in a house on the site that Wilde wrote *The Importance of Being Earnest*. It is jarring and ironic that a lover of all that was beautiful and graceful should be commemorated on the side of so unsightly a building. Indeed, the plaque might have been better placed on the low retaining wall in front of the block, which is all that remains here from Wilde's time.

However, since we know from Wilde's letters and from old directories that the Haven was No. 5 – and since, as we have seen, the west side of the Esplanade had just two houses (Nos 9/9a and 10), which were built later – it seemed clear, from studying old photographs and visiting the location, that the block on the east side of the street had comprised eight houses numbered 1–8; and that No. 5 must have been in the centre. (Although the front doors to the houses are not clearly visible in the old photographs, the overhanging porches are wide enough to allow for the possibility that there were two front doors under each, side by side, one serving a bow-windowed house and one a plain-fronted house.)

Prior to the plaque being placed on the block in 1994, Kim Leslie, former director of the West Sussex Blue Plaque Scheme, had researched the question of which house the Haven had been; and in late 2010 he helpfully sent me photocopies of the material he had used in reaching his conclusion – which was the same as my initial conclusion, namely that the house where Wilde had stayed was a narrow house in the centre of the block. John Wagstaff, writing in *The Wildean*, No. 5 (1994), expressed the same opinion: 'No. 5 was squeezed into the centre of the terrace.'

However Leslie, Wagstaff and I were all wrong.

The main source for Leslie's conclusions had been the *Worthing & District Blue Book* of 1919–20. This listed two houses on the west side, as now (although at that time they were named, not numbered). On the right side, eight houses were listed, Nos 1–8. From this, Leslie made the reasonable assumption that the west-facing block that appears on old photographs and postcards consisted of the eight houses of the Esplanade. Accordingly, he marked up a photograph of the building into eight divisions, chopping the terrace up into seven narrow houses (alternately with and without first-floor bow windows), with an eighth, slightly larger house at the sea end, with a curved balcony on its first floor.

The fact that a very modest, narrow, plain-fronted house was thus putatively

The Location of the Haven

allocated to Wilde for his 1894 stay did give some pause for thought. Although Wilde had written to Bosie, just before he left London for Worthing, 'The house, I hear, is very small and I have no writing room', this 'very small' house nevertheless needed to be large enough to accommodate a party of six – Wilde, Constance, Cyril, Vyvyan, the Swiss governess and Arthur the valet – in addition to two resident servants and the child of one of them. In a house with just two front windows (one on the first floor and one on the second) and two or three at the back, this seemed a tight fit. Nonetheless, the rest of the evidence appeared conclusive.

Then, on 28 March 2011 – I give the date because of the odd coincidence that it was the (not widely commemorated) 120th anniversary of Alphonse Conway's baptism at St Andrew's Church, Worthing – I was studying the detailed 1896 Ordnance Survey map of Worthing for other purposes, when I noticed something to which I had not previously paid attention.

Wherever there were terraces on the map, there were dividing lines to mark out the individual houses. In every case these delineated a single dwelling. This was clear from comparing terraces on the map with the number of houses shown for the same terraces in old street directories. However, in the case of the block that Leslie, Wagstaff and I believed to be the 'complete' Esplanade in 1894 (thus, Nos 1–8), there were just four houses marked out with lines – and the Ordnance Survey mapper would obviously not have applied a different principle to this one terrace.

It thus appeared that the west-facing block familiar from old photographs and postcards comprised four houses rather than eight; and indeed that they were houses of reasonably generous proportions.

I then revisited the 1927 edition of *Kelly's Directory* and was struck by something odd and unexpected: Nos 1–4, The Esplanade had disappeared since 1919–20. Only Nos 5–8 were now listed for the west-facing side of the street.

The only explanation for this – other than demolition, which could be ruled out by reference to old photographs – was that the houses that had originally been numbered as Nos 1–4, The Esplanade had been the houses in two blocks that appear on the 1896 map to the east of the main west-facing terrace and are visible in old pictures; and that at some point between 1919–20 and 1927 these houses had been renumbered as part of Brighton Road. In other words, the Esplanade in 1894 had consisted not of just the west-facing block, but of three blocks in all – two of them situated to the east of the main block, with their north sides abutting Brighton Road and their south sides looking out over the sea. This deduction was not contradicted by the appearance of the blocks, since the two smaller blocks were of the same period and design as the west-facing terrace. The best evidence suggests that all were built around 1881.

Since the north sides of the second and third blocks faced onto Brighton Road, it was a logical decision on the part of Worthing Council – at some point when the town's street numbering was being rationalised – to give these houses Brighton Road addresses, in order to avoid the messy situation of there being four stray houses facing the sea which did not have a proper street address. It was inappropriate for these houses to have the address 'The Esplanade' when they were located not on the street bearing that name but north of the seafront promenade that ran between Farncombe Road and Windsor Road, which, confusingly, bore the same name. (This confusion was eliminated some years ago when the promenade ceased to be called the Esplanade.)

If the central and eastern blocks comprised part of the Esplanade, however, the numbering of the houses in those blocks would have had to have been from east to west, as otherwise No. 1, The Esplanade would have been next to No. 5. Although unconventional, east–west numbering was not an impossibility.

The one piece of incontrovertible proof that these deductions were correct would have been an old town plan of the type the borough council would be expected to have maintained for rating and other purposes – a plan that included all house numbers. However, enquiries of the relevant department at Worthing Council drew a blank. It was therefore necessary to search for indirect evidence in the comprehensive collection of Worthing directories held on microfiche at the town's library.

Importantly for our purposes, the old directories provided confirmation that the Esplanade had indeed consisted not just of the west-facing block but also of the two blocks to the east. This was demonstrated by the fact that, between the 1918–19 and 1921 directories, the addresses 1-4, The Esplanade had disappeared and the houses had been reallocated Brighton Road numbers: helpfully, they were still listed under the Esplanade in 1921, even though they now had Brighton Road addresses.

In addition, the deduction that the numbering of the second and third blocks started at the eastern end was shown to be correct from the fact that the 1918–19 *Blue Book* has No. 2, The Esplanade named as Pyrford and No. 1 as Beach Lawn – and that in the 1938–39 *Blue Book*, Pyrford is listed as 106 Brighton Road and Beach Lawn as 108 Brighton Road. Thus No. 1, The Esplanade (Beach Lawn) was situated to the east of No. 2 (Pyrford).

Frustratingly, however, the central piece of evidence was elusive, since the listing practices of the two directories (*Kelly's* and the *Blue Book*) differed, making it unclear whether the numbers given for the west-facing block started at the Brighton Road end (thus 5–8, from north to south) or at the sea end (thus 8–5). Either was possible in the context of the second and third blocks, since from No. 4 the numbering might have continued in a westerly direction along Brighton Road or in a south-westerly direction along the sea-front. (These four substantial semi-detached houses probably had doors at both front and back.) The position of the buildings relative to each other, as shown on the 1896 plan, suggested the first as the more logical option. However, in view of the fact that logic had not been present when the numbering 1–4 had been introduced on an east-to-west basis, an appeal to logic could not be regarded as conclusive.

However, three important further clues were found in the old directories.

Long's Worthing Directory of 1891 lists a 'wall letter box' located between Nos 5 and 4, The Esplanade. Since we have now established that No. 4 was at the west end of the central block, then, if No. 5 was the house at the sea end of the west-facing terrace, this postbox would have been located in an improbable position, tucked away on the seafront just before the last two buildings in the town; and indeed no old photographs of the Esplanade taken from the south show a postbox in the low wall or indeed a position it could have occupied. The more likely location for the postbox was on Brighton Road, where it would have been convenient also for the other terraces at the eastern edge of the town and for passers-by. Thus it must be regarded as probable that this was where the postbox was, and that No. 5 was therefore located at the Brighton Road end of the west-facing terrace.

Two other two pieces of evidence in the 1938–39 edition of the *Blue Book* point to the same conclusion. The compiler is unusually clear and precise about the sequence of houses in the Esplanade. He lists as 'left from New Parade' Nos 9, then 9a, then 10 – and this sequence remains the same today in the important respect that No. 10 is at the Brighton Road end (although, oddly, No. 9a is south of No. 9). On the other side of the street the compiler lists as 'left from Brighton Road', 5, 6, 7 and 8. This strongly suggests that No. 5 was at the Brighton Road end of the terrace.

The second piece of evidence is the names that the two houses that concern us were using by 1938: No. 5 was called Esplanade House and No. 8 (which between 1899 and at least 1923 had been known as Ormonde) was Wide Horizon – an apt name for the curved-balcony house at the sea end, but an absurdity for the house at the Brighton Road end, whose view since about 1898 had been only of other houses and a short stretch of Brighton Road.

These three pieces of evidence proved all but conclusively that No. 5 had been the house at the northern end of the terrace, on the corner of Brighton Road.

Importantly, there was nothing to contradict this conclusion in the evidence from Marie Stopes's diary account of a conversation she had with Bosie on 18 March 1939:

> He told us that they [Wilde and Douglas] were staying in rooms with a balcony in Worthing. The house was then called, I think, the Haven, and Lord Alfred had recently been down and found it, though the name of the street and the house have both been changed. But he found an old fisherman who remembered it [the house] under its old name. The beautiful large room he and Wilde had, had been spoiled by partitioning, but otherwise the house was unchanged.

(There are a couple of minor oddities here – Bosie's having apparently said that he and Wilde were 'staying in rooms'; and the somewhat misleading concept that he and Wilde 'had' a beautiful large room. These must be due either to Marie Stopes's misremembering some of the conversation when she wrote up her diary, or to Bosie's having airbrushed Wilde's family holiday of 1894 out of the picture in order to put himself at the heart of the period when *The Importance of Being Earnest* was being written.)

We know that by 1939 the house was no longer called the Haven – indeed the name seems to have disappeared early in the twentieth century – so Bosie's experience of the changed house name makes sense. As for the change in street name, Bosie's puzzlement at the time of his 1939 visit was presumably due to the fact that, as we have seen, two of the Esplanade blocks (houses 1–4) – although not the block where Wilde's house was – had been given Brighton Road addresses and numbers. Since Bosie could not find his way to the Esplanade without asking directions, it is evident that his memory of the location after forty-five years was in any case somewhat hazy.

The beautiful large room with the balcony to which Bosie refers might seem a good match for the curved-balconied house at the sea end of the block, but the pictures of the Esplanade terrace in the centre of this book show that all the other houses had balconies accessible from the second floor. In addition, by the time of the 1923 edition of *Kelly's Directory*, No. 5 consisted of 'apartments', and the conversion of the house into flats would almost certainly have involved alterations, including the partitioning to which Bosie referred.

At the same time as my research was taking place at Worthing Library, another important clue was on its way. Donald Mead, editor of *The Wildean*, had mentioned a photograph in the possession of John Stratford, treasurer of the Oscar Wilde Society. Donald knew that this photograph, taken in the early 1940s, showed Bosie at the Esplanade, but did not know in front of which house it showed him standing. This piece of additional evidence would be invaluable, since Bosie's position in the photograph – while it could not in itself serve as total proof – would be a very strong indication.

It seemed appropriate to pass on to Donald Mead the conclusions generated by the research at Worthing Library before either of us had sight of the Bosie photograph. I therefore e-mailed him to say that the evidence of the investigation appeared to have established beyond doubt that the Haven had been the house at the northern end of the west-facing terrace on the corner of Brighton Road. We then awaited the arrival of the photograph, in the hope that the often ambivalent Bosie had stood unambiguously in front of a specific house – and that it was the same house that all the other evidence suggested must have been the Haven.

As illustration 23 shows, Bosie did not fail us. In addition, the name 'Esplanade House' is prominently displayed above the first-floor bay window; and that, as we have seen, was the name that No. 5 had by 1938. Everything hung together.

Quod erat demonstrandum.

APPENDIX F

Alphonse Conway's First Name

Although Alphonse was Alphonse Conway's correct first name, Oscar Wilde always referred to him as 'Alphonso'.

There are two possible explanations for this. One is that Alphonse had, out of caprice, decided to call himself Alphonso, and introduced himself as such; and that Oscar never knew that this was not his real name. The other, more likely explanation – and we will proceed on this assumption – is that this was an affectionate name that Wilde gave the boy soon after they met, and that he always used that name thereafter, including when introducing him to others. As John Wagstaff pointed out in *The Wildean* in January 1995, Wilde similarly seems to have used the name 'Ernesto' for Ernest Scarfe, with whom he had been involved earlier that year – that variant appearing in the letter Wilde wrote to Lord Alfred Douglas the day before he left for Worthing.

Most twentieth-century biographers of Wilde, such as Hesketh Pearson, H. Montgomery Hyde and Rupert Croft-Cooke, seem to have known that Conway's real name was Alphonse, since they used that version, even though they were aware that the Plea of Justification used 'Alfonso'. Since the name Alphonse appears nowhere in any written evidence known to Wilde's biographers, that name must have entered the historical record from someone who was in Worthing during the holiday of 1894 – probably Bosie.

'Alphonse' is thus the version that H. Montgomery Hyde uses in *The Trials of Oscar Wilde* (1948). Although some of Hyde's source material certainly used 'Alphonso' – as already indicated, it was the version used during the libel trial – Hyde standardised to what he evidently knew to be the boy's real name. Hyde again used 'Alphonse' in his *Oscar Wilde* (1975), but for some reason had defected to 'Alphonso' by the time of his *Lord Alfred Douglas* (1984).

Some more recent writers, including Richard Ellmann, Merlin Holland and Neil McKenna, have preferred to use 'Alfonso'. This is presumably because, until Alphonse's baptism and census records became available, the Plea of Justification was the most authoritative document available – and indeed the inclusion there of Alphonse's second name, Harold, may have added to the impression that it gave the definitive version of the boy's first name.

This is the sole occurrence of 'Alfonso' in any of the documentation of the period. The spelling used in the official transcript of the libel trial is 'Alphonso' (e-mails from Kathryn Johnson, Curator, Modern Drama Collections, British Library, 29 July and 1 October 2010). This is also the spelling used in the boy's witness statement (private information from Neil McKenna).

Wilde himself was the first to use the boy's first name in court – in response to Edward Carson's question 'What was his Christian name?' – and it is perhaps surprising that he chose the form 'Alphonso'. But Wilde had seen the Plea of Justification, where 'Alphonso' – in this one case spelt 'Alfonso', as we have seen – was used rather than 'Alphonse', so perhaps he thought it best to follow suit and use the name that Alphonse had apparently given. Or perhaps, since he had always used 'Alphonso' himself, this version was instinctive. In any case, he had more important things to concentrate on during his cross-examination than addressing a minor error of nomenclature.

Certainly 'Alphonso' is the spelling Oscar himself used in writing, since it appears in the 'storm letter' to Bosie of 10 September 1894 and in the inscription Oscar wrote in the copy of *Treasure Island* that he gave Alphonse, which was found after the Second World War among the possessions of Detective-Inspector Brockwell, who had been in charge of the Wilde case. When Merlin Holland quotes this dedication, he applies his principle of standardising to 'Alfonso' ('Misspelled names have been altered according to official records', Holland, *Irish Peacock and Scarlet Marquess*, p. xli). However the British Library, which now has the torn-out title page – the book itself was thrown away by Inspector Brockwell's granddaughter – has confirmed that Wilde clearly wrote 'Alphonso' (e-mail from Kathryn Johnson of the British Library, 29 July 2010).

There remains the question of why 'Alphonso' – or in one instance 'Alfonso' – was used during the legal proceedings, rather than 'Alphonse'. The answer is probably that, initially addressed by that name when Queensberry's detectives confronted him, Alphonse was too intimidated and embarrassed to correct the assumption the detectives had made. The detectives' having presumably used this version of the name when they first met Alphonse supports the theory (see Chapter 5) that their information about Wilde's friendship with Alphonse came from servants at the Haven, who would have heard Wilde use that version. The form 'Alphonso' would have been known only to those who had heard Wilde use it during or after the Worthing holiday.

APPENDIX G

Alphonse Delahay

On 24 June 1878, at the Old Bailey – seventeen years before Oscar Wilde was convicted in the same court – a thirty-one-year-old man called Alphonse Delahay was sentenced to seven years' penal servitude for stealing 'two sealskin jackets, a cashbox, six shares in the Union Bank of London, and other articles' from a house in Camden Town where his accomplice, Maurice Blanc, aged forty-one, had been lodging. It appears from the report of the trial that Delahay was the receiver of the stolen goods rather than the actual thief. His long sentence in part reflected the fact that he also 'pleaded guilty to a conviction of felony at Liverpool in October, 1874'. Blanc, who had no previous convictions – and who, unlike Delahay, admitted his part in the Camden Town crime – was given two years without penal servitude.

(Interestingly, the two men whose names appear just above Delahay's on the list of that day's sentences at the Old Bailey – a list arranged in order of length of sentence – were both sentenced for buggery, Conrad Ettingshausen to twenty years and Marques Manuel to ten. Unless there were major exacerbating circumstances in the cases of Ettingshausen and Manuel, this is suggestive of the kind of sentence Oscar Wilde might have received had he been charged with and convicted of that offence.)

It was stated in court that, when arrested and charged by Inspector Dodd, Delahay had said, 'Me, me? You mistake. I am only two week [sic] from Brussels.' Perhaps Delahay genuinely spoke little English. However, he seems to have spent a fair amount of time in England – after all, he was in Liverpool four years earlier – so it is possible that he was play-acting the confused foreigner. It is true that he relied during the trial upon a written defence which had to be translated – presumably from French – but on the other hand he knew enough English to be able to challenge Inspector Dodd's evidence and force him to accept that one particular item had not in fact been in his possession when he was searched. ('I am in error,' Dodd admitted. 'You had a chain but no watch.')

In his statement, Delahay claimed that Blanc's wife – who was also charged in connection with the theft, but was found not guilty – had 'asked him [Delahay] to keep a box for him [Blanc] containing some kitchen utensils, as he [Blanc] was going to Paris and that he [Delahay] had no idea of the contents'. The box contained the stolen items. With Brussels and Paris associations to choose from, we may assume that Delahay and Blanc were either Belgian or French.

Confirmation of Delahay's age is provided by the 1881 census. In that year Delahay was serving his sentence in HM Convict Prison, Portsmouth. He is listed as unmarried and thirty-four years old. The old convict prison – not to be confused with HMP Kingston, a later Portsmouth prison, which closed in 2013 – was on Anchor Gate Road, Portsea, a site now within the Royal Naval dockyard. It had been built in 1852 to house convicts who had previously been kept on prison ships in Portsmouth Harbour, and held about 1,000 prisoners.

The reason that Alphonse Delahay is of interest to us is that he is – from among the few men with the first name Alphonse who, the censuses tell us, were in southern England at the right time – the most plausible candidate to have been the father of Alphonse Conway.

We would not expect there to be any information in the historical records linking a woman and the father of her illegitimate son (see page 71 for the evidence that Conway was almost certainly illegitimate), except perhaps in the baptismal record and the birth certificate – and there is no direct link between Alphonse Delahay and Sarah Conway. However, there is intriguing circumstantial evidence.

The first is the direct minor fact that Alphonse Conway's father's name is shown as Alphonse on the baptismal document.

But there are indirect facts that also make for a decent match. Delahay was the right age to have had a relationship with Sarah, since in 1878 he was thirty-one, three years older than her; he certainly spent some time in the south of England; and his being in prison from 1878 until (probably) 1885 make him a good candidate for a father who was absent when his son was a young child.

Certainly there is nothing implausible in Sarah's having met and become involved with a man who spent some of his time in London, as Delahay did. Indeed, if the evidence in Appendix H is correct, then she was herself living in London in the 1870s. Although Delahay seems to have moved around England, perhaps in connection with his work – as we shall see, he was a civil engineer as well as a thief – he seems to have known London quite well; and indeed he apparently returned there after his release from prison, as we shall also see.

Sarah Conway, like many young women from the provinces, probably initially went to London to find employment in domestic service. Indeed, most of the women who kept small seaside lodging houses in the second half of the nineteenth century – as Sarah did at three different locations in Worthing between 1883 and 1895 – originally learnt their housekeeping skills as servants in the households of the upper and middle classes. Alphonse was born in Bognor (in 1878), but this does not contradict his having been conceived in London – there is nothing surprising in a woman returning to her home area for the birth of a child, particularly if the father was by then absent.

Beyond these areas of general semblance, there are two interesting points of closer possible connection between Sarah and Alphonse Delahay.

The first is that Delahay's occupation is given in the 1881 census as 'civil engineer'. According to Wilde, cross-examined by Edward Carson on 3 April 1895 during the Queensberry libel trial, Alphonse had told him that his father had been 'an electrical engineer who had died young'. This of course is not the same thing, but the coincidence of the word 'engineer' is suggestive, not least because it is an unexpected occupation for the father of a boy of Alphonse's class (or indeed for a part-time felon). In any case, Alphonse may have either confused or embroidered what his mother had told him about his father's job. Or Wilde, always prone to haziness over unimportant details, may have misremembered what Alphonse told him. Certainly Alphonse Delahay was the only Alphonse registered in England in 1871 who was an engineer of any type – although it remains puzzling that a man with so respectable an occupation should have become involved in petty crime, in at least two locations in England.

The second point of connection is the date of Delahay's conviction and sentence – 24 June 1878. This was just sixteen days before Alphonse Conway was born, and, if Delahay was indeed his father, this would provide a compelling reason why Sarah did not have her son christened immediately after his birth. She would have wanted to avoid awkward questions from the vicar or the parish clerk – embarrassing enough in the case of illegitimacy, but worse still with the addition of a father who was a recently convicted criminal.

The name Alphonse Delahay occurs in one other place in the available records, and since – at least in an English context – it is a most unusual name, it is likely that the Alphonse Delahay whose death occurred in Camberwell, London at some point in the second quarter of 1885 is the same man, in spite of the fact that his age is shown as forty-five and the convict would have been about thirty-eight. However, in the absence of any certain information as to a dead person's date of birth – and of course no birth certificate would have been available for someone born abroad – the age of death recorded would have been an estimate. A lengthy sentence of penal servitude would have been very ageing, so, if they were the same man, it is entirely possible that the recently released convict looked much older than his years. The fact that forty-five is a round figure is also supportive of the possibility that the age was an estimate.

If he served his full sentence, the convict Delahay would have come out of prison a few days before the end of June 1885 – in which case he died very soon after his release, perhaps either by his own hand or at the hands of some fellow criminal he had wronged.

As we saw in Chapter 5, Alphonse Conway was finally baptised when he was twelve years old, on 28 March 1891, eight days before the date of the 1891 census. If Delahay was indeed Alphonse's father, Sarah was not technically a widow, as she indicated in the census. However, she was 'nominally' a widow to the extent that the father of her son was by then dead. Conway was a legitimate surname for Sarah herself to use, since it was her maiden name (although, as we shall see in Appendix H, her official name at this time may have been Cook). But, since we are confident that Alphonse's father's name was not Conway, Alphonse's legal surname was not Conway either.

That Alphonse Delahay was Alphonse Conway's father is demonstrably no more than an interesting – although plausible – hypothesis. Delahay is certainly the best available candidate, but the evidence falls a long way short of proof, and it is unlikely that further information will come to light either to confirm or to contradict the theory. However, if Delahay was indeed Alphonse's father, the irony of her son's having – like herself – been seduced by a man who was subsequently convicted at the Old Bailey and sent to prison must have been savagely unwelcome to Sarah.

APPENDIX H

Alphonse Conway and the Australian Connection

In March 2010, Michael Seeney, vice-chairman of the Oscar Wilde Society, received an e-mail from an Australian whom we shall call MM. In the course of researching his family history, MM had discovered that the Alphonse Conway of whom he had read in a biography of Oscar Wilde was apparently a distant relation of his. The e-mail was passed on to me because an article I had written about Conway had been published six weeks earlier in *The Wildean*, although MM was not aware of this.

There followed an extensive e-mail correspondence, during which MM provided me with a wealth of interesting material gleaned during the course of his researches into his family's history. What follows is a digest of the information he gave me, filtered through – and interpreted in the light of – my own knowledge of Alphonse Conway's story.

This investigation must come with a caution, for we are dependent on the 'two Sarahs' in this story – MM's, whom we are about to encounter, and the Sarah Conway we are already familiar with – being the same person. The evidence is compelling, but, since we are in part reliant on long-ago family memories, it is possible that there is a flaw in the structure.

If everything coheres, however, the grandmother of Alphonse Conway was a woman called Elizabeth Jones who, in the fourth decade of the nineteenth century, was living with her husband Thomas Jones in Petworth in West Sussex. And it was there in 1833 that she gave birth to the only child of the marriage, a girl called Mildred. Thomas died when Mildred was about ten, and six years later – in 1848 or 1849 – Mildred's mother, by then aged over forty, had another daughter, Sarah, this time illegitimate. The oral history in MM's family was that the father was a local man called Conway. This was probably the John Conway mentioned in Chapter 6 of this book. Although she was initially known by her mother's surname of Jones, Sarah later used her father's name – this being the surname she used in her teens, and again in her thirties and forties. We also saw in Chapter 6 that Alphonse's mother, Sarah Conway, was born in Petworth about 1849. It is surely all but inconceivable that there were two different Sarah Conways born at the same time in the same small Sussex town, especially since Conway seem to have been a very rare name in Petworth.

In 1854, a man called Charlie Mathews visited England. Mathews was of English parentage, but had been born and brought up in Australia, where he made a great deal of money in the goldfields of Victoria. While visiting relations in Sussex, he met and fell in love with Mildred Jones, Sarah Conway's half-sister. The pair wanted to get married, but Mildred's mother was opposed to the idea, because marriage would mean that Mildred would disappear to the other side of the world. So Charlie and Mildred eloped.

When Mathews died in Australia in 1899, his estate was worth the considerable sum of about £88,000. Mildred, who inherited half the money, set about making her own will and tried to make contact with Sarah, whom she had not seen for over forty years. They had, however, corresponded at some point – it is thought in the 1880s or 1890s. Members of MM's family are clear that at the period of this correspondence Sarah was living in Sussex, was calling herself Conway, and had a son. This matches perfectly with the Sarah Conway who was Alphonse's mother who had been in the town from about 1883.

When Mildred was preparing her will in 1900, the most recent address she had for Sarah was in Worthing, but, despite several letters to that and other addresses, Sarah proved elusive. One of the letters was returned unclaimed, while the others remained unanswered. Thinking that Sarah might no longer be alive, Mildred made no mention of her in the will, and she died in 1910 without hearing any news of her half-sister.

We do not know why the correspondence had ceased but, since the sisters had clearly not fallen out, a possible reason was that, in the aftermath of the shame and disruption that the Oscar Wilde scandal brought on Sarah and Alphonse, Sarah felt too embarrassed to communicate with her only living relation. To a twenty-first-century eye this may seem far-fetched, but it is difficult for us to imagine the opprobrium attached to homosexuality in the aftermath of the Oscar Wilde trials – to say nothing of the particular shame of having been intimately associated with Wilde himself. Even twenty years later, the secretly homosexual E. M. Forster was having his title character in *Maurice* – a novel that he did not dare publish in his lifetime – declare, 'I am an unspeakable of the Oscar Wilde sort.'

If embarrassment was indeed the reason that Sarah stopped writing to Mildred, then the last address Mildred had would have been 1 Bath Place in Worthing. It is entirely likely that Sarah left no forwarding address when, in 1895, she and Alphonse fled from there to Shoreham and subsequently, as far as the available records are concerned, disappeared totally, perhaps having changed their names.

Mildred Mathew's great-great-granddaughter remembers her own grandmother (Mildred's granddaughter) showing her some of Sarah Conway's letters in the early 1950s. She was astonished that an adult could make as many errors of spelling and grammar as Sarah apparently did, but it was explained that, when Sarah was a child, education in England was not compulsory and many poor children had little or no schooling.

Sarah Conway's half-sister Mildred died in 1910. Her personal effects, including Sarah's letters, remained the family until 1976, when, following the death of her granddaughter, they were burnt without the knowledge of the rest of her relations by someone who had married into the family. Therefore a wealth of evidence about Alphonse Conway's mother and – almost certainly – about the boy's own childhood and adolescence went up in smoke in the Blue Mountains, about sixty miles west of Sydney, on a random and regrettable day in 1976.

*

We now return to nineteenth-century England, where Elizabeth Jones, mother of Mildred and Sarah – who, as we have seen, was widowed about 1843 – had in due course remarried. Her new husband was not John Conway, the father of her younger daughter, but a man called Christopher Cooper.

Throughout most of her childhood Sarah had continued to be known as Jones, which was her widowed mother's surname at the time of her birth. However, at some point in her teens she apparently decided to take her father's name of Conway. Later still, she appears to have adopted her mother's second husband's name of Cooper, and this was the maiden name she was using when she got married. She married at a reasonably young age, since by the time of the 1871 census, when she was twenty-three, she is shown as the wife of James Cook, a coachman and domestic servant. They were living at Phillip Terrace, Paddington. Sarah's birthplace appears in the census as Vetworth (*sic*).

In December 1875, Sarah's mother, Elizabeth Cooper (formerly Jones), made a will. By then she was again a widow, and she was herself living in London. She left most of her estate to Sarah rather than to Mildred – probably partly because she would have been closer to the daughter who lived in England, and partly because Mildred was well off, whereas Sarah was not. So Elizabeth bequeathed relatively minor items such as table linen and silverware to Mildred, but the bulk of the estate (£285) – together with her furniture and such household goods as had not been left to Mildred – went to 'my daughter Sarah Cook, the wife of James Cook of Paddington'. There was also a legacy to 'my grandson Frederick James Cook, infant son of my daughter Sarah Cook' – the sum of £50, to be placed in trust for his future education expenses. No child of the couple is listed in the 1871 census, so it is reasonable to assume that Frederick was born between then and Elizabeth's making her will in December 1875.

The sudden appearance in the story of Sarah's husband James Cook and infant son Frederick Cook seemed to bring this investigation to an abrupt and puzzling end. There had been compelling evidence that the two Sarah Conways were the same person – and yet how could a woman who in 1875 had been married to a man called Cook and been the mother of a son called Frederick James be the same woman who, living in Worthing in the 1890s, was calling herself Conway and had a son called Alphonse Harold, born in 1878?

There seemed no way round this – even though the rest of evidence was persuasive, and, as already suggested, it seemed inconceivable that that there could have been two different Sarah Conways born in the same year in Petworth. Nonetheless, the two sets of facts appeared to be irreconcilable, and for this reason MM's and my correspondence came to an end for some six months.

Then one evening I was re-reading the numerous e-mails that contained the component parts of this complex story when there occurred to me a couple of explanations that would allow all the available facts to cohere. One of these explanations – that Frederick Cook had died in infancy – had to be dismissed when further information came to light, but the other made a very comfortable fit, and contradicted neither the existing facts nor further facts that were about to be discovered by MM.

It must, however, be noted that, by following this theory, we are entering into Sarah's life a major life event for which there is no direct evidence. Nonetheless it is only by introducing this event that we can construct a bridge between the two Sarah Conways who much other evidence suggests were the same person.

What if there had been an estrangement between Sarah and her husband, perhaps caused by her having an affair with – and becoming pregnant by – Alphonse's father? Since Sarah would then have been branded a scarlet woman, James Cook would have had no difficulty in retaining custody of their son if he had wished. Equally, following the acrimonious collapse of her marriage, Sarah would not have wanted herself to retain (or her second son to be given) the name of Cook – so it is entirely plausible that she then reverted to the name of Conway, gave birth to Alphonse and, in due course, moved to Worthing.

At this point it was desirable to try to establish what had happened to Sarah's elder son, Frederick James Cook, born at some point between 1871 and 1875, since – if the facts hung together – he was Alphonse Conway's half-brother. Again there proved to be an Australian connection, for MM went back to his investigations and he was able to obtain the death certificate of Frederick James Cook, who had died in Australia. Australian death certificates are more comprehensive than British ones, and Frederick Cook's contained much useful information.

Frederick Cook, a 'retired clerk' and the son of James Cook, 'car man', and Sarah Cook, *née* Cooper, died on 1 June 1950 in Melbourne, Australia at the age of seventy-seven. He had thus been born in 1872 or 1873. He had been married twice, first in London at the age of about twenty-three and secondly almost immediately on his arrival in Australia in 1918 at the age of forty-five. The first marriage had produced no children; the second a son, who predeceased his father, and a daughter. If there are no flaws in the information and the deductions in this article, these children were Alphonse Conway's half-nephew and half-niece.

Frederick Cook's emigration to Australia cannot have had anything to do with the fact that his Aunt Mildred had gone there many years before and that he had numerous relations in the country, since there is no knowledge or memory of him among any of the members of MM's extended family. This would support the case for his having been brought up by his father since the age of six or seven. It is equally true, however, that even if he had subsequently been in touch with his mother – although perhaps only in adulthood – he would probably never have known his Aunt Mildred's address. As we have seen, Sarah had lost contact with her half-sister by 1900, when Mildred wrote her will – indeed by 1895, since we know that the last address Mildred had was a Worthing address. This was many years before Frederick's emigration to Australia in 1918. Even in the age of the internet, it is difficult to track down long-missing relations. One hundred years ago the task would have been Herculean.

We do not know whether Frederick and Alphonse knew each other. We have posited that Frederick's parents' marriage broke up and that he remained with his father, James Cook, and therefore perhaps disappeared from his mother's life, at least for a while. During the Queensberry libel trial Oscar Wilde said that Alphonse had told him he was 'the only child'. Wilde's statement makes it unlikely that Frederick stayed with his mother after the marital breakdown we have conjectured, since in that case he would have been part of Sarah Conway's household in Worthing, certainly during the 1880s, and therefore known to a half-brother who was only five or six years younger. In addition, Frederick is not listed in Sarah's household in the 1891 census. However, by then he would already have been eighteen or nineteen, and thus, even if he had been in Worthing during the previous decade, old enough to have left his mother's home. As we have seen, the sketchy 'memory-record' handed down through MM's family was that in the 1880s or 1890s Sarah was living in Worthing and 'had a son'. This information does not rule out the possibility of there having been another son who either had left home or had not been in his mother's life since the age of seven. If the two Sarahs were the same woman, however, the son mentioned in the letters from Worthing was certainly Alphonse rather than Frederick.

Late in 2011, MM was able to establish from research in Australian online databases that Frederick Cook's daughter, whom we will call CS, was still alive and living in a retirement village in a suburb of Melbourne. He discovered her address and learnt that she had a married son, GS. She had been twenty-nine at the time of her father's death in 1950 and was therefore now in her early nineties. If the disparate evidence set out in this article hangs together, then – as the daughter of Alphonse's half-brother, Frederick – CS is the granddaughter of Sarah Conway and Alphonse Conway's 'half-niece'.

MM was due to make direct contact with CS and her family at the start of 2012, but I never heard from him again. The e-mail correspondence had been lengthy and friendly, so there seemed only two possible interpretations for this sudden silence. One was that MM had died over Christmas and New Year 2011/12. The other was that the outcome of his meeting with CS and her family was such that he felt unable to tell me what he had found out. This interpretation would suggest that CS and her family were indeed Alphonse's close relations and did not wish to let what they knew about their family's history enter the public domain.

There is, of course, a third possible reason for the silence – that, for some bizarre reason, MM had over an extended period fed me a carefully constructed fantasy of extraordinary complexity, and that the process had now run its course. Once such a suspicion breaks in, mental question marks begin to proliferate. For example, it is, on the face of it, a curious coincidence that an enquiry about Alphonse Conway should have reached the Oscar Wilde Society just six weeks after my article was published. There is also something almost over-neat about the fact that investigation into the later life of Frederick Cook should have established that he too had ended up in Australia, and about the ease with which MM was able to identify and locate Frederick's daughter. The office at the retirement village in Melbourne seems to have been surprisingly well-informed – and indeed surprisingly communicative to a stranger contacting them by telephone – on the subject of CS, down to the fact that her son's wife was very interested in family history and that the whole family, including CS, were apparently 'off to the coast' for a couple of weeks over the Christmas period.

Nonetheless, the length and tone of MM's e-correspondence with me made such an interpretation of his disappearance improbable. Anyone amusing themselves by sowing false historical seeds would not – to mix a metaphor – need to construct so vast and elaborate an edifice. Also, concocting complex fantasies requires exceptional memory and powers of organisation, and there were no contradictions of any significance in MM's account, although it is true that, as time passed, he appeared to retreat from one or two assertions that he had made early in the correspondence. Finally, while much of the historical linkage had to be taken on trust, there was one detail that not only was easily verifiable but also could not have been found by someone looking for a random resident of Petworth to link into Sarah's story – that is, the record of Sarah Cook's having been born in the misspelt 'Vetworth'.

Therefore, having set down these caveats, we shall proceed to the end of the story on the assumption that the information MM gave was true and accurate.

We can only speculate about what CS – seemingly Alphonse Conway's half-niece – and her son GS knew of Alphonse. If CS's father Frederick never saw his own mother after the age of seven, then of course CS would not even have known that she had an Uncle Alphonse. However, it is improbable that CS's father never told her anything about his own mother – even if he had not seen her since his parents' marriage ended and his memories were only of when he was a young child.

In any case, the theory that Sarah's son Frederick may not have seen his mother after the age of about seven is only one theory, and it runs counter to the more likely option that there was some subsequent contact with her. It is, for example, possible that Alphonse did not know of the existence of his half-brother at the time that he knew Wilde, but that Alphonse's own disgrace made his mother thereafter feel comfortable about revealing her own chequered past. Alphonse was almost a man by now, and old enough to be told awkward facts about his background. If there was indeed contact between Frederick and his mother in the second half of the 1890s, then Frederick would probably have known of his half-brother's association with Wilde, not least because of the disruptive effect it had on their mother's life. However, this might have been sufficiently dark a family secret not to be divulged to the next generation, and thus to CS – although the passage of time (Frederick Cook died half a century after Wilde's summer in Worthing) might have dulled the sense of embarrassment and increased the temptation for Frederick to share so remarkable a family story with his daughter and the rest of the family.

As already suggested, the most obvious interpretation of the fact that MM felt unable to communicate to me the result of his meeting with CS and GS is that they did not wish whatever information they had to be made public. Perhaps they already had some knowledge of what happened to Sarah and Alphonse after 1895. Perhaps the Wilde connection was also known to them – or perhaps it came as fresh and unwelcome news.

One strong possibility must be that Sarah and Alphonse themselves emigrated to Australia in 1895 or soon after, which would be one reason – a change of name would be another – for their disappearance from the English archival records. Since Sarah had corresponded with her half-sister in Australia, she would have been aware of the opportunities available in that country, and she and Alphonse would have been able to put half the world between themselves and the Wilde scandal. However, if they did emigrate, they clearly did not make contact with Mildred, since, as we have seen, there was no communication between the sisters after the correspondence faded away at some point before Sarah and Alphonse left Worthing. It is, however, possible that – rather than Sarah's having been too ashamed to remain in contact with her sister, as we suggested earlier – Mildred's address simply got lost in the chaos of their departure from Worthing and that, if Sarah and Alphonse did go to Australia, they did so partly because they entertained the hope that they might find Mildred. Even if Sarah had forgotten the street address, she would have remembered the name of the city where her half-sister lived.

Another piece of evidence that supports the theory that Sarah and Alphonse went to live in Australia was the emigration to that country of Sarah's elder son, Frederick, in 1918. Until then he had presumably stayed in England – where he had a wife and a job – but if (as appears to be the case) his first wife died around 1918 it would have made perfect sense at that point to go to the country where his mother and half-brother were already living.

If Alphonse did go to Australia after the Wilde scandal, then there could be children of his who are still alive – although they would be at least in their nineties – and there could certainly be living grandchildren. We are able to be detached about Alphonse's relationship with Wilde, but members of his immediate family may, even now, be less relaxed – this history would, after all, be very close to them.

As already suggested, the most obvious interpretation of the lack of any information having been made available from people who are probably close relations of Alphonse Conway is that there are indeed facts of substance known to them. If so, it is just possible that whatever it is they know may one day be published.

It is tantalising and frustrating that this investigation should have ended one step away from potentially fascinating information – one step away from someone still living who is seemingly the niece of Alphonse Conway, and the granddaughter of the intriguing and elusive woman who was variously Sarah Jones, Sarah Cooper, Sarah Cook, Sarah Conway and possibly, after 1895, Sarah Something-Else-Altogether.

APPENDIX I

The Ballad of Worthing Beach

For the author of a serious biographical book to print his own verses – even in an appendix – exposes him to the risk of disobliging comment.

However this book – like the eight articles in *The Wildean* from which much of it derives – consists mainly of a dense and fact-heavy record of events. Where atmosphere is present, it arises naturally out of the letters and texts quoted; there has been little or no attempt to add colour. The largely light-hearted verses that follow, first published in *The Wildean* in July 2012, were written to redress the balance. The piece is partly biographical narrative (hence the notes at the end), partly flight of fancy, and partly melancholy commentary on the Wilde story.

The metre was chosen with recitation in mind. The poem is therefore best read slightly aloud, with a one-second pause between each verse.

I

The story this ballad will tell
Began quite remarkably well
– But the early part lacked
The Faustian pact
And the sudden descent into hell.

When writers sit back on their laurels,
They forget that the world thrives on quarrels
And that nothing provokes
Respectable folks
More greatly than sub-standard morals.[1]

Oscar Wilde, the star of his age,
Saw the world as his personal stage.
He endeavoured to fashion
Fine poems from passion
– And he lived what he wrote on the page.

It's a fair proposition to say
Doubts started with *Dorian Gray*
– A Wilde can of worms
With (to use modern terms)
A sub-text quite palpably gay.

The verdict of history shows
That the themes were much more than a pose
– But even in theory
They caused bitter fury
And were seen as pure poison in prose.[2]

As Greek love grew ever more rife,
The Establishment sharpened its knife.
Though not wholly deserved,
Foul cells were reserved
For those who mixed art up with life.

So the blithe primrose path Wilde was
  treading
Was a cut-off relentlessly heading

To the less flowery trail
Via Pentonville jail
To wretched confinement in Reading.³

II

If he fancied a scullion or waiter
While dining with Ruskin or Pater,
Wilde stopped taking part
In discussion of art
And focused on what might come
  later.

Thus (fluid on matters of class)
When he glimpsed an ephebe through
  a glass
Of absinthe or hock,
To no-one's great shock
He invariably made a deft pass.⁴

Few things can more totally change us
Than perilous comfort from strangers
So sensible shepherds

Shun tigers and leopards,
Knowing feasting with panthers holds
  dangers.⁵

If love is a sweet-scented posy,
Wilde gave that rich garland to Bosie,
And he never once thought
It would end up in court,
For the sky at first dawn had been
  rosy.

The regrettable fact is that Wilde
Was intensely, insanely beguiled.
The young lord was lazy⁶
And, bluntly, half-crazy
– But he charmed the weak-willed
  when he smiled.

III

These are factors we cannot ignore
As we come to the year '94,
When a great play was written
On the south coast of Britain
In a tall terraced house near the
  shore.⁷

(The play that was *Earnest* became
The object of worldwide acclaim
– A near-perfect fit
Between stagecraft and wit,
And the rock of Wilde's literary fame.)

Though many think Worthing is worth
More than half of the treasure on
  earth,⁸
A petulant lord
Can quickly get bored
– Accidie being present from birth.

So Oscar, spurred on by his lordling,
Set off for the sands without dawdling
– They'd thought it their duty
To admire male beauty

Ever since they were members of
  Magdalen.⁹

As they stroll on the beach or the
  dunes,¹⁰
It is popular songs Bosie croons,¹¹
But cultured old Oscar
Hums *Carmen* or *Tosca*,¹²
Not cacophonous music-hall tunes.

Of what did they talk as they trod
Near the kingdom of haddock and
  cod?¹³
The importance they placed
On aesthetics and taste?
Or the doubtful existence of God?¹⁴

But the chat was not purely didactic,
For the lovers compared sexual
  tactics¹⁵
And the merits of each
Of the boys on the beach
– By whom they were greatly
  distracted.

IV

There now enter this tale – lawks-a-
  mercy! –[16]
Alphonse Conway and Stephen and
  Percy[17]
– Though nothing occurred
With the second and third
(Odysseus had only one Circe).[18]

But Wilde is hoping to spend
Special time with a new special friend.
Since the boy that he wants
Is the pliant Alphonse,
There is only one way it can end.

When in lust, Oscar rarely delayed
And they met up along the Parade.
Was it quite life-enhancing
On the quiet road to Lancing?[19]
Or did Alphonse regret that he stayed?

In truth it is probably best
That these matters aren't closely
  addressed
– So we draw a grey veil
Over part of this tale,
And the dark Sussex night hides the rest.

Moral lessons are outside the reach
Of this ballad of old Worthing beach.
Though Wilde's sexual flaws
Flouted ethics and laws,
At this point it is pointless to preach.

All summers have Shakespeare's short
  lease[20]
And both sunshine and passion soon
  cease.
Things that fade fast
Become shapes in the past
– We must leave the long-dead to their
  peace.

V

So Oscar and Alphonse soon parted,
But the waters ahead were uncharted
– Dice started to roll
Quite out of control[21]
And a tragic momentum had started.

The lines of men's lives aren't drawn
  straight;
Random angles and turnings await.
Short hours of affection
Take unwelcome directions
When they play second fiddle to fate.

Lord Queensberry – that infamous
  brute[22]
Whom Oscar had threatened to shoot
If he came to his premises –
Was now Wilde's nemesis
(Dwarf trees may bear poisonous fruit).[23]

And Worthing erupted with scandal,
Too much for poor Alphonse to
  handle.
The rest of his history
Is shrouded in mystery,
All trace of him snuffed like a candle.[24]

A literary footnote at most,
He left no more mark than a ghost.
He'd been flattered and kissed,
But now vanished like mist
In the dawn on the cold Sussex coast.

Oscar Wilde atoned for his crimes
And retreated to warm foreign climes.
Though his spirit was scarred,
Old habits died hard
– He bought love *à la Grecque* many
  times.

What a man loves he finally slays
With the kiss for which treachery
  pays.
Though Irish by birth,
Wilde lies in French earth
In a tomb in sad Père Lachaise.

La vie, à l'opinion des sages,
N'est plus qu'un très bref orage.
– Donc peut-être son esprit
Entend toujours les cris
Des beaux garçons qui jouent sur la
  plage.[25]

Notes

Most of these notes are straightforward references or amplifications. A few, however, consist of commentary on the poem as though written by a second party.

1. 'A giant among pygmies, Mr Wilde has naturally been cordially hated by all the mean and little people, and they now think to increase their own size and importance by belittling his.' *London Figaro*, 11 April 1895.
2. When *The Picture of Dorian Gray* was first published (in the July 1890 issue of *Lippincott's Monthly Magazine*), most of the reviews were virulently hostile. The *Daily Chronicle* described it as 'a poisonous book, the atmosphere of which is heavy with the mephitic odours of moral and spiritual putrefaction'.
3. Oscar Wilde spent four weeks on remand in Holloway between his arrest and the end of the first criminal trial. After sentence, he spent a month in Pentonville, four and a half months in Wandsworth, and eighteen months in Reading. HMP Reading closed permanently on 22 November 2013.
4. This is questionable. Most of Wilde's literary friends, certainly including Ruskin and Pater, would have been shocked if they had seen Wilde proposition a restaurant employee. Any pass Oscar made would therefore indeed have needed to be exceptionally deft.
5. 'It was like feasting with panthers. The danger was half the excitement.' (*Complete Letters*, p. 758.)
6. 'You had been idle at your school, worse than idle at your university.' (*Complete Letters*, p. 685.)
7. *The Importance of Being Earnest* was largely composed at the Haven, 5, The Esplanade, Worthing, where Wilde stayed between 10 August and 4 October 1894.
8. The unusually high estimation in which the author holds the town of Worthing is not universally shared.
9. By his own admission, Bosie engaged in homosexual activity as a schoolboy at Winchester, and there is evidence that Wilde was aware of that side of his own nature during his schooldays. In both cases, however, it was during their time at Oxford that their sense of duty with regard to male beauty hardened into a philosophical position.
10. There are no dunes at Worthing, but perhaps the two poets were enjoying their singing and their conversation so much that they walked along the coast as far as the beach at Goring, where there are dune-like features.
11. Bosie's taste for popular music is twice documented in 'De Profundis': 'I accepted your passion for going to music-halls' (*Complete Letters*, p. 692); 'There was no harm in your seriously considering that the most perfect way of passing an evening was to have a champagne dinner at the Savoy, a box at a music-hall to follow, and a champagne supper at Willis's as a bonne-bouche for the end' (*Complete Letters*, p. 771).
12. The author is in error here, since Puccini's *Tosca* had its first performance in January 1900, over five years after Wilde was in Worthing. He may be confusing *Tosca* with the same composer's 1893 opera *Manon Lescaut*.
13. In referring to the sea as 'the kingdom of haddock and cod', the author seems to be consciously imitating the high-flown language of much late nineteenth-century verse (not excluding that of Wilde and Douglas).

14. Bosie wrote in a letter to More Adey soon after Wilde's death, '[Wilde] was as a matter of fact the most complete sceptic imaginable, and would never have bowed his intellect to any dogma or any form of religious belief however fine.'
15. By then Wilde and Douglas were lovers only of others, their relationship seemingly having had a sexual dimension for just a few months in 1892. However, Wilde wrote in 'De Profundis' that Bosie's conversation constantly revolved round sex. ('Fascinating, terribly fascinating though the one topic round which your talk invariably centred was …', *Complete Letters*, p. 692.)
16. 'Lawks-a-mercy' is a variant of 'Lord have mercy', occurring – for example – in James Joyce's *Ulysses*, Episode 14: 'Lawksamercy, doctor, cried the young blood in the primrose vest, feigning a womanish simper and with immodest squirmings of his body.'
17. Alphonse Conway and his friends Stephen and Percy (whose surnames are not known) were the three boys Wilde and Bosie regularly took out on boating expeditions during the summer of 1894. Alphonse noticed that Percy was 'the Lord's favourite', a remark Wilde quoted in one of the letters he wrote Bosie from Worthing (*Complete Letters*, p. 602).
18. Circe, described in Homer's *Odyssey* as 'the loveliest of all immortals', initially turned Odysseus and his men into pigs when they turned up on the island of Aeaea where she lived. This change was later reversed, and she and Odysseus then lived on terms of intimacy for a year.
19. According to Alphonse Conway's statement to the Marquess of Queensberry's solicitors, Wilde asked Alphonse to meet him on the Parade one evening in late August 1894, walked with him along the road in the direction of Lancing, and suddenly kissed him. Seduction followed.
20. Shakespeare, Sonnet 18, line 4: 'And summer's lease hath all too short a date.'
21. 'In your [that is, Bosie's and Queensberry's] hideous game of hate together, you had both thrown dice for my soul, and you happened to have lost' (Wilde to Bosie, *Complete Letters*, p. 709).
22. During the Queensberry libel trial, Wilde claimed that when the Marquess of Queensberry paid a visit to his house on 30 June 1894 he had said to him, 'I don't know what the Queensberry rules are, but the Oscar Wilde rule is to shoot at sight'; and that he had told his servant that Queensberry was 'the most infamous brute in London'. Queensberry, however, said that Wilde had shown him the white feather (Ellmann, *Oscar Wilde*, p. 396).
23. Queensberry was 5 feet 8 inches tall, and thus 7 inches shorter than Wilde. Although Bosie's notorious telegram to Queensberry on 2 April 1894 read 'What a funny little man you are', Bosie himself was only an inch taller than his father.
24. By the time of the criminal trials, Alphonse and his mother had left Worthing and were briefly living in Shoreham. After that, both disappear from the historical record.
25. 'Life, in the opinion of wise people, is no more than a very brief storm – so perhaps his spirit still hears the shouts of good-looking boys playing on the beach.'

Sources of Illustrations

1. Oscar Wilde and Lord Alfred Douglas (© National Portrait Gallery)
2. Oscar Wilde (1889) (© National Portrait Gallery)
3. Oscar Wilde (1892) (© National Portrait Gallery)
4. Lord Alfred Douglas in Egypt, from the frontispiece to Lord Alfred Douglas's *Lyrics* (1935)
5. Page of letter from Oscar Wilde to Lord Alfred Douglas (by courtesy of the William Andrews Clark Memorial Library, University of California, Los Angeles)
6. Oscar, Constance and Cyril in 1892 (Merlin Holland's collection)
7. Constance Wilde (full face) (Merlin Holland's collection)
8. Constance Wilde (profile) (Merlin Holland's collection)
9. Page of letter from Constance Wilde to Lady Mount Temple (scan provided by the Broadlands Archive, University of Southampton; reproduced by courtesy of Merlin Holland)
10. Cyril Holland (Merlin Holland's collection)
11. Vyvyan Holland (Merlin Holland's collection)
12. The Marquess of Queensberry (photograph) (Merlin Holland's collection)
13. The Marquess of Queensberry (cartoon), reproduced in H. Montgomery Hyde's *Trials of Oscar Wilde* (1948)
14. The Marquess of Queensberry (silhouette) (© National Portrait Gallery)
15. Robert Ross (Merlin Holland's collection)
16. Frank Harris (Merlin Holland's collection)
17. Wilfrid Scawen Blunt, reproduced in Wilfrid Scawen Blunt's *My Diaries: 1888–1914* (1932)
18. Lord and Lady Mount Temple (Merlin Holland's collection)
19. Sir Edward Clarke (© National Portrait Gallery)
20. Edward Carson (© National Portrait Gallery)
21. Mayor, aldermen and councillors, from *A Descriptive Account of Worthing* (1895) (Geoffrey Godden's collection)
22. The Haven, detail from Wells Series postcard (author's collection)
23. Lord Alfred Douglas outside the Haven (reproduced by kind permission of the Literary Estate of Lord Alfred Douglas)

24. The Haven from Brighton Road, from a Mezzotint Co. postcard (author's collection)
25. Bandstand in grounds of Warwick House, from Henfrey Smail's *Warwick House* (1952)
26. Lifeboat Demonstration (author's collection)
27. The New Theatre Royal, from Robert Elleray's *Worthing: A Pictorial History* (1977)
28. Pavilion at sea end of pier (author's collection)
29. Marine Hotel, from a Lévy Sons & Co. postcard (author's collection)
30. Royal Albion Hotel, Brighton, from a modern postcard (Collectorcard, Croydon)
31. Metropole Hotel, Brighton (author's collection)
32. The Esplanade from the south-west (Francis Frith Collection)
33. The Esplanade from the east (author's collection)
34. The Esplanade from the north-west, from a postcard published by Loader's Photo Stores, Worthing (author's collection)
35. Worthing College, from a Wells Series postcard (author's collection)
36. Beach House (www.westsussexpast.org.uk)
37. Warwick House, from Henfrey Smail's *Warwick House* (1952)
38. High Street, from Edward Snewin's and Henfrey Smail's *Glimpses of Old Worthing* (1945)
39. Cook's Row, from Edward Snewin's and Henfrey Smail's *Glimpses of Old Worthing* (1945)
40. Cannon Inn, from Edward Snewin's and Henfrey Smail's *Glimpses of Old Worthing* (1945)
41. Warwick Street from the east (author's collection)
42. Newington's, from *A Descriptive Account of Worthing* (1895) (Geoffrey Godden's collection)
43. Warwick Street from the Town Hall (author's collection)
44. The Town Hall, from a Lévy Sons & Co. postcard (author's collection)
45. South Street (www.westsussexpast.org.uk)
46. East Parade, from a Victoria Series postcard (author's collection)
47. Pier Kiosks, from a Lévy Sons & Co. postcard (author's collection)
48. Pavilion and paddle steamer (www.westsussexpast.org.uk)
49. Royal Hotel (www.westsussexpast.org.uk)
50. Royal Hotel with boys (www.westsussexpast.org.uk)
51. Cambridge Terrace with boys (www.westsussexpast.org.uk)
52. West Parade, from a Wells Series postcard (author's collection)
53. Montpelier Terrace and Cambridge Terrace (www.westsussexpast.org.uk)
54. Scene west of the pier (www.westsussexpast.org.uk)
55. Marlborough House and the bandstand (www.westsussexpast.org.uk)
56. Ladies on the seafront (www.westsussexpast.org.uk)

The full credit represented by 'www.westsussexpast.org.uk' is 'West Sussex County Council Library Service, www.westsussexpast.org.uk'.

Where images derive from old postcards, the date given in the captions does not come from the postmark on the postcard – if there is one – since postmark dates cannot date a postcard reliably. Firm dates are given only where exact date information is known, usually from knowledge of when a publisher took a particular set of postcard photographs. Where an approximate date is given, it is unlikely to be more than two or three years out.

Acknowledgements

My greatest debt is to Donald Mead, chairman of the Oscar Wilde Society and editor of *The Wildean*, who accepted for publication between 2011 and 2013 the eight articles that form the basis of much of this book, and then made himself freely available for advice while I was writing the rest. He kindly agreed to read the material he had not previously seen, pointed out some errors and infelicities, and provided me with a number of helpful references.

I am much indebted also to Merlin Holland, Oscar Wilde's grandson, for providing me with ten pictures from his collection, for giving me permission to quote extensively from the letters of Oscar and Constance Wilde and from the transcript of the Queensberry libel trial, and for helping me with various queries.

I am grateful to Robert Elleray, Geoffrey Godden, James Gregory, Steve Jebson of the Met Office, Kathryn Johnson of the British Library, Kim Leslie, Neil McKenna, Franny Moyle, J. D. Murphy and Colin Peters for helpful information or other assistance.

For providing pictures and permission to use them, I am indebted to Emma Butterfield of the National Portrait Gallery, Martin Hayes of West Sussex County Council Library Service (www.westsussexpast.org.uk), Scott Jacobs of the William Andrews Clark Memorial Library, University of California, Los Angeles, and Julia Skinner of the Francis Frith Collection.

Finally I would like to thank Nicola Gale, my patient and authoritative editor at Amberley, and her colleague Alex Bennett, who copy-edited this book and its predecessor *Jane Austen's Worthing: The Real Sanditon*, and is, quite simply, a master of his trade.

The Author

Antony Edmonds was born in Southsea in 1951 and educated at Churcher's College, Petersfield and Magdalen College, Oxford. He has published numerous articles in *The Wildean*, the journal of the Oscar Wilde Society, and writes regularly on literary and historical subjects for *Sussex Life* and the *Worthing Herald*. His previous books, *Worthing: The Postcard Collection* and *Jane Austen's Worthing: The Real Sanditon*, were published by Amberley in 2013.

Index

Adey, More 16, 98, 216 n.14
Albermarle Hotel, London 64
Albert Victor, Prince 130
Albion Hotel, Brighton see Royal Albion Hotel
Alexander, George 28, 98, 109, 110, 111, 121, 122, 127, 163 n.28, 171, 177
'Alexander, Mrs' see Fraser, Mrs Caroline
Algiers 126
Allen, William 129
Assembly Rooms, Worthing 35, 37, 40, 42, 43, 44, 150, 154 n.1, 155 n.8, 171
Athens 25, 140, 149,
Atkins, Frederick 136, 142, 169 n.60
Augusta, Princess 117, 165 n.15, 165 n.16
Avondale Hotel, London 126
Aynesworth, Allan 121

Babbacombe 21, 32, 88–9, 100, 106, 107, 161 n.11, 172
Bath Place, Worthing, No. 1 37, 72, 78, 80, 159 n.23, 206
Bedales School 35
Beerbohm, Max 120
Benson, E. F. 119
Biskra 126
Blunt, Wilfrid Scawen 59, 60–1, 170
Bognor 70, 202
Bosie see Douglas, Lord Alfred
Bracknell 115, 116, 165 n.13
Brighton 27, 28, 48, 49, 56, 57, 58, 66, 67, 68, 77–9, 107–8, 114, 118, 119, 125, 155 n.2, 155 n.8, 158 n.23, 164 n.50, 172, 174 n.31, 175 n.36, 182, 188–9, 191
Brighton Road, Worthing 44, 57, 194–8
Brockwell, Detective-Inspector 80, 159 n.24, 200
Browning, Oscar 24–5
Buckingham Road, Shoreham-on-Sea, No. 5 80

Bunbury, Captain 114
Bunbury, Henry S. 115
Bunbury, Mr (magistrate) 115

Café Royal, London 29, 176
Carson, Edward 69, 75–8, 81, 82, 133–6, 138, 141, 142, 155 n.8, 159 n.11, 175 n.34, 184–192, 200, 202
Charles, Mr Justice 140
Chesterton, G. K. 100
Clapham Junction 144
Clarke, Sir Edward 31, 75, 143, 188, 190–1, 192
Cleveland Street, London 130–1, 134, 157 n.16, 167 n.13
Cliburn, Robert 129
Collins, Mr Justice 184
Colman, Edward and Sheila 68, 158 n.28
Conway, Alphonse
  acquaintance with Constance Wilde 74–5, 104–5, 191, 192
  ambition to join Merchant Navy 75, 79, 186, 191
  appearance 73–4, 81–2
  at the Haven 74–5, 76, 79, 159 n.22, 185–6, 192
  at the Wilde trials 80, 81, 84
  birth and baptism 69–70
  character 186, 189–90
  correct first name 70, 199–200
  education 73, 186
  employment selling newspapers 75, 184–5, 191, 192
  first meeting with Wilde 74, 185, 191–2
  interest in the theatre 43, 77, 155 n.8, 186
  overnight stay in Brighton 77, 188–9
  parentage 70–1, 202–4
  possible emigration to Australia 210–11
  possible half-brother 207–11
  presents from Wilde 76–7, 80, 187–8, 192

probable illegitimacy 70–71
  seduction by Wilde 75–6, 83–4, 186
Conway, John 70, 205, 207
Conway, Julia Sarah 69–73, 84, 85–6, 202–4, 205–11
Cook, Frederick 207–10
Cook, James 207–8
Cooper, Christopher 207
Cortis, Alderman 39–41
Cowper, Jessie 107, 164 n.47
Cowper-Temple, William see Mount Temple, Lord
Crabbet Park 60
Criterion Theatre, London 123
Croft-Cooke, Rupert 63
Cromer, Lord and Lady 25
Custance, Olive 148

Dansey, Claude 20, 24–5
Dansey, Colonel 25
Delahay, Alphonse 201–4
Dieppe 13, 36, 52, 65–6, 146, 172, 174 n.31, 175 n.32, 177, 179–81
Douglas, Lord Alfred
  and Oscar Wilde 13, 15, 16–17, 18–21, 22, 25–6, 36, 66–7, 107–8, 118–19, 120, 125–6, 127–8, 132, 134, 139–40, 142, 146, 148
  in North Africa 126
  in Worthing 59–68, 118–20, 170–2
  marriage 148
  presence during the writing of *Earnest* 118–19
  pilgrimage to Stratford-upon-Avon 60–1, 170
  relationship with his father 18, 26, 61–2, 216 n.21, 216 n.23
  in Goring-on-Thames 21–2, 24, 118
  attitude to money 16, 17–18, 127
  relationships with boys 16, 19–20, 24–5, 42, 65, 67, 85, 126
  at Oxford 16, 17, 21, 26, 129, 157 n.16
Douglas, Lord Percy 147, 157 n.19
Douglas, Raymond 148
Dowson, Ernest 13,
Drumlanrig, Viscount 125–6

Egypt 25, 89
Ellmann, Richard 9, 69, 79, 117
Euston, Earl of 130, 134
Eyton, Canon Richard 99–100

Fenn, Arthur 31, 32–4, 110, 120, 153 n.12, 153 n.17, 170, 172
Foldy, Michael S. 140–1
Ford, Emily 107, 164 n.38
Fraser, Bruce 39, 154 n.2
Fraser, Captain A. B. S. 38–40, 41, 49, 51, 52, 54, 56, 57, 117, 154 n.2
Fraser, Captain C. E. 38, 52, 56, 154 n.2

Fraser, Cecil 39, 154 n.2
Fraser, General Alexander 38, 39, 154 n.2
Fraser, Mrs Caroline 38, 39, 117, 154 n.2

Gide, André 126
Gill, Charles 136, 167, n.13
Goring-by-Sea 215, n.10
Goring-on-Thames 9, 21–2, 24, 33, 81, 85, 113, 118, 138, 139
Grainger, Walter 20, 22, 33, 73, 81, 85, 131, 138–9, 145, 154 n.19
Grossmith, George 155 n.7
Grossmith, Weedon 43, 155 n.7

Hammond, Charles 130
Harris, Frank 12–13, 16, 146–7
Haven, The 22, 27, 29–33, 44, 57, 62, 63, 64, 66, 67, 74, 75, 76, 79–80, 82, 91, 95, 96, 103, 105, 117, 150, 170, 172, 173, 179, 180, 186, 193–8, 200
Haymarket Theatre, London 21, 122, 123
Hewitt, Father John 100
Hichens, Robert 119, 160 n.2, 166 n.23
Holland, Cyril see Wilde, Cyril
Holland, Lucian 147
Holland, Merlin 10, 147, 200
Holland, Otho see Lloyd, Otho
Holland, Vyvyan see Wilde, Vyvyan
Holloway Prison 19, 112, 215 n.3
Hotel d'Alsace, Paris 147
Hove 38, 68
Humphreys, Arthur 14, 31, 88, 89–99, 101, 162 n.16, 162 n.17, 170, 171
Humphreys, Charles 127, 163 n.29
Hyde, H. Montgomery 69, 83, 156 n.2, 199

Isaacson, Colonel 146
Ives, George 80, 81

James, Henry 111
Johnson, Lionel 15
Jones, Elizabeth 205, 207
Jones, Mildred 205–7, 208, 210, 211
Jones, Thomas 205

Keane, Lady 116
Kearley, Detective-Inspector 79

La Napoule 146–7
Labouchere, Henry 129
Lancing 68, 186
Lancing (road to) 74, 76, 84, 186, 214, 216 n.19
Lane, John 16, 117
Law, Arthur 43, 155 n.6
Leslie, Kim 193, 194
Lewis, George 16
Lilley, Rev. Alfred Leslie 65, 99–102, 104, 163 n.38, 171
Little College Street, London 131

Littlechild, Chief Detective-Inspector 79
Littlehampton 65, 76, 83, 171, 178, 180
Lloyd, Otho 13, 22, 31, 35, 36, 88, 104–5, 168 n.54
Lockwood, Sir Frank 81, 137, 142–3, 167 n.13
Lord, Henrietta 29
Lord, Miss 29, 30, 79, 170

Magdalen College, Oxford 17, 115, 147, 213
Marine Hotel, Worthing 51, 63–4, 74, 76, 150, 171, 186
Marlborough College 131
Mason, Charles Spurrier 109, 124, 164 n.2, 166 n.1
Mathews, Charlie 206
Mathews, Elkin 16, 117
Mathews, Mildred see Mildred Jones
Mathews, Willie 167, n.13, 192
McKenna, Neil 10
Mead, Donald 198
Mendelssohn, H. S. 87–8, 160 n.1
Metropole Hotel, Brighton 66, 79, 158 n.24, 164 n.50, 172
Mount Temple, Lady 21, 32, 88–89, 100, 102, 103–104, 105, 106, 107, 160 n.3, 161 n.7, 161 n.8, 161 n.9, 162 n.13, 172
Mount Temple, Lord 88–9, 161 n.9, 161 n.10
Myers, Frederic 97, 162 n.25

Nelson, Major 146
Newhaven 66, 172, 177
Newlove, Henry
Newton, Arthur 130, 167 n.13
Nicholson, John Gambril 111
Noel, Conrad 101, 163 n.35

Old Monk's Farm, Lancing 68, 158 n.28
Olympian Quartet 40–42, 155 n.5, 171, 179

Palmer, Albert 110
Palmerston, Lord 88, 161 n.9, 161 n.10
Paris 15, 26, 28, 96, 147, 202
Parke, Ernest 130, 134
Parker, Charles 117, 124, 135, 136, 140, 149, 169 n.60, 191, 192
Pater, Walter 98, 103, 164 n.31, 213
Pearson, Hesketh 122
Pentonville Prison 213, 215 n.3
Percy (boy in Worthing) 42, 65, 73, 74, 75, 76, 79, 87, 157 n.19, 159 n.11, 171, 178, 214
Petworth 70, 205, 207, 210
Pier Pavilion, Worthing 46, 50, 52, 53, 150, 182
Piper, Alderman 40, 48
Portsmouth 77, 189, 202

Queensberry, Lady 18, 25, 115
Queensberry, Marquess of 9, 18, 26, 29, 32, 33, 61–2, 68, 79, 80, 81, 85, 121, 125, 126, 127–8, 130–4, 139, 142, 143, 147, 153 n.18, 165 n.13, 166 n.7, 192, 214, 216 n.21, 216 n.22, 216 n.23

Reading Prison 13, 16, 20, 23, 98, 139, 144, 146, 148, 213, 215 n.3
Rosebery, Earl of 125–6, 143, 166 n.4
Ross, Robert 12, 23–5, 32, 112, 127, 136, 138, 146, 147–8, 151 n.1
Royal Albion Hotel, Brighton 56, 77–9, 159 n.17, 172, 189, 190
Royal Hotel, Worthing 48, 50, 52
Ruskin, John 89, 162 n.12, 213

Sanger, 'Lord' George 46–7, 156 n.11
Sanger, 'Lord' John 46–7, 156 n.11
Savoy Hotel, London 21, 64, 67, 112, 136, 168 n.47, 215 n. 11
Scarfe, Ernest 138, 152 n.4, 199
Shaw, George Bernard 158, n.26
Shelley, Edward 16, 69, 81, 136, 169 n.60, 185, 188
Sherard, Robert 132, 142
Shoreham-on-Sea 73, 80, 206
Smith, Charlotte 39, 154 n.2
Somerset, Lord Arthur 130
Somerset, Lord Henry 157, n.16
St Andrew's Church, Worthing 69, 195
St James's Place, London 26
St James's Theatre, London 111, 122
Stanhoe Hall Hotel, Worthing 52, 117, 165 n.17
Stephen (boy in Worthing) 63, 65, 74, 75, 76, 82, 87, 150, 159 n.11, 171, 178, 180, 214
Stevens, John 148–50, 169 n.57
Steyne Hotel, Worthing 50
Stopes, Marie 119, 197
Stratford-upon-Avon 60–1, 170
Sutcliffe, Tom 149–50
Swiss Governess 31, 60, 117, 170, 173 n.2, 176–7, 195

Tankard, Herbert 168 n.47
Taylor, Alfred 79, 82, 84, 124–5, 130, 131, 142, 152 n.4, 164 n.2, 166 n.1, 191
Tite Street, Chelsea, No. 16 14, 15, 22, 26, 32, 33, 62, 67, 127, 152 n.11, 161 n.7, 161 n.8, 172
Tollemache, John 88
Trinity College, Dublin 11, 100, 115
Turner, Reginald 120, 147, 166 n.25

Veck, George 130

Wagstaff, John 114, 179, 193, 194, 195, 199
Walker, Miss 30

Waller, Lewis 123
Wandsworth Prison 144, 215 n.3
Warman Terrace, Worthing, No. 2 70, 72, 80
Warwick House, Worthing 43–4
Wells, H. G. 122
Western Terrace, Worthing, No. 2 71, 72
Wilde, Constance
  and Arthur Humphreys 89–99
  and Cyril and Vyvyan 34–5
  and Georgina Mount Temple 88, 106–7
  and Leslie Lilley 99–101
  and Lord Alfred Douglas 25–6, 64–5, 87
  attitude to religion 14, 92, 99, 102, 104
  choice of reading matter 102–4
  health 87, 106, 107
  interest in spirituality 102, 104, 162 n.25
  knowledge of Wilde's sexuality 22–3, 104–6
  letters from Worthing 88
  marriage 11–14, 23, 64, 87, 89, 94, 104
Wilde, Cyril 13, 21, 31, 32, 34–5, 40, 49, 65, 74–5, 81, 84, 105, 106, 147, 150, 154 n.21, 170, 171, 172, 173 n.2, 173 n.4, 177, 180
Wilde, Lady 28, 36, 95, 107–8, 171
Wilde, Oscar
  and Alphonse Conway 43, 50, 56, 69, 73–77, 79, 81, 82–6, 135–6, 141, 145, 155 n.8, 171–2, 184–92, 199–200
  and Arthur Humphreys 90, 91, 92, 98–9
  and Constance Wilde *see* marriage
  and Cyril and Vyvyan Wilde 34, 35, 40, 63, 74, 105, 177, 180
  and George Alexander 28, 109, 110, 111–12, 113, 121, 122–3, 177
  and Lord Alfred Douglas 13, 15, 16–17, 18–21, 22, 25–6, 36, 66–7, 107–8, 118–19, 120, 125–6, 127–8, 132, 134, 139–40, 142, 146, 148
  and Robert Ross 12, 147
  and the Marquess of Queensberry 9, 26, 33, 126, 127–8, 131, 132–3, 134, 142, 153 n.18
  and Walter Grainger 22, 33, 73–4, 81, 85, 131, 138–9, 145
  at the Lifeboat Demonstration 37, 49–50
  at the Venetian Fete 37, 38, 52, 53–6, 182–3
  at the Worthing Annual Regatta 37, 51
  attitude to religion 14, 216 n.14
  attitude to scandal 7–9
  attitude to social class 33, 134–9
  criminal trials 16, 20, 21, 81, 82, 112, 123, 129, 130, 131, 132, 133, 136–7, 139–40, 141–3
  Greek love 23, 139–41
  in exile in Europe 9, 13, 132, 146–7
  in Goring-on-Thames 21–2, 33, 113, 118, 138–9
  in North Africa 126
  in prison 19, 98, 112, 145–6, 215 n.3
  letters from Worthing 28–9, 35, 36, 40, 62, 63, 65, 73, 76, 109–110, 120–1, 160 n.2, 176–81
  marriage 11–14, 23, 64, 87, 89, 94, 104
  money problems 13, 16, 17–18, 28, 77, 109–110, 125, 127, 146, 176, 177
  Queensberry libel trial 22, 32, 61, 80–2, 122, 130, 132–3, 141, 184–92
  sexuality 12, 13, 22–3
  trip to Dieppe 36, 65–6, 172, 174 n.31, 177, 190
Wilde, Oscar (literary works)
  A Woman of No Importance 21, 109, 113
  An Ideal Husband 7, 21, 28, 113, 122, 123, 126
  'De Profundis' 13, 17, 18–19, 57, 59, 66, 67, 118, 119, 124, 125, 128, 132, 142, 146, 148, 153 n.18, 158 n.23, 158 n.24, 164 n.50, 167 n.22, 174 n.31, 215 n.11, 216 n.15
  Intentions 14
  Lady Windermere's Fan 7, 15, 110, 113
  Lord Arthur Savile's Crime and Other Stories 14
  Oscariana 62, 88, 90, 92, 95, 96, 97, 98, 102, 103, 157 n.11, 161 n.6, 170, 171, 173 n.9, 173 n.13
  Salome 15
  The Ballad of a Fisher Boy 146–7
  The Ballad of Reading Gaol 146, 147
  'The Critic as Artist' 14
  'The Decay of Lying' 14
  The Duchess of Padua 11
  The Happy Prince and Other Tales 14
  The House of Pomegranates 14
  The Importance of Being Earnest 9, 17, 22, 28, 32, 39, 62, 67, 77, 109–123, 126, 127, 150, 166 n.31, 171, 172, 177–8, 194, 213
  The Picture of Dorian Gray 12, 14, 15, 212, 215 n.2
  'The Soul of Man under Socialism' 8, 14, 134, 144
  Vera, or the Nihilists 11
Wilde, Vyvyan 13, 14, 21, 32, 34–5, 49, 63, 74, 75, 99, 113, 147, 154 n.21, 170, 172, 173 n.2, 173 n.4, 177, 180
Wills, Mr Justice 130, 143
Winchester College 17
Wood, Alfred 20, 32, 33, 129, 134, 140, 169 n.60
Wortham, Biscoe Hale 24–5
Wyndham, Charles 123